FiNALEonline.de

FiNALEonline ist die digitale Ergänzung zu deinem Abiturband. Hier findest du eine Vielzahl an Angeboten, die dich bei deiner Prüfungsvorbereitung zusätzlich unterstützen.

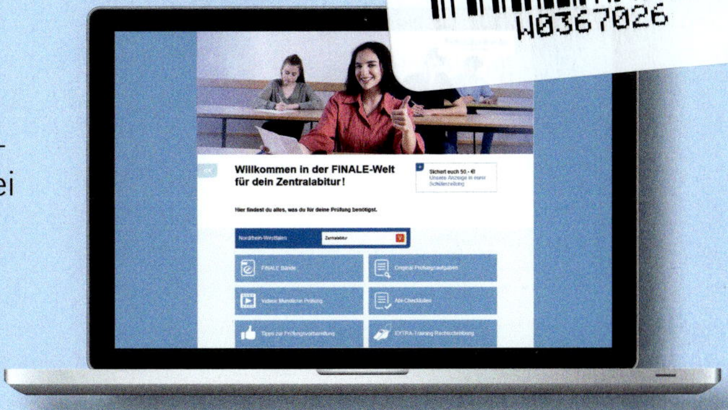

Das Plus für deine Vorbereitung:

- Original-Prüfungsaufgaben mit Lösungen (bitte Code von Seite 2 eingeben!)
- EXTRA-Training Rechtschreibung
  So kannst du einem möglichen Punktabzug bei deinen Abi-Klausuren vorbeugen.
- Videos zur mündlichen Prüfung
- Tipps zur stressfreien Prüfungsvorbereitung
- Abi-Checklisten mit allen prüfungsrelevanten Themen

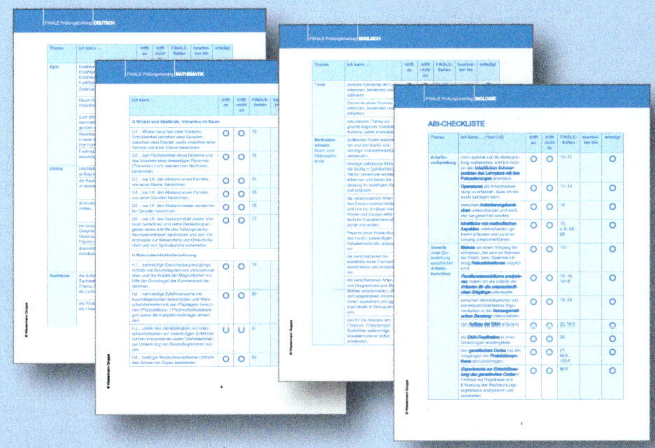

Abi-Checklisten

Sie helfen dir, den Überblick über den Prüfungsstoff zu behalten.

FiNALEonline.de

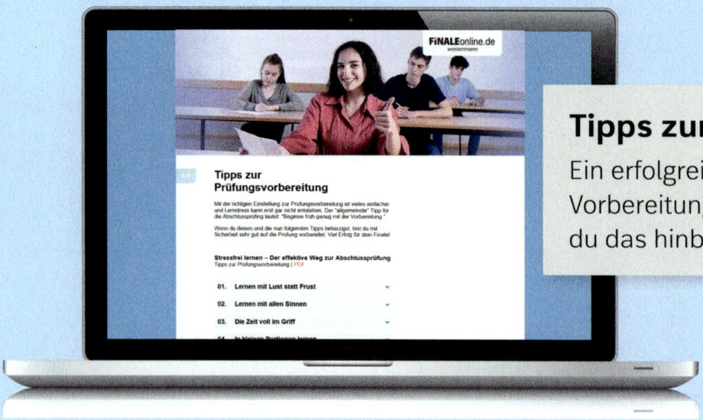

Tipps zur Prüfungsvorbereitung
Ein erfolgreiches Abitur erfordert eine gezielte Vorbereitung ohne unnötigen Lernstress. Wie du das hinbekommst, erfährst du hier!

Videos zur mündlichen Prüfung
Nur wenige Abiturienten wissen genau, wie sie abläuft, die „Mündliche“. Die Videos geben dir Einblick in den Ablauf der Prüfung und Tipps für die richtige Vorbereitung.

Die Kombination aus FiNALE-Buch und FiNALEonline bietet dir die optimale Vorbereitung für deine Prüfung und begleitet dich sicher zu einem erfolgreichen Abitur 2022!

www.finaleonline.de

westermann

FiNALE Prüfungstraining

Zentralabitur 2022

Englisch

Niedersachsen

FiNALEonline.de

Liebe Abiturientin, lieber Abiturient,

FiNALEonline.de ist die optimale Ergänzung zu diesem Abiturtrainer. Hier finden Sie:

- die Original-Prüfungsaufgaben 2021 nach Eingabe des Codes:
  EN8R6S8
- eine Abi-Checkliste für die effektive Zeitplanung
- allgemeine Tipps zur Prüfungsvorbereitung

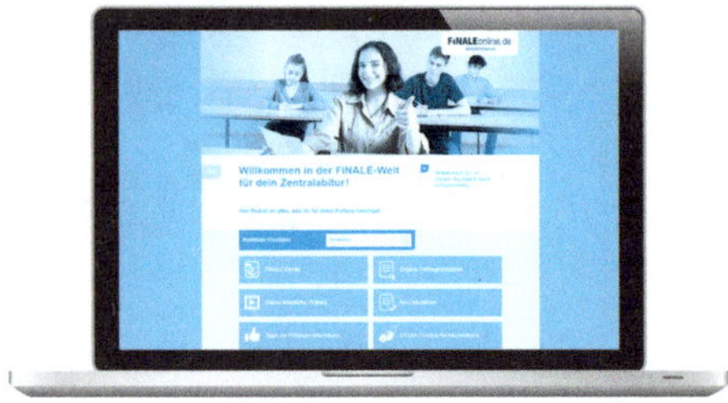

Einfach mal reinschauen: www.finaleonline.de

Autorinnen: Isabel Wagemann-Steidel und Ortrud-Christine Rotzoll sowie Lara Jost

westermann GRUPPE

Bildnachweis:
Peter Wirtz Fotografie, Dormagen: Titel, 2.1. |toonpool.com, Berlin, Castrop-Rauxel: Popa Matumula 161.1.

Druck 1/Jahr 2021

Redaktion: lüra – Klemt & Mues GbR, Wuppertal
Kontakt: finale@westermanngruppe.de
Layout: Druckreif! Sandra Grünberg, Braunschweig
Umschlaggestaltung: Gingco.Net, Braunschweig
Umschlagfoto: Peter Wirtz, Dormagen
Druck und Bindung: westermann druck GmbH, Braunschweig

ISBN 978-3-7426-**2237**-2

Inhaltsverzeichnis

Textgestaltung

Ausdrucksvermögen/Verfügbarkeit sprachlicher Mittel

Beispiele für Prüfungsaufgaben

Aufgaben mit Beispiellösungen

Aufgaben mit Bewertungskriterien

Aufgaben zur Sprachmittlung mit Beispiellösungen oder Bewertungskriterien

Original-Prüfungsaufgaben 2020 und 2021

Arbeiten mit *Finale*

Finale Prüfungstraining Englisch möchte Ihnen eine praxisnahe Hilfe zur Vorbereitung auf die Abiturprüfung sein. Im Praxis-Teil finden sich daher – neben den Original-Prüfungsaufgaben 2020 – zu allen geforderten Themenbereichen weitere authentische Aufgaben, die in ihrer Form den Vorgaben entsprechen. Wir verzichten hier auf eine Differenzierung nach Kursen mit grundlegendem beziehungsweise erhöhtem Anforderungsniveau. Im Abitur unterscheiden sich die Aufgaben einerseits durch den Textumfang, andererseits durch den Schwierigkeitsgrad des Textes für Übungstexte keine große Rolle. Auch als Schülerin oder Schüler in einem Kurs mit grundlegendem Anforderungsniveau sind Sie durch den Englischunterricht mit längeren und komplexeren Texten vertraut. Als Schülerin oder Schüler eines Kurses mit erhöhtem Anforderungsniveau können Sie eine Textanalyse auch an kürzeren, einfacheren Texten üben. Dieser Band bietet Ihnen Informationen zum Abitur 2022. Vieles gilt für beide Jahrgänge, sodass in den Kapiteln oft nicht unterschieden wird. Es gibt allerdings Unterschiede bei den verbindlichen Materialien. Bei den vorgestellten Materialien wird daher jeweils angegeben, für welchen Abiturjahrgang sie relevant sind. Zudem gibt es getrennte Übersichten, damit Sie leichter zu Ihren Themen finden.

Zwei Aufgaben im Kapitel „Beispiele für Prüfungsaufgaben" werden kleinschrittig erarbeitet und schließen mit einer Musterlösung. Dies soll für Sie eine exemplarische Hilfe sein auf dem Weg vom Ausgangstext über das Textverständnis, die Methodik der Textanalyse und die Evaluation hin zur Gliederung und sprachlichen Darstellung des Zieltextes. Den weiteren Aufgabenbeispielen folgen Bewertungskriterien ganz in der Form, wie Ihre Lehrerinnen und Lehrer sie zur Korrektur der Abiturarbeiten an die Hand bekommen. Sie dienen Ihnen zur Selbstkontrolle in Ihrem fortschreitenden Prüfungstraining. Geschrieben wurde dieses Buch im Jahr 2021, damit es frühzeitig zur Vorbereitung auf das Abitur 2022 beitragen kann. Die zu diesem Zeitpunkt aktuellen Abituraufgaben 2020 werden jeweils mit Musterlösung angeboten. Sobald die Original-Prüfungsaufgaben des Jahres 2021 freigegeben sind, können Sie sie unter www.finaleonline.de abrufen.

Das Kapitel „Basiswissen" bietet Ihnen eine kompakte Übersicht über die für das Zentralabitur vorgegebenen Themen. Es hilft Ihnen, das im Unterricht erworbene Wissen zu strukturieren und in seinen Grundzügen abzurufen. Um den Umgang mit dem thematischen Vokabular zu vertiefen, ist dieser Teil in englischer Sprache geschrieben und wird durch Glossare zum thematischen Vokabular ergänzt.

Die sprachliche Leistung spielt in der Fremdsprache bei aller inhaltlich-thematischer Kompetenz immer noch die herausragende Rolle. Ein sicherer Umgang mit den Strukturen und Wörtern der englischen Sprache ist also unabdingbar. Deshalb haben wir in *Finale* ein ganzes Kapitel zur sprachlichen Leistung aufgenommen.

Wir wünschen Ihnen viel Erfolg!

Informationen und Tipps zur Prüfung

Das Kerncurriculum (KC) für die Sekundarstufe II

Mit der Einführung des neuen Kerncurriculums für die gymnasiale Oberstufe entwickelt sich der Englischunterricht auf moderne Weise weiter – so, wie es mit dem entsprechenden Kerncurriculum für die Klassen 5–10 bereits angelegt wurde. Das KC für die Oberstufe führt die im KC für die Sek I angelegten Grundlagen fort, sodass ein nahtloser Übergang in die Qualifikationsphase erfolgen kann. Grundlegend ist auch in der Sekundarstufe II der Gemeinsame Europäische Referenzrahmen *CERF (Common European Framework)*.
Im Zentralabitur **2022** wird die Prüfung aus folgenden **drei Bestandteilen** bestehen (s. auch S. 8):

1. Hörverstehen (30 Minuten),
2. Sprachmittlung (60 Minuten), sowie
3. einer Textaufgabe (auf erhöhtem Niveau: 210 Minuten, auf grundlegendem Niveau: 130 Minuten). Für die Textaufgabe besteht weiterhin die Wahlmöglichkeit zwischen zwei Vorschlägen.

Die folgende Zusammenfassung der wichtigsten Anliegen des neuen KC gibt Ihnen eine Orientierung über die im Abitur von Ihnen erwarteten Kenntnisse und Kompetenzen.

Die Kompetenzorientierung

Kompetenzen

Das Abitur in Niedersachsen ist nicht nach Inhalten ausgerichtet, sondern es wird eine kompetenzorientierte Prüfung abgenommen. Inhalte sind selbstverständlich immer noch wichtig, sie ergeben sich aus den im Unterricht verpflichtend zu behandelnden Materialien. Die inhaltliche Grundlage sind die Themenfelder, die das Kerncurriculum für die Sekundarstufe II ausweist.

Der Englischunterricht soll es ermöglichen, Fremdes und Anderes zu erfahren und durch Perspektivenwechsel andere Weltsichten zu verstehen, um Perspektiven zu koordinieren und Empathie zu entwickeln.

Hierzu müssen die Inhalte „meaningful“, also für die Lernenden von Bedeutung und außerdem in einem interkulturellen Sinne relevant sein. Hierbei wird ausdrücklich von einer erforderlichen Verstehensanstrengung ausgegangen, sodass Aufgaben nicht einfach nur mit bereits vorhandenem Weltwissen oder Allgemeinbildung gelöst werden können. Gefordert sind somit interaktive fremdsprachliche Prozesse, die sinnvolle diskursive Handlungen notwendig machen. Auf diese Weise sollen Reflexion und Selbstreflexion ermöglicht werden.

Um kompetent sprachlich und interkulturell kommunikativ handeln zu können, müssen Wissen und Können mit einander verknüpft werden. Inhalte werden in ihrer Bedeutung relativiert, da die Kompetenzen zwar an Inhalten erworben werden, dieses jedoch exemplarisch geschieht, sodass in der Abiturprüfung keine speziellen Inhalte wie etwa „India“ oder „The American Dream“ im Mittelpunkt stehen. Gefragt sind vielmehr methodische Problemlösungsstrategien, denn die erworbenen Kompetenzen werden auf neue Situationen, Themen und Kontexte transferiert. Sprachliche, pragmatische oder soziokulturelle Strukturen müssen in den einzelnen Prüfungsteilen erkannt und im Sinne eines kompetenten Umgangs mit der Fremdsprache beherrscht werden.

Wichtig ist hierbei der Hinweis, dass laut KC der Erwerb interkultureller Kompetenzen nicht mit der erfolgreich bestandenen Abiturprüfung endet, sondern ein Leben lang fortgesetzt wird.
Für Schülerinnen und Schüler bedeutet dies, dass sie laut KC nicht nur auf vorhandenes Wissen zurückgreifen müssen, sondern dass sie sich weiterführendes Wissen selbst beschaffen und entsprechende Zusammenhänge erkennen können. Weiterhin sollen sie in der Lage sein, Handlungsschritte zu planen und Lösungen auf kreative Weise zu erproben. Die verfügbaren Kenntnisse, Fähigkeiten und Fertigkeiten sollen dabei zum Einsatz kommen, das gewonnene Ergebnis soll anhand angemessener Kriterien selbst überprüft/evaluiert werden.

Diese Erweiterung der Kompetenzfelder wird nicht nur in den Unterricht, sondern vor allem auch in die Abiturprüfung einfließen.

TIPP Further reading

1. *Kerncurriculum für das Gymnasium – gymnasiale Oberstufe*
   Herausgegeben vom Niedersächsischen Kultusministerium (2009 und 2017), 30159 Hannover, Schiffgraben 12
   Das Kerncurriculum ist auch als PDF-Datei auf dem niedersächsischen Bildungsserver abrufbar: http://www.cuvo.nibis.de
2. *Gemeinsamer Europäischer Referenzrahmen*
   Autoren: John Trim/Brian North/Daniel Coste in Zusammenarbeit mit Joseph Sheils. Langenscheidt, ISBN: 978-3-468-49469-7
3. Materialien für kompetenzorientierten Unterricht, hrsg. vom Niedersächsischen Kultusministerium (2010), und Materialien zur Sprechprüfung (2014) auch online unter www.nibis.de
4. Bildungsstandards für die Allgemeine Hochschulreife, als PDF zu finden unter http://www.nibis.de/uploads/1gohrgs/files/englisch/Bildungsstandards_allg_Hochschulreife.pdf

Kompetenzerwerb

Der Erwerb der für die Abiturprüfung erforderlichen Kompetenzen wird bereits in der Sekundarstufe I grundgelegt. Dennoch ist es ratsam, sich in Bezug auf die Abiturklausur rechtzeitig mit den strukturierten Kompetenzanforderungen vertraut zu machen. Das erworbene Wissen soll in der Abiturarbeit abgerufen und in verschiedenen Zusammenhängen genutzt werden können. Am Ende der Einführungsphase soll hier das Niveau B1+ nach dem Gemeinsamen Europäischen Referenzrahmen erreicht werden. Im Folgenden werden die wichtigsten Kompetenzen kurz dargestellt.

Abitur 2022

In der Abiturprüfung wird es zwei Prüfungsteile geben:

1. a) Hörverstehen (30 Minuten)
1. b) Sprachmittlung (60 Minuten)
2. Textaufgabe (130 Minuten gA / 210 Minuten eA)

Hörverstehen

Im Abitur 2022 wird es einen Hörverstehensteil geben, der 30 Minuten in Anspruch nehmen wird. Sie sollten dabei imstande sein, wesentliche Inhalte eines authentischen Hörtextes zu verstehen.

Als Material für die Prüfung können Hörvorlagen z. B. aus Radiosendungen, Reden, Interviews oder Gesprächen herangezogen werden. Die Länge der einzelnen Vorlagen wird fünf Minuten in der Regel nicht überschreiten. Das Hörverstehen wird mittels geschlossener und halboffener Aufgabenformate überprüft, denkbar wären also diese Aufgabenformate:

- Multiple Choice (mit drei oder maximal vier Alternativen pro *item)*
- Zuordnungsaufgaben
- Kurzantworten (mit 1–5 Wörtern)
- Gelenktes Notizenfertigen (Vervollständigung von Sätzen, Tabellen, ...)

Richtig/Falsch-Fragen zum Ankreuzen wird es nicht geben, die Ratewahrscheinlichkeit wäre zu groß.

TIPP zum Punktesammeln

Wichtig: Sollten Kurzantworten gefordert sein, zählen Rechtschreib- und Grammatikfehler nicht, solange erkennbar ist, was ausgesagt werden soll! Die geforderte Wortzahl ist unbedingt zu beachten!

Die Datei mit den Höraufgaben läuft bis zum Ende, ohne angehalten zu werden. Sie enthält daher auch alle Zeitintervalle, die zum Lesen der Aufgabenstellung benötigt werden. Die Texte werden zweimal angehört.
Um 05 Punkte zu erreichen, müssen 45 % der items richtig gelöst werden, für 11 Punkte mindestens 75 %.

Sprachmittlung (Mediation)

Im Abitur 2022 wird im ersten Prüfungsteil auch die Kompetenz Sprachmittlung geprüft. Hier kommt es darauf an, den Inhalt eines deutschsprachigen Textes sinngemäß, adressatengerecht und kontextgebunden in englischer Sprache wiederzugeben. Die entsprechenden Merkmale der geforderten Textsorte müssen beachtet werden. Der Adressat muss in die Lage versetzt werden, den Text für seine Zwecke nutzen zu können. Je nach Text kann es sinnvoll sein, kulturelle Besonderheiten zu berücksichtigen, indem man zusätzliche Erläuterungen anfügt. Unbekannte Wörter und Wendungen müssen gegebenenfalls umschrieben und sprachliche Strukturen vereinfacht werden.
Sprachmittlung (*mediation*) darf also keinesfalls mit Übersetzung (*translation*) verwechselt werden. Entscheidend ist für die Sprachmittlung allein die korrekte Wiedergabe wesentlicher Inhalte in sprachlich angemessener und idiomatisch richtiger Weise.
Für den Prüfungsteil Sprachmittlung gilt als Bewertungsgrundlage: Der Inhalt wird mit 40%, die Sprache mit 60% bewertet. Das Beispiel auf Seite 10 zeigt eine mögliche Aufgabenstellung. Zusätzlich finden Sie im Kapitel „Beispiele für Prüfungsaufgaben" weitere Sprachmittlungsaufgaben (S. 151, 168, 171).

Leseverstehen

In der Abiturprüfung 2022 wird es keine Aufgaben zum Leseverstehen geben, da man sich bundesländerübergreifend auf das Aufgabenformat „Sprachmittlung“ verständigt hat. Dennoch müssen die erworbenen Kompetenzen auf der Niveaustufe B1+ während der Qualifikationsphase dahingehend erweitert werden, dass das Niveau C1 erreicht wird, um selbstständig einen längeren, anspruchsvolleren fiktionalen oder nichtfiktionalen Text zu verstehen, ihm gezielt Detailinformationen zu entnehmen und unbekanntes Vokabular zu erschließen. Die Arbeit sowohl mit einem Wörterbuch muss also beherrscht werden, ebenso wie die unterschiedlichen Arbeitstechniken etwa des intensiven und extensiven Lesens.
Sie müssen außerdem in der Lage sein, sprachliche und gestalterische Merkmale eines Textes zu erfassen und somit die Wirkungsweise eines Textes analysieren können.

Den Erschließungstechniken wie *skimming* (globales Leseverstehen, Erkennen der Hauptaussage des Textes), *scanning* (detailliertes, genaues Lesen) und *careful reading* (Suchen nach spezifischen Informationen) kommt dabei große Bedeutung zu. Weiterhin sollten unbekannte Wörter auch ohne Zuhilfenahme eines Wörterbuches erschlossen werden können.

Sprechen

Die Kompetenz „Sprechen" ist für die schriftliche Abiturprüfung ohne Bedeutung. In einer P5-Prüfung (oder: in einer mündlichen Nachprüfung im schriftlichen Prüfungsfach) wird hingegen sowohl monologisches als auch dialogisches Sprechen geprüft. Beim monologischen Sprechen muss man über einen Zeitraum von ca. zehn Minuten frei und zusammenhängend über ein vorgegebenes Thema reden, das auf der Grundlage von Prüfungsunterlagen, zumeist einem Text, zu erschließen ist. In der Regel wird zunächst eine kurze Zusammenfassung des Textmaterials erwartet, bevor die weiteren Aufgaben abgearbeitet werden. Hierbei soll laut KC korrekt und flüssig gesprochen werden. Der Prüfling soll in dem sich anschließenden Prüfungsgespräch zeigen, dass er flexibel und spontan auf den Prüfer reagieren und seine eigenen Argumente begründen kann.

Insgesamt soll das Prüfungsgespräch so natürlich wie möglich und idiomatisch korrekt geführt werden, wobei der Prüfling zeigen soll, dass er Verständnisschwierigkeiten in der Zielsprache ausräumen und Wortschatz- und Grammatiklücken überbrücken kann. Die mündliche Prüfung dauert in der Regel 20 Minuten, die maximale Dauer beträgt 30 Minuten.

Schreiben

Ausschlaggebend beim Schreiben ist die sogenannte kommunikative Absicht, es muss deutlich werden, welchem Zweck der Text dienen soll. Es wird erwartet, dass die Schülerinnen und Schüler selbstständig Texte verfassen, die adressatengerecht und sinnvoll strukturiert sein sollen. Die Abiturklausur wird aus einer großen Bandbreite möglicher Themen ausgewählt, die sich auf fachliche oder auch persönliche Fragestellungen beziehen können. Hierbei müssen Planungsstrategien, beispielsweise die Mindmap, ebenso bekannt sein wie Vorgehensweisen zur Gliederung, Bearbeitung und kritischen Beurteilung der eigenen Texte. Die Grundlage der schriftlichen Abiturprüfung können auch sogenannte mehrfach kodierte Texte sein. Hierzu zählen zum Beispiel Karikaturen, Bilder, Statistiken oder Diagramme.

Auf die Bewertung der sprachlichen Leistung im Rahmen der sogenannten **Integrativen Sprachentwicklung** wird später noch eingegangen (s. S. 131).

Beispielaufgabe Mediation

You and your English exchange partner have seen Baz Luhrmann's film *Romeo and Juliet* (1996). Your friends want to know how the film was received in Germany. You found the review printed below. Write an e-mail of not more than 250 words to your exchange partner summarizing in English the most important aspects of the review.

„Romeo und Julia“-Kritik – Shakespeare in modernem Gewand

[...] Wenn man sich mit den prägendsten und bekanntesten Personen der Weltliteratur beschäftigten will, dann stößt man auf die üblich Verdächtigen, was in diesem Fall jedoch in keiner Weise negativ gemeint ist, denn hier besteht die Ausnahme, das Popularität wirklich gleichbedeutend mit Qualität ist. Wir sprechen also von Menschen wie Johann Wolfgang von Goethe, Friedrich Schiller, Lord Byron, Edgar Allan Poe, Charles Baudelaire und John Keats. Männer, deren Ruf als Dramatiker, Philosophen, Lyriker, Dichter, Denker oder ganz einfach Autoren auf der ganzen Welt zu Recht bekannt ist. Jedoch wurde eine Person bewusst noch nicht genannt. Eine Meister, dessen Name und Werke überall ein Begriff sind, selbst wenn man sie nie gelesen hat. Die Rede kann natürlich nur vom Engländer William Shakespeare sein, und wenn man an Shakespeare denkt, dann kommt einem auch unweigerlich seine frühe Tragödie „Romeo und Julia“, geschrieben 1597, in den Sinn. Aber wen interessieren nun, aus der Sicht der Filmwelt, noch die Verfilmungen von Shakespeare? Wahrscheinlich nur die Literaturfanatiker und Shakespeare-Fans, doch auch die sehen der unzähligsten Verfilmung inzwischen schon mit einem genervten und gelangweilten Blick entgegen. Was muss ein Regisseur also tun, um den Stoff wieder massentauglich zu machen? Baz Luhrmann hat mit seiner „Romeo & Julia“-Interpretation im Jahre 1996 einen mehr als ansprechenden Weg gefunden.

Die Geschichte rund um die beiden Liebenden sollte ja bekannt sein, deswegen darf die Inhaltsangabe in diesem Fall ruhig etwas knapper ausfallen. Es ist Liebe auf den ersten Blick, so viel steht fest, als Romeo und Julia sich das erste Mal in die Augen sehen und gegenseitig ihre Herzen verschenken. Das Problem dabei ist nur, das Julia der Familie Capulet angehört und Romeo den Namen Montague trägt. Diese beiden Familien sind verfeindet und eine offene Liebe wäre unmöglich. Doch auch wenn es Unterstützer gibt, ist das nicht zu schaffen und die verbotene Liebe wird immer weiter aufgedeckt. Es kommt zur Katastrophe, in der Romeos Freund Mercutio und Julias Cousin Tybalt verwickelt sind. Die Folge bedeutet Verbannung für Romeo, und Julia steckt mitten in der aufgezwungenen Hochzeit mit Paris, den ihre Eltern für sie bestimmt haben. Doch das ist noch lange nicht das Ende der problematischen Liebe und es soll noch viel schlimmer werden ...

Der interessanteste Aspekt ist die Aufmachung des Films. Luhrmann hat das Setting, die Kulissen und den äußeren Ton vollkommen in die Moderne verlegt. Wir finden uns in der fiktiven amerikanischen Küstenstadt Verona Beach wieder. Die Sonne brennt, die Stadt ist schmutzig und die brodelnden Schwingungen, ob der Gewalt oder Liebe wegen, liegen standhaft in der Luft. Luhrmann entfernt sich von jeder Altertümlichkeit und der frische Stil weiß in seiner Ungewöhnlichkeit voll zu überzeugen. Kameramann McAlpine hält das Geschehen in knallbunten Fotografien fest und lässt den Film nicht selten, auch dank seiner schnellen Schnitte und Überzogenheit, wie ein typischen Musikvideo aussehen, wobei dabei auch der gemischte Soundtrack seinen Teil zu dem Eindruck beiträgt, denn der Mix aus Rock, Pop und kraftvoller Oper ist schon eine Sache für sich, mit der man sich natürlich erst mal anfreunden muss. Schauspielerisch wurden dementsprechend auch reine und unverbrauchte Gesichter gesucht, die genau in die neue Form passen. Mit Leonardo DiCaprio als Romeo hat man schon einmal den richtigen Schauspieler auf der männlichen Seite und auch Julia wurde mit Claire Danes passend besetzt. Dabei kommt es gar nicht unbedingt auf das Schauspiel selbst an, sondern auf die Harmonie zwischen Danes und DiCaprio, und die ist durchgängig so glaubwürdig, dass man ihnen die Gefühle einfach abkauft. [...]

https://cinemaforever.net/romeo-julia-usa-1996-kritik-william-shakespeare-modernem-gewand/

Beispiellösung

Dear Mike,

In your last e-mail you wanted me to tell you what German audiences think about the 1996 film version of "Romeo and Juliet". I managed to find a suitable film review on the Internet which represents the general attitude quite well.

The author points out that Shakespeare is one of the most outstanding writers in world literature, even though most people have never read any of his plays. Still, everyone has, at least, heard of "Romeo and Juliet", which he wrote around 1597. Since the plot of this tragedy is so well-known, nobody is really interested in yet another film version of the family feud with its tragic ending. That's why Baz Luhrmann interpreted Shakespeare's play in a completely new way - and with considerable success. He did, of course, keep the story line the same. Romeo and Juliet, members of rivalling Montague and Capulet families of Verona, fall in love at first sight, but their forbidden love inevitably leads to catastrophe.

There are, however, differences compared to other movies dealing with Shakespeare's drama, and this 1996 version has a refreshing effect on the cinemagoer. In Luhrmann's adaptation the action is not set in Italy but in a fictitious, hot and dirty American town called Verona Beach. The soundtrack is a composition of rock, pop and opera, which takes some getting used to. The cameraman, McAlpine, uses fast cuts and colourful photographs to make the film look like a music video. The chemistry between the actors seems perfect. They act their roles in remarkable harmony.

I wonder whether you agree with the author of this review. I would really appreciate it if you could let me know what people in Britain think about the film.

I'm looking forward to hearing from you soon.

Love

Valerie

Bewertung für die Aufgabe zur Sprachmittlung

Diese Übersicht ist ein Auszug aus der Bewertungskala des Niedersächsischen Kultusministeriums.[5]

Punkte	Sprache (60%)	Inhalt (40%)
15–13 P.	Die Zielsprache wird nahezu durchgängig korrekt und treffsicher verwendet: Geringfügige sprachliche Mängel beeinträchtigen die Verständlichkeit nicht. Thematischer und funktionaler Wortschatz werden idiomatisch und treffend verwendet. Die Darstellung enthält alle durch die Aufgaben geforderten charakteristischen Textmerkmale. Bei der Gestaltung des Textes werden die sprachlichen Anforderungen der Situations- und Adressatenorientierung nahezu vollständig umgesetzt.	Alle Aspekte der Aufgabenstellung werden beachtet. Alle im Sinne der Aufgabenstellung wichtigen Informationen werden präzise und situations- bzw. adressatenorientiert wiedergegeben. Ggf. werden relevante kulturspezifische Erläuterungen präzise formuliert, wie z. B die Erklärung von Eigennamen oder kultur-spezifischen Begriffen. Die Darstellung und die Gliederung sind klar und logisch.
06–04 P.	Die Zielsprache wird in Teilen korrekt verwendet: Die sprachlichen Erfordernisse der Aufgabenstellung werden teilweise beachtet und umgesetzt. Zahlreiche Mängel beeinträchtigen die Verständlichkeit so, dass einzelne Aussagen nicht erfassbar sind. Thematischer und funktionaler Wortschatz werden nur lückenhaft verwendet. Die Darstellung enthält wenige durch die Aufgabenstellung geforderte charakteristische Textmerkmale. Bei der Gestaltung des Textes werden die sprachlichen Anforderungen der Situations- und Adressatenorientierung in Teilen korrekt umgesetzt.	Die Aspekte der Aufgabenstellung werden teilweise beachtet. Wenige im Sinne der Aufgabenstellung wesentlichen Informationen werden wiedergegeben; der Situations- bzw. Adressatenbezug wird nur ansatzweise beachtet. Die Darstellung und die Gliederung sind in Ansätzen logisch und zusammenhängend.

5 Niedersächsisches Kultusministerium, ANLAGE 1 Bewertungsskala Sprachmittlung Erlass vom 02.11.2015 – 33-82102-03/15 i. d. F. vom 16.2.2017

Verknüpfung der Themenfelder und Lektüren

Die curricularen Vorgaben für die Oberstufe sehen die Behandlung von **verpflichtenden Themenfeldern** vor, die im jeweiligen Abiturdurchgang durch verpflichtend zu behandelnde Materialien ergänzt werden. Die verpflichtenden Materialien sollen vor einem thematisch breiteren Hintergrund erarbeitet und in diesen eingebettet werden. Die folgende Übersicht hilft, dies zu veranschaulichen.

Verbindliche Themenfelder für 2022

Auf alle genannten Themenfelder muss im Laufe der vier Semester eingegangen werden. Aufgrund von Corona wurde für das Abitur 2022 entschieden, für das Fach Englisch der Behandlung der verbindlichen Materialien sowie der verbindlichen Unterrichtsaspekte Vorrang vor der Behandlung weiterer Themen der Themenfelder zu geben.

Beliefs, values and norms in society: Tradition and change • Britishness • the American Experience • postcolonial/neo-colonial experiences • migration effects on the world of work	**Individual and society** • identity • ethnic, cultural and linguistic diversity • gender and sexual diversity	**Globalisation** • effects on the world of work • impact on personal lives • global responsibility concerning e. g. politics, the environment, economy • English as a global language
Erhöhtes Niveau (eA) **Shakespeare** • the world that made him • modern adaptations	**Die Lektüren/ Materialien müssen mit diesen Themen verknüpft werden.**	**Science and technology** • chances and risks • visions of the future • the media, e. g. the influence of the media on public opinion and personal life • the digital revolution

Das Curriculum ist vor allem auf eine Vernetzung der Themen ausgelegt, wie sie sich durch die jeweiligen literarischen Texte, Sachtexte, Songs, Filme oder Dokumentationen ergibt. Im Folgenden werden die verbindlichen Texte für den Abiturdurchgang 2022 aufgelistet und thematisch verortet, sodass Sie in der Lage sind, die sich anbietenden Vernetzungen nachzuvollziehen. Die jeweiligen Niveaustufen werden mit gA (grundlegendes) und eA (erhöhtes) Anforderungsniveau abgekürzt.

Verbindliche Materialien 2022

Die Reihenfolge, in der die Materialien behandelt werden, ist nicht festgelegt. Auch gibt es keine feste inhaltliche Bindung der Lektüren an die Themenfelder. Die hier genannten Verknüpfungen sind daher nur Vorschläge.

Material	**inhaltliche Schwerpunkte**	**thematische Verknüpfungen**
Roman: Sindiwe Magona, *Mother to Mother*	*apartheid in South Africa, ethnic and cultural diversity, justice, personal guilt and accountability*	Individual and society Beliefs, values and norms in society
Short Story: Andrea Levy, “Loose Change” (2005)	*belonging and identity, post-colonial experience, ethnic and cultural diversity*	Beliefs, values and norms in society Individual and society
Short Story: Shereen Pandit, “She Shall Not Be Moved” (2005)	*belonging and identity, post-colonial experience, ethnic and cultural diversity, racism*	Beliefs, values and norms in society Individual and society Globalisation
Film: *Gran Torino*	*search for values and beliefs, personal life and happiness, second generation immigrants, gang culture in the USA, violence, cultural clashes*	Individual and society Beliefs, values and norms in society Globalisation
zusätzlich für erhöhtes Anforderungsniveau		
Short Story: Jhumpa Lahiri, “The Third and Final Continent” (1999)	*belonging and identity, displacement, post-colonial experience, ethnic and cultural diversity, migration*	Beliefs, values and norms in society Individual and society Globalisation
Short Story: Qaisra Shahraz, “The Escape” (2009)	*belonging and identity, displacement, post-colonial experience, ethnic and cultural diversity*	Individual and society Globalisation Beliefs, values and norms in society

Drama: William Shakespeare: *Richard III*, dazu Film: "Richard III" (Richard Loncraine 2012)	*the pursuit of power, the role(s) of women, fate vs. free will*	Shakespeare
		Individual and society
Roman: Mary Shelley, *Frankenstein* (1831)	*ethics of science, the role of nature, dreams of happiness, questions of human identity*	Individual and society
		Science and technology

Hinweis

Die Lektüren werden in diesem Band an der Stelle thematisiert, an der sie inhaltlich am naheliegendsten zu verorten sind. Grundsätzlich bietet jedes der Materialien verschiedene Zugangsmöglichkeiten an, sodass es unter unterschiedlichen Gesichtspunkten behandelt werden kann. Dies wird im Folgenden exemplarisch verdeutlicht.

Beispielhafte Verortung von Materialien

Anhand des folgenden Beispiels soll deutlich werden, dass keines der Materialien nur einen einzigen thematischen Zugang zulässt, sondern vielmehr vielseitige Diskussions- und Interpretationsanlässe eröffnet. Allen Materialien ist gemein, dass sie interkulturelles Verständnis und das Bewusstsein für globale Probleme schärfen können. Diese übergeordnete Betrachtung der Texte und Filme bildet den Schwerpunkt in diesem Band. Eine inhaltlich detaillierte Thematisierung der Materialien erfolgt im Unterricht und kann mithilfe von Sekundärliteratur oder Informationen aus dem Internet vertieft werden. Hier soll in erster Linie der Blick für den größeren Zusammenhang geschärft werden, in dem die Texte zu verorten sind.

Material	Mögliche thematische Erarbeitung
Film: ***Gran Torino*** (gA + eA) Grundlegende Kenntnisse zum Verständnis des Films: – individual and society	**Individual and society:** Der Film *Gran Torino* (2008, Regie Clint Eastwood) spielt in einer vom wirtschaftlichen Niedergang gezeichneten Vorstadtsiedlung in Detroit. Der Hauptfiguren sind der US-amerikanische Koreakriegsveteran Walt Kowalski, ein ehemaliger Ford-Mitarbeiter, der ein von rassistischen Vorurteilen geprägtes Weltbild pflegt und Thao, der zu den aus Südostasien eingewanderten Hmong in seiner Nachbarschaft gehört. Im Verlauf des Films entwickelt sich der rassistische Walt Kowalski zu einem ungewollten Helden, der auf seine Art Thao als Vaterfigur dient und ihm letztlich bei der Identitätsfindung und Integration in die US-amerikanische Gesellschaft hilft.

	Walt Kowalskis ganzer Stolz gilt seinem 1972er Ford Gran Torino, der der letzte Beweis für die einst blühende Wirtschaft und das gute Leben in Detroit ist. Als Thao im Rahmen eines Initiationsritus versucht, den Wagen zu stehen, kann Walt Kowalski dies mit Waffengewalt verhindern. Später setzt er auch auf Waffengewalt, um Thao und seine Familie vor einer Gang zu schützen. Walt Kowalski lässt während der Filmhandlung zwar nicht vom Waffengebrauch ab, aber sein Verhalten gegenüber Thao, der die bisher von Walt Kowalski verachteten „Schlitzaugen" symbolisiert, wandelt sich zum unterstützenden „Helfer".
– beliefs and values – cultural and ethnic diversity – the role of gang culture and violence	**Beliefs, values and norms in society:** Der Katholik Walt Kowalski übt seinen Glauben nicht aktiv aus und lässt Pater Janovich dies auch unmissverständlich spüren. Erst zum Ende des Films geht Walt zum Pater, um die Beichte abzulegen. Er tut dies, weil er seinen Tod plant. Dass er einen Maßanzug bei seinem Tod trägt, zeigt, dass er trotz aller Rauigkeit doch an gesellschaftlichen Wertvorstellungen festhält. Sein gewaltsamer Tod durch die von ihm provozierte Schießerei der Vorstadt-Gang, die Thaos Familie und das Viertel tyrannisiert, lässt sich als Sühne für seine Schuld, die er am Tod eines koreanischen Teenagers trägt, deuten.
– globalisation	**Globalisation** Themenbereiche der Globalisierung lassen sich in den Aspekten der Auswirkungen des Koreakrieges und der Wirtschaftskrise von 2008 finden. Die Teilnahme Walt Kowalskis am Koreakrieg und seine ihn prägenden Eindrücke wie das ihn plagende Schuldgefühl, eine am Kriegsgeschehen unbeteiligte koreanische Jugendliche getötet zu haben, sowie die Auswirkungen für die pro-amerikanischen Hmong sind Folgen der globalen Vernetzung. Die ethnische Gruppe der Hmong, die auf Seiten der US-Amerikaner gegen Nordvietnam gekämpft hatten, fanden Zuflucht in den USA, wo sie oftmals Ausgrenzung erfuhren. Die Wirtschaftskrise von 2008 traf Detroit, zuvor ein industrieller Ankerpunkt der US-amerikanischen Autoproduktion, hart. Massenentlassungen und Rückbau der Automobilproduktion erfolgten, was den wirtschaftlichen und sozialen Niedergang der Region bewirkte.

Basiswissen

Das folgende Kapitel gibt einen Überblick über die curricularen Themenfelder des Oberstufenunterrichts ohne konkrete Semesterzuordnung. Das Ziel dieses Vorgehens ist es, einen Gesamtüberblick über die inhaltlichen Kenntnisse zu bieten, die im Zentralabitur z. B. auch für Hörverstehen und Mediation vorausgesetzt werden. An geeigneten Stellen wird darauf hingewiesen, wie die verbindlichen Lektüren thematisch im größeren Kontext verortet werden können. Die Zuordnung in fünf große Themenfelder entspricht den Vorgaben für das Abitur 2022 (s. S. 14). Fast alle Unterkapitel in diesem Buch entsprechen dem geforderten Basiswissen für beide Jahrgänge. Darüber hinaus wird auf weitere Lektüren, Filme und andere Materialien hingewiesen, die in vorherigen Abiturdurchgängen relevant waren und/oder sich als „Klassiker" zur näheren Auseinandersetzung mit dem Thema eignen.

Beliefs, Values and Norms in Society

Britishness

People outside of Britain often refer to the British as the English – two terms which are often falsely regarded as being synonymous. This stereotypical perception may have its roots in the history of the British Isles as well as the history of the British Empire. Here, the dominance of English culture can certainly still be seen. In the following chapter a general overview will be given with regard to the correct terms to use when speaking of "the British" as well as the main cultural values and norms which have shaped British society.

Common Stereotypes

British people, but in particular the English, are considered to be well-mannered and polite. A common example named in this context is that British people apologize both when they accidentally run into someone and when they are run into. The British are also renowned for their sense of irony and for their small talk which they usually begin by talking about the weather, especially when they meet someone they don't know. Some consider the English to be snobbish and arrogant, but also very hospitable. Both the British and the Irish are famous for their pub culture. More stereotypes could be listed, but being what they are – clichés – all of them must be carefully examined.

TIPP Further reading

The peculiar ways of the English are humorously depicted in *Watching the English* by Kate Fox (2004), a sociological approach to (stereo-)typical English behaviour and "Englishness".

Geographical and Political Distinctions

There are several phrases commonly used to refer to the English-speaking area in Europe. They are explained here.

- **Great Britain:** refers to the main island including England, Scotland and Wales;
- **The United Kingdom** (of Great Britain and Northern Ireland): the political term meaning England, Scotland, Wales and Northern Ireland; the terms "Britons" and "The British" are commonly used synonymously to describe the nation and its people;
- **Scotland, Wales and Northern Ireland** were and are centrally governed by London, but have all gained rights of self-government (S & W: 1999, NI: 2006);
- the **Republic of Ireland:** independent from the United Kingdom since 1921; as a result of the independence treaty, the island of Ireland was divided into Northern Ireland (which still belongs to the UK) and the Republic of Ireland.

English Cultural Dominance and its Historical Roots

- The **name "England"** is derived from the Angles, a Germanic tribe which settled the island during the 5th and 6th centuries.
- On the island of Great Britain, England gained dominance over Welsh and Scottish territories, which had been settled by Celtic tribes; over the centuries, all three parts of Great Britain became a political union which still bears traits of its cultural diversity (this can be observed in language, cultural heritage and political concessions).
- At the beginning of the 16th century, England gained world-wide influence during the **Age of Discoveries:** English merchants followed the great explorers; English settlers founded colonies in North America and other newly-discovered parts of the world, while the British East India Company set out to exploit the wealth of the newly established Asian colonies economically.
- The growing territorial expansion during the 16th and 17th centuries led to the development of the **British Empire,** which – at its height – included approximately one quarter of the world's land.
- The Empire lost its influence as the former colonies began to seek independence.
- The earliest colonies to obtain independence from Britain were the thirteen northern American colonies, which in 1776 formed the United States of America.
- During the 19th and 20th centuries most of the other colonies gained independence by peaceful or violent means (the most important ones being India, South Africa, Australia and the Republic of Ireland); some former colonies joined the Commonwealth of Nations – an organisation which promotes trade and cultural relations between its members.

Because of the long history of Britain as the world's ruling colonial power, British culture has influenced societies worldwide. Its cultural effects can be observed in many nations: Australia recognizes Queen Elizabeth as Queen of Australia, represented by the Govenor-General; driving on the left is the rule in many former colonies and many still use English as their official language, etc.

Democracy and Monarchy

Despite being a monarchy, the United Kingdom has a long history of parliamentary structures (first attempts to assert popular power date back to the Magna Carta of 1215 and the Bill of Rights of 1689). Britain has no written constitution, and its legislature is based on laws passed by parliament. Parliamentary sovereignty is the leading norm and the monarch no longer plays an active role in legislative processes. Parliament constitutionally consists of the Crown (the monarch formally heads Parliament), the House of Lords (the aristocracy) and the House of Commons. Parliament, however, is controlled by the Prime Minister and his or her cabinet. The Prime Minister and his or her government have gained the executive powers of the monarch and act in his/her name.

The Issue of Class

Britain is considered to be an extremely class-conscious society. The definition of "class" can very generally be put as a distinction in social standing which developed in feudal times and became more diversified during the Industrial Revolution. Social differences can be defined in terms of heritage (aristocratic vs. common birth), educational, professional and financial standing. Class distinctions into upper, middle, lower and, since the Thatcher Era of the 1980s, a new upper and an underclass, have their origins in the emergence of new working and entrepreneur classes during the Industrial Revolution.

The British class system is no longer "closed", meaning that it offers chances for upward or downward movement (social mobility). Education or professional success allows members of lower classes to move upwards on the metaphorical "social ladder". Thus, people are no longer bound to the class they were born into.
Class is generally associated with certain stereotypical traits. The various classes differ with regard to habits and attitudes, as can be observed in everyday life, for instance, in where people live, what they eat, the way they dress, spend their free time, which newspapers they read and which TV programmes they watch, which schools their children attend, the vocabulary they use and what accent they speak with. British people are very aware of these class differences.
Class differences are most easily observed in the British educational system, which is still divided into public schools (which in fact means "private") and state schools. British public schools control admission by means of tuition fees and application procedures, but grants and scholarships can be applied for. Attending one of these schools is still to some extent a requirement for admission to the so-called "Oxbridge" universities. Thus social mobility is essentially a matter of financial and educational background.

Britain and the EU

The UK was a member of the EU from 1973 to 2020, but during this period the scepticism of certain political and public circles towards Europe never ceased.
On June 23, 2016 a referendum was held about Britain's membership in the EU: 51.9% voted to leave the EU, 48.1% to remain. The UK finally left the EU after long and complex negotiations on January 31, 2020. Brexit is the UK's attempt to break free from unwanted EU rules and regulations in order to re-establish national sovereignty. Its supporters hope the UK will shed what they see as its EU-regulated and hampered shell in order to negotiate free trade agreements with other countries that will provide it with a better economic and social future.
Others fear that there will be significant economic drawbacks, as the UK is no longer a member of the European single market. This may lead to higher prices of goods on both sides of the Channel, despite the new EU-UK Trade and Cooperation Agreement. Another problem is the question of Northern Ireland. The Republic of Ireland is still part of the EU, but the Brexit deal avoids a "hard border" between the Republic and the Six Counties of Northern Ireland and establishes a de facto customs border between the two islands. This is a major problem for the anti-EU Protestants in Northern Ireland. Peace-threatening conflicts between certain elements in the Republic of Ireland and Northern Ireland have rekindled, though such conflicts had been settled by the Good Friday Agreement in 1998. Brexit has partially aroused feelings of insecurity in Northern Ireland concerning its future. A well-wrought solution to Northern Ireland's special situation is yet to come.
In the Brexit referendum Scotland voted with a significant majority to "remain". Some politicians – and many Scottish people – would now like a second referendum on Scottish independence: i. e. to leave the UK in order eventually to rejoin the EU. This is unlikely, however, to be agreed by the present government in London.
In the course of time, Brexit may turn out to be a success story, but the people's will in the referendum vote was strongly influenced by populist politicians. Many British people do not like the new regulations and consequences of Brexit, as they bring changes for the worse, such as visa requirements, export restrictions, reduced research funding, or the UK's withdrawal from the Erasmus study program.

Internationally, Britain has established a strong connection with US foreign policies (for years it has been engaged both in Afghanistan and Iraq), which partly results from its alliance with America during the Second World War and the subsequent formation of NATO. However, unlike former American administrations, which often regarded the United Nations as a weak institution, Britain regards the UN as an important framework for promoting international foreign policy. Like the United States, Britain is a permanent member of the UN Security Council.

Glossary of Common Political Terms (BE)

administration	Verwaltung (im AE auch: Regierung)
Act (of Parliament)	(verabschiedetes) Gesetz
bill	Gesetzesvorlage
chamber	Kammer (z. B. House of Commons)
checks and balances	Gewaltenteilung (in der Politik)
constituency	Wahlkreis
constituent	Wähler
domestic/foreign policy	Innen-/Außenpolitik
Foreign/Home Secretary	Außen-, Innenminister
election	Wahl
electorate	Wählerschaft
representative	hier: Volksvertreter
MP (Member of Parliament)	Abgeordneter
Speaker	Vorsitzender des Unterhauses
(hereditary, life) peer	(erbliches, lebenslanges) Mitglied des Oberhauses
in office	im Amt
to hold office; to take office	amtieren; ein Amt antreten
to stand down	zurücktreten
universal suffrage	allgemeines Wahlrecht

The American Experience

The United States of America came into being as a reaction to a lack of political influence. As colonies of the British Empire, the original thirteen states, which had been settled by British citizens, had to pay taxes to the motherland. Yet their interests were not represented in parliament; hence the famous slogan "No taxation without representation." Instead of granting their overseas citizens a say in their own affairs, the British crown continued to impose taxes, which led to several uprisings that eventually turned into outright war between the colonies and their motherland. The imbalance of power led the American settlers to declare their independence in 1776. The famous document, originally written by Thomas Jefferson and signed by representatives of the American people (today called the "Founding Fathers"), questioned the rights of the British King, George III, and included the following statement, which would later become the basis of democratic thought and popular emancipation from the ruling aristocracy: "We hold these truths to be self-evident, that all men are created equal, that they are endowed by their Creator with certain unalienable Rights, that among these are Life, Liberty and the pursuit of Happiness."

This concept of equality and equal opportunities became the key to America's later self-perception and national identity and led the US to emerge from the War of Independence (1771–1776) as the world's first modern democracy. In its time (and long before the French Revolution), the concept of equality, as expressed in these lines, was revolutionary.

The American Constitution

- written in 1787
- new ideas of a democratic state stated in the **preamble** of the constitution: "We the People of the United States, in Order to form a more perfect Union[5], establish Justice, ensure domestic Tranquility, provide for the common defense, promote the general Welfare, and secure the Blessings of Liberty to ourselves and our Posterity, do ordain and establish this Constitution for the United States of America."

The Bill of Rights

- the first ten amendments to the American Constitution
- written because some delegates feared that the new American government would threaten everyone's chance of achieving personal freedom and the pursuit of happiness
- The First Congress of the United States originally proposed twelve amendments in 1789, ten of which were added to the constitution as a preamble
- amendments known as the Bill of Rights
- guarantee America's citizens certain unalienable rights, e.g. freedom of religion, freedom of speech and the press as well as the right to bear arms

The American Dream/American Nightmare

The American Dream:

There is no single definition of what the American Dream actually is, as it varies for each and every American. The term was first used by James Truslow Adams, an American historian, in his book *The Epic of America*, in 1931: "[The] American Dream [is] the dream of a land in which life should be better and richer and fuller for every man with opportunity for each according to his ability or achievement."

In order to understand how people who had grown up in a monarchy and were used to being subjects of a king or queen could come to the conclusion that they possessed equal rights, one must consider the motives which led the early settlers to leave Britain.

5 Barack Obama took up the idea of "a more perfect union" in a speech he delivered on May 28, 2008, in which he elaborated on the issues of race and inequality in the USA.

The Puritans, religious values, New Canaan

- The first English settlers to arrive on American soil were religious outcasts, Protestants who had wanted to cleanse the Anglican Church from remaining Roman Catholic influence. These **Puritans**, as they called themselves, were persecuted in England and thus left for the colonies. Other religious sects like the Quakers, Baptists and Methodists followed.
- September 1620: a group of 102 people left England for America, sailed on a ship called the Mayflower, which arrived 65 days later in a bay they called Plymouth Bay.
- Between 1620 and 1640 thousands of Puritans emigrated to New England and founded the first settlements in Plymouth and Massachusetts Bay. To them America was God's promised land, a **"New Canaan"**, a reference to the biblical country to which Moses led his people to free them from slavery in Egypt. In America the Puritans hoped they would be able to follow their religious beliefs and live freely.
- Puritan values such as integrity, virtue, the right to education, individual freedom and communitarianism still constitute central aspects of American self-perception.
- At the same time, the Puritans imposed strict moral rules on their communities and today Puritan is a term associated with extreme conservatism and prudishness.

American values and beliefs

The key to the image of the United States as the country of unlimited opportunities, where each and every person can turn from "dishwasher to millionaire", from rags to riches, lies in these early visions of individual freedom, opportunity and self-reliance which led millions to emigrate to the former British colonies. These ideals shape the American Dream, which is not one single concept, but a combination of individual goals and general values.

- **Individualism/self-reliance:** The underlying belief is that everyone is responsible for their own fate and has the liberty to determine their way of life.
- **Opportunity:** If a person is given the chance to take matters into his or her own hands, he or she will prosper. If that person fails, however, he or she has not worked hard enough.
- **Freedom:** This has two faces. On the one hand, it allows all individuals to pursue their own vision of happiness without being controlled by a central government. On the other, this belief also led to a general scepticism towards any kind of federal interference in individual affairs. Even today, Americans still tend to be sceptical of decisions made by the central administration in Washington D.C., suspecting it of limiting their communal, state or personal rights.
- **Community:** Individual hardships such as unemployment are seen as personal failures, yet the local communities readily offer help to those in need. Because of this communal spirit, federal programs of social welfare and common health care often meet with opposition as they are seen as an intrusion into personal rights.

The American Dream is still alive, and each year many people come to the United States to pursue it, although the number of people able to obtain a "green card" has always been limited and many immigrants today arrive illegally. After the original settlement period, the main waves of immigration entered the US between the middle of the 19th until the beginning of the 20th century, when the United States was in need of workers and a sufficient number of people to settle new territories in the west. Millions of mostly European immigrants arrived at Ellis Island, New York, were inspected and continued on to the city of New York and later to places across the entire country. German immigrants, for example, settled mostly in the Midwest, as can still be observed when looking at city names on a map.
The first thing many immigrants saw when they came by ship to New York City during the 19th and the first half of the 20th century, was the Statue of Liberty, which is located on Liberty Island.

The Statue of Liberty

- given to the USA as a gift by France in 1886 to celebrate the first 100 years of American independence from Britain (the centennial)
- a robed woman, holding a lighted torch in her right and a tablet in her left hand, showing the date of the Declaration of Independence (July 4, 1776)
- underneath her right foot the remains of broken shackles can be seen
- one of the most famous American icons, symbolizing enlightenment, independence, liberty and freedom
- the theme of Emma Lazarus's famous poem "The New Colossus" (1883), which can be seen on a bronze plaque inside the statue

Ellis Island

- the place where most immigrants first set foot on American soil
- an island of hopes but also an island of tears for a number of immigrants, as some of them were detained there for legal or medical reasons or even sent back to their home countries; for the majority the gateway to a new – better – life
- a federal immigration station from 1892 to 1954

The American Dream today

- The American Dream itself has come to be seen more critically.
- A considerable number of critics regard the American Dream as an illusion, as not everyone has access to the opportunities usually associated with it.
- Examples of American nightmares include the Vietnam War, September 11, 2001, and the financial crisis starting in 2008.

The Frontier Experience

Since its independence in 1776 the country had continually acquired larger territories to the west. To put it simply, both the Pacific and the Atlantic coast had been settled and explored, yet the middle of the vast continent was still mostly open territory which remained unknown. The fringe between the settled and unknown territories, more commonly called the "Wild West", not only refers to the geographical border between wilderness and civilization, but also to the social and political aspects which characterized these areas.

The **westward movement** of the early settlers was not a federally organized enterprise. Instead, the federal government simply assigned the right to obtain land in the west to people who were willing to take on the challenge of discovering these unknown lands. While the **pioneers** moved westward in covered wagons, law enforcement and legal order were slow to follow. This left the frontier zone both in a state of lawlessness and unlimited opportunity for anyone willing to take the risk of entering a region inhabited only by Indians.

Essential text – The Turner Thesis (1893):

Frederick Jackson Turner defined the "frontier experience" as the key which determined the American belief in freedom and unlimited opportunities. The abundance of land in the west and the experience of unlimited space provided the psychological basis for the American conviction that anything can be achieved. Once the west had been explored, the U.S. sought to overcome new frontiers. Thus, the frontier experience was later also considered an explanation for American endeavours to overcome frontiers in a much broader sense (be it in areas of technological advancement or by landing on the moon).

Manifest Destiny

The term "Manifest Destiny" was coined by the American journalist John L. O'Sullivan in 1839.

- stands for the belief that America is the one nation ordained by God to expand across the North American continent
- according to John L. O'Sullivan: "[America is] the nation of progress, of individual freedom, of universal enfranchisement." According to him the American people had been chosen "… to establish on earth the moral dignity and salvation of man – the immutable truth and beneficence of God."[5]
- America = a country that is superior to all other countries
- stresses the virtue of the American people, as they are the ones to establish moral rules and values across the globe. American patriotism is deeply rooted in the concept of "Manifest Destiny".
  A picture that illustrates the idea of the "Manifest Destiny" is the allegorical representation of the new west in the painting *The American Progress* by John Gast (1872).

5 from: "The Great Nation of Futurity," *The United States Democratic Review,* Volume 6, Issue 23, pp. 426 – 430.

Gran Torino (film, gA, eA)

Directed by Clint Eastwood, the film Gran Torino was released in 2008, at the beginning of a major financial crisis which brought dramatic changes in economies worldwide. Banks collapsed and people lost their homes, jobs and hope. The film is set in a run-down part of Detroit, once the proud and wealthy centre of the U.S. motor industry, now dominated by poverty and shattered dreams.
The protagonist of the film, Walt Kowalski, a disillusioned, racist veteran of the Korean War, is played by Eastwood himself. After the death of his wife, Walt has become an outsider in his part of town. The sole object of his pride is his Gran Torino, a big 'muscle car', built at the beginning of the 1970s when Walt still worked at the Ford Motor Company in Detroit. Walt is a Catholic, but does not go to church any more. His neighbours, a family of Asian immigrants, belong to the ethnic group of the Hmong. Walt despises these people, but when the son of the family, Thao, tries to steal Walt's car because he is under pressure from a gang, Walt resolves to help the boy. He also helps Thao's sister Sue against three young men. The family is so grateful and friendly that Walt reluctantly begins to change his behaviour towards them. He becomes a friend and father figure to Thao. When the family is attacked by the gang and Thao and Sue are injured, the victims do not go to the police (there are no witnesses). Thao wants revenge, but Walt wants to prevent Thao from becoming a killer. Walt himself faces the gang unarmed, provokes them and gets shot, sacrificing himself in order to protect the family. He leaves his Gran Torino to Thao.
Eastwood weaves several complex topics into a moving story: migration, racism, gang culture and violence, war trauma, a dying city and culture, the loss of religious beliefs and the collapse of the American Dream on the one hand, and an individual's alternative to growing racism, hatred and isolation on the other.

Main Characters and their Profiles

In the following the three main characters are described with 10 adjectives to give you a short yet descriptive overview of their personality.

Walt	lonely, conservative, masculine, racist, self-reliant, practical, conscience-stricken, determined, considerate, caring
Thao	insecure, soft, torn, lost, weak, a push-over, persistent, willing, self-confident, positive
Sue	strong, assimilated, friendly, self-confident, open, considerate, courageous, intelligent, emancipated

Background information

Motor city ("Motown") Detroit – from boom to bust

Several factors led to Detroit's fate and its fall from being "motor city" to a broken shell of its former glory. (cf. https://archive.nytimes.com/www.nytimes.com/interactive/2013/08/17/us/detroit-decline.html)

reliance on single industry	– by 1950, the population figures had reached almost 1.85 million – the Big Three auto companies: Ford, General Motors and Chrysler attracted many workers – decentralization halted the boom: strikes led by the unions, the refusal by blacks and whites to work side by side – automation (replacing assembly-line jobs with machinery) cost tens of thousands of jobs – foreign competition threatened profit – lack of industrial diversity made Detroit suffer more than other cities
racial tension	– 1950: population was 16% black – 1967: population was approx. 33% black – today: population is about 82% black – fear and hatred have remained since the 1967 riots and have hindered growth
failed leadership	– city leaders supposedly involved in corruption, others ignored deep-rooted structural problems (e. g. Coleman A. Young, Kwame M. Kilpatrick)
no efficient transit system	– the focus was on the car industries, investments went into roads and highway construction rather than public transportation – lack of effective connective between class, race, age, etc.
consequences of poverty	– 36% of the population is below the poverty level – fewer taxpaying residents leads to reduced social services – city's unemployment rate is approx.19% – plans to cut pensions – growing gang violence

Angry white men

In the first half of the movie the protagonist Walt Kowalski is shown as a typical "angry white man". This stereotype refers to a group of white males without higher education who were once blue collar workers but face unemployment or minimum wage jobs. Especially in the so called "rust belt" (former industrial region in the north east, covering Ohio, Pennsylvania, Wisconsin and Michigan which was hit hard by the financial crisis in 2008 und suffered economic collapse) many feel abandoned by the government and overwhelmed by the changes that are taking place throughout society. They believe in a strong national identity, the concept of American mascu-

linity as personified by Clint Eastwood as "The man with no name" or "Dirty Harry". Globalization, emancipation, multicultural society and gun control laws are not part of their favoured lifestyle. Instead they direct their anger often towards immigrants, African Americans, homosexuals.
Deindustrialization had a massive negative impact on the lives of the working class (see table on Detroit, above) and their fear of identity loss. Their anger, ignored or underestimated for years, finally led to a wave that carried populist President Donald Trump into the White House in 2016.

Angry white male

A politically reactionary white man, especially from the dispossessed U.S. working classes, who is angry about his (real or imagined) loss of status or position in life: *the simple, knee-jerk reaction of the angry white male ...*

blue-collar mentality

of or relating to wage-earning workers who wear work clothes or other specialized clothing on the job, e.g. mechanics, longshoremen, miners

American masculinity

For many years the concept of American masculinity seemed to consist of the following traits:
- the strong-and-silent type
- being a protector and provider
- being stoical and brave at all times (not expressing emotions)
- using violence to deal with problematic issues

Many "angry white men" still strongly believe in this concept. However, currently there seems to be a crisis with regard to the concept of American masculinity. The ambiguity can be summarized by what Marke Green, executive editor of "The Good Men Project", says about it. He believes that the crisis can only be addressed if society realizes that American culture has turned its masculinity into a "narrow, conformist, violent, bullying version" of itself. (cf. https://goodmenproject.com/featured-content/the-american-man-is-in-crisis-snsw/)

Gran Torino focuses on two very different concepts of masculinity: the old concept as desribed above and a more reflective, caring version with a sense of responsibility for past and present actions.

History of the Hmong

The story of the Hmong people is a tragic story that is seldom openly discussed in the U.S. Here you can find information about their origin and why the Hmong came to the States.

- Who: one of the most recent Asian immigrant groups to come to the USA
- Origin: they originate from the northern mountain regions of Laos
- Why: during the Vietnam War, Hmong villagers fought for America against the North Vietnamese in what has been called a „secret war" in Laos
- after the war, Laos was taken over by Pathet Lao communists
- Hmong were persecuted due to their support of U.S. involvement
- Hmong and other Laotian exiles escaped to Thailand
- Hmong achieved refugee status because of their war efforts on behalf of the U.S., as well as their need to escape the communist regime in Laos

The trauma of war or PTSD = post-traumatic stress disorder

Post-traumatic stress disorder (PTSD)

A condition of enduring anxiety after experiencing – or being close to someone who has experienced – shock, acute danger, or other frightening or threatening ordeals. PTSD can occur in adults or children and is more common in female than male victims of violence. It may be associated with narcotics or alcohol dependency.

Many war veterans suffer from PTSD. War veterans from the Korean War (1950-1953), also known as the "The Forgotten War" or "The Unknown War" because World War II or the Vietnam War overshadowed it, frequently suffer not only from PTSD but also from lack of recognition for what they sacrificed and endured while serving their country.

Background Information and *Gran Torino*

Background Information	*Gran Torino*
Detroit	– Walt worked for the automobile industry – he experienced the better times of Detroit – he is now stuck in a multi-cultural, impoverished neighbourhood – his neighbourhood is being bullied by a gang
angry white man	– first half of the movie: Walt's world has collapsed completely but he refuses to move house – his anger is directed toward his coloured neighbourhood – Walt's racial slur
blue collar mentality	– Walt: used to be hard-working, well-paid member of car industry and proud of his job: still keeps his Gran Torino

American masculinity	– the Grand Torino expresses Walt's masculinity – Walt was a soldier in the Korean War – in the first half Walt represents the typical angry white man, believing in traditional American masculinity – in the second half he represents more progressive traits: being a mentor to Thao – the main traits remain till the end: being protective, brave, solving an issue with violence – Thao represents the opposite: he likes gardening, lets his sister "boss him around" – Thao's journey into American masculinity: gets a job as a constructor (considered typically male), has a girlfriend (dates Youa) and finally inherits Walt's Gran Torino (complete American identity)
the Hmong	– Walt's neighbours are Hmong – culture clash becomes obvious in the first half
PTSD	– Walt fought in the Korean War – he killed 13 people, among them an innocent Korean teenager – most likely suffers from PTSD – his Asian neighbours trigger old memories and guilt

Main themes

family	Walt	– estranged from his own family – his sons show a lack of respect towards him
	Thao and Sue	– part of extensive Hmong family – Thao has a difficult position in his female-dominated family, no male role model
	Walt → Thao	– Walt becomes a father figure for Thao
racism in multicultural society/ cultural clash	Walt	– "white flight" from Highland Park – uses racial slur
	Sue and Thao	– social norm of staying with one's own people (Sue is an exception: she is dating a white boy)
guilt and redemption	Walt	– killed 13 people in the Korean War, among them an innocent teenager – responsible for the spiral of violence and its impact (drive-by shooting, rape) – sacrifices his life in order to atone for past and present guilt

American masculinity	Walt Thao	– stereotype of angry white man – develops another kind of masculinity, although certain traits remain – almost opposite to the concept of American masculinity – is "manned up" by Walt (job, girlfriend, car)
(gun) violence		– Walt has at least two guns – Latino and Hmong gangs use guns

Symbols and motifs

the Gran Torino

- represents conservative American values
- the "muscle car" stresses Walt's (American) masculinity
- symbolizes its owner's status as "outdated model"
- represents the growing bond between Walt and Thao

lighter and silver star medal

- stands for Walt's Korean war experiences
- symbol of his ever-present guilt
- at the end Walt uses the lighter to provoke the gang into shooting him, thus changing the symbol of guilt into one of redemption

cross

- symbol of Walt's salvation

Motif: life and death

- are juxtaposed (funeral vs. birth ceremony, Walt's death vs. peaceful life for Thao and Sue)
- the film is framed by two funerals
- Father Janovich often focuses on "life and death"
- Walt's war experience
- final shootout

dilapidation vs. refurbishment

- street in disrepair symbolises the loss of values and traditions
- Thao's job of refurbishing houses symbolises the gaining of self-confidence
- Thao and Walt working together and helping each other with repairs: symbolises their friendship

The US as a World Power

The United States of America has become the foremost world power after the end of the Cold War with the Soviet Union. Because of once having been a colony ruled by a foreign nation, it chose to stay out of global politics for over a century. Its involvement in two world wars in the first half of the 20th century led to a change in its foreign policy from isolationism to interventionism.

When, after WW II, the US and its allies found themselves in a worldwide struggle for influence and power with the Soviet Union, the American ideal of freedom and democracy turned into an outright ideology opposing the communist system. In 1947, President Truman formulated the so-called **Truman Doctrine,** which would define US foreign policy: Truman stated that it was "the policy of the United States to support free peoples who are resisting attempted subjugation by armed minorities or by outside pressures." The main aim of the US in the years 1947–1989 was to restrict the expansion of the Soviet Union.

This period also shaped post-Cold War US policy and led it to develop new concepts of preemptive intervention to protect its national security (as in the wars in Afghanistan and Iraq). The key to American foreign policy is its self-image as a nation offering the promise of freedom and democracy; a promise whose roots lay in the concept of Manifest Destiny (see p. 26).

US foreign policy has repeatedly been criticized as being hypocritical in the sense that the nations and peoples the US military supposedly sought to set free from oppressors were then in fact subjected to American interests. Indeed, some overt and covert international interventions especially in Central and South America and the Middle East can be seen as mainly motivated by commercial interests and matters of national security (by securing natural resources, controlling the influx of drugs into the US etc.) rather than the altruistic aspiration of bringing peace and democracy.

From a German perspective, however, the role of the US and its allies during the Second World War must be considered as that of a liberator without whom our nation might never have grown to become an internationally accepted democracy.

Glossary of Common Political Terms (AE)

amendment (to the constitution)	Zusatzerklärung zu der Verfassung; die ersten zehn *amendments* sind im *Bill of Rights* verfasst
constitution	Verfassung
unalienable/inalienable rights	unveräußerliche Rechte
Civil Rights Movement	Bürgerrechtsbewegung
Declaration of Independence	Unabhängigkeitserklärung
equality, emancipation	Gleichheit, Befreiung/Emanzipation
freedom (of speech, of the press, religious freedom)	(Rede-, Presse-, Religions-) Freiheit

from rags to riches	Redewendung: vom Tellerwäscher zum Millionär
the Founding Fathers	die Gründungsväter, die Unterzeichner der Unabhängigkeitserklärung
"In God we trust"	offizieller Wahlspruch der USA: „Wir vertrauen auf Gott."
the Promised Land the land of milk and honey God's own country the New Canaan	das gelobte Land das Land, in dem Milch und Honig fließen Gottes eigenes Land das neue Kanaan alles Bezeichnungen für Nordamerika (später die USA)
pioneer	Pionier
pioneer spirit	Pioniergeist
pursuit of happiness	das Streben nach Glück
to attain self-fulfilment	sich selbst verwirklichen
success	Erfolg
failure	Misserfolg, Versagen
to pledge allegiance to the flag	den Fahneneid leisten Ausdruck des amerikanischen Patriotismus, wird u. a. in Schulen an offiziellen Feiertagen gesprochen: "I pledge allegiance to the flag of the United States of America, and to the republic for which it stands, one nation under God, indivisible, with liberty and justice for all."
to prosper	Erfolg haben, gedeihen
to settle	(be)siedeln
settler	Siedler
settlement	Siedlung
to be persecuted	verfolgt werden
religious/political persecution	religiöse/politische Verfolgung
to immigrate	einwandern
immigrant	Einwanderer
immigration	Einwanderung
influx of immigrants	Zustrom von Einwanderern
Immigration Act	Einwanderungsgesetz
multiculturalism	Multikulturalität
naturalization	Einbürgerung
assimilation	Assimilation, Angleichung an Bestehendes

Post-colonial/Neo-colonial Experience

This chapter will outline the main aspects of two issues:
- How did Great Britain influence other nations as an empire? What consequences does its role as a former empire have for the UK?
- What consequences does its role as a former colony have for the US? How does its society deal with its minorities?

Keywords:

Post-colonialism: term first used in the middle of the 20th century; refers to the time after the British had left the colonies, i. e. after their formal rule over the colonies had come to an end.
Political independence did not necessarily lead to economic independence. The withdrawal of the British often resulted in problems for the ex-colonies, e. g. in difficulties in setting up a functioning government which guaranteed the people the freedom they dreamed of.

The Commonwealth: a group of 52 states; many former British colonies joined at the end of the decolonization process; aims at racial equality and national sovereignty. The British Queen is the head of the Commonwealth.

From Empire to Commonwealth

- At the beginning of the 17th century Britain started to expand its empire worldwide.
- The colonizers had a huge impact on the colonies and their people, bringing new traditions, values and beliefs with them.
- After the Second World War the British Empire changed rapidly.
- Most British colonies had become independent from Britain by 1970, but a large number of them stayed closely connected with their former colonizer by joining the Commonwealth.
- While the British ruled the colonies, their culture, values, traditions and language were regarded as superior to those of the colonized.
- This often caused a feeling of displacement and rootlessness on the part of the colonized, as they grew up being constantly reminded of their inferiority.
- Now, after independence, they faced the difficult task of recreating their own identity, bridging the gap between their country's native traditions and values and British ones.
- As people from member countries of the Commonwealth were allowed to emigrate to Britain, many people did so in the second half of the 20th century.
- First they were welcomed, as workers were needed after the Second World War, but in the 1970s, when more and more workers faced unemployment because of the economic crisis, immigration came to be seen more critically.
- Much post-colonial writing – written both in the former colonies and in Britain – deals with the issue of being caught between two cultures or of trying to find one's identity.

Minorities in the UK

Nationalization and Immigration Acts:

Imperial Act (1914): People from the colonies were given British citizenship.
British Nationality Act (1948): New status of Citizen of the United Kingdom and Colonies (CUKC) came into effect for those living within the Commonwealth. This preserved their existing status as British subjects whilst allowing them national citizenship of their own country of origin. However, this did not apply to countries that had gained independence by that date.
Immigration Act (1962, 1971): These acts, passed to counter increasing immigration, tightened the law on immigration of British subjects from other parts of the Commonwealth. Immigrants had to prove strong links to the UK (partiality) in order to be able to live and work in Britain.
British Nationality Act (1981): Today's nationality law differentiates between several forms of citizenship, in particular for those living in the overseas territories. Only those with British citizenship, and some Commonwealth citizens, are still automatically entitled to reside in the United Kingdom.

- About 12.4 % of the population in the UK were born abroad (2013), the non-UK born population decreased from 9.4 million in 2017 to 9.2 million in 2020 and the non-British population decreased from 6.2 million to 6.0 million. Poland remains the most common non-UK country of birth, taking over from India in 2015 (which reflected longer-term migration trends); Polish has been the most common non-British nationality in the UK since 2007.[5]
- Between the 1960s and 1980s many Indians, Pakistanis and Bangladeshis immigrated to Britain. They now form the largest immigrant communities.
- Many of them settled in the Midlands or in towns in Lancashire, Yorkshire and Strathclyde, where they worked, for example, in the textile industry.
- The highest percentage of ethnic minorities can be found in the London area.
- In recent years, the UK has constantly tightened its laws on immigration.
- The main immigrant groups to Britain – from India, Pakistan, the Caribbean, Africa, Southeast Asia and recently Eastern Europe – differ widely in culture, religion and language.
- **Ethnic diversity** enriches Britain, not only when it comes to music, fashion and food.
- Many embrace the opportunities and advantages of ethnic diversity (such as the former Foreign Secretary Robin Cook, who said that Chicken Tikka Masala " ... is now a true British national dish..."[6]).
- Others fear that "Britishness" will eventually be lost; they interpret multiculturalism as meaning that various cultures coexist peacefully, but without having a common basis of shared values.

5 For these statistics look at https://www.ons.gov.uk/peoplepopulationandcommunity/populationandmigration/internationalmigration/bulletins/ukpopulationbycountryofbirthandnationality/2017
6 https://www.ons.gov.uk/peoplepopulationandcommunity/populationandmigration/internationalmigration/bulletins/ukpopulationbycountryofbirthandnationality/yearendingjune2020#main-points and at https://migrationobservatory.ox.ac.uk/resources/briefings/migrants-in-the-uk-an-overview/

- **Second generation immigrants,** i. e. children born to parents who immigrated to Britain prior to (or shortly after) their children's birth, faced and still face a variety of problems:
  - They often experience a clash of cultures. Outside their parents' home they adopt a western lifestyle similar to that of their white friends and classmates. At home, however, they live according to values, beliefs and traditions typical of their parents' home countries, which many of these children and teenagers have never visited. Quite often they do not speak their parents' language any more, either. For some, the transition between these two different lifestyles is not easy.
  - They have difficulty when it comes to living up to the expectations of their parents, friends, teachers, etc.
  - They often have to face discrimination and overt racism.
  - According to a 2007 poll, about a third of British Asians felt it necessary to "act and think white" in order to fit into British society. About the same number did not feel British, but believed they needed to be a "coconut", meaning to be brown on the outside but white on the inside[7].
  - Therefore, defining one's identity and becoming confident in both cultures has been a central issue for most second generation immigrants.

Today, the third or fourth generation slowly but surely become more integrated into the British society and have arrived in British politics and public positions like the mayor of London Sadiq Khan.
The large number of immigrants from the EU, mostly coming from Eastern Europe after the opening of the borders in 2004 and subsequent years, have had less problems to adapt to British society. However, their being in Britain is also seen highly critical by the British public and was one reason for the Brexit vote in the 2016 referendum. In 2021 it is still unclear what their status in Britain will be in future.

In literature, this clash of cultures is portrayed most prominently by British writers such as Hanif Kureishi, Farrukh Dhondy, Zadie Smith and Salman Rushdie.

Post-colonial Literature or New English Literature:

The literature which deals with the consequences of the British Empire is called post-colonial literature or New English literature. Its authors reflect their nations' history as parts of the former British Empire and the role of the individual in these contexts. The main issues which are reflected in post-colonial literature are: social and cultural changes/conflicts, exploitation and the misuse of power, cultural alienation and integration of the individual torn between the values of the former colonizers and his or her traditional values and beliefs.

3 See BBC poll, 30 July 2007, http://news.bbc.co.uk/2/hi/uk_news/6921534.stm

Examples of Post-Colonial Societies: India, Australia, South Africa

At its height, the British Empire encompassed about a quarter of the world's land and dominated its crown colonies politically, economically and culturally. One must distinguish two types of colonies:

- those which were mainly colonized by the British with a relatively small indigenous population (such as Australia), sometimes also called the "white" colonies
- those colonies with a large indigenous population (such as India)

The decline of the British Empire resulted from internal demands for more independence from the Crown (the earliest colonies to leave were those in Northern America, see chapter I). In most cases this progression from colonial rule to independence was achieved peacefully. But in those countries with a large indigenous population, the way to independence was often paved with rebellion and violent conflict. In the following, the route to independence of three former colonies of the British Empire will be described briefly.

India

India became independent in 1947 and was the first non-white colony to gain complete independence from Britain.

- British influence in India started as early as the 16th century with the founding of the British East India Company. Because of its spices, cotton and tea, India was mainly a trading colony.
- 1858: The British Crown took over the areas ruled by the British East India Company, and in 1876 Queen Victoria became Empress of India. The time of British rule is also called the Raj (Hindu for "reign").
- August 15, 1947: The Indian Empire became independent, but was divided into the Union of India and the Dominion of Pakistan.

The case of India is unique in the way it gained complete independence from the British Empire at a rather early date by non-violent means. In India, the British rulers were by far in the minority, and dissatisfaction with British rule led to a national independence movement headed by Mahatma Gandhi. At first, he demanded equal civil rights for Indians in their own country and accused the British of mistreatment and oppression of the Indian people. Gandhi's struggle sparked a nationwide independence movement. His key to achieving independence was the revolutionary concept of civil disobedience. Being in the majority, the Indians were able to halt all social and economic life by simply refusing to comply with the British. Gandhi's aim was to achieve independence by non-violent means. After many years of struggle and several years spent in prison, Gandhi achieved his goal. Being unable to rule the country any longer, the British complied with India's demand for independence and thus lost one of their most important colonies.

Gandhi's concept of non-violent resistance became a role-model for other leaders of oppressed peoples and minorities. Leaders like Nelson Mandela (in South Africa) and Martin Luther King (in the US) considered him to be their inspiration to fight peacefully for racial equality and civil rights.

Australia

- dominion status in 1901, formally independent in 1931
- Australia's eastern half was claimed by the British in 1770 and most of the original settlers were prisoners shipped from England to the colony of New South Wales, which was founded in 1788.
- Australia's history as a penal colony for Britain resulted from the fact that the country was relatively poor in resources and from the overflow of criminals in British prisons.
- The Australians did not seek independence from Britain by violent means and indeed kept close political and constitutional ties to the United Kingdom until the last century. Australia gained the rights to self-government in 1901 and is today a fully independent nation although the British Queen is formally still head of state; she is represented by the Govenor-General in Australia.
- Most of the Australian population is white and of European descent (mostly British and Irish), but after World War II, Australia opened its borders to immigrants and experienced a large influx of nationals from Europe and Asia. Today, nearly two out of seven Australians were born overseas.

Background Information: The Aboriginals/The Stolen Generation(s)

Australia's Aboriginals (or: Aborigines) settled the continent 40,000 years ago. Their number was comparatively small and the white settlers regarded the indigenous people as inferior and barbaric. Their semi-nomadic way of life and the absence of large settlements made it easy for the settlers to take away their land to build their own settlements and farms and raise cattle. The Aboriginals found it increasingly difficult to maintain their traditional way of life. For the centuries to come they were to be oppressed and discriminated against by the white population. This oppression reached its climax in the racist ideology which led to the implementation of a child removal programme executed between about 1880 and 1960. This state-supported programme allowed the abduction of Aboriginal children from their families, supposedly to protect them from bad living conditions. These children were put under church or social care and raised according to white values and traditions, thus eradicating the indigenous traditions. It is estimated that more than 100,000 children were put under such guardianship. Not until 2008 did the Australian government headed by Prime Minister Kevin Rudd apologize for these actions.

South Africa

The Republic of South Africa is a parliamentary representative democratic republic and a multi-racial southern African country with a population of more than 50 million. After transition from white minority rule under apartheid, a system of state-enforced racial segregation and socio-economic discrimination, the nation held its first free elections in 1994.
South Africa has the largest, most diversified and most highly industrialized economy in Africa, which has achieved moderate economic growth in recent years.
Due to its political and commercial ties across Africa and its active role within the African Union, South Africa has a considerable influence on the continent, especially in southern Africa. As a strategic partner of the USA, it plays a leading role in trade and investment, and democracy and youth leadership development, as well as peace and international security.

The following **issues** are **of high importance:**

- bilateral political and trade and investment ties
- development cooperation
- conflict mitigation and development across Africa
- anti-apartheid struggle
- HIV/AIDS, COVID-19 and other health challenges
- education and skills shortage
- corruption
- poor rural infrastructure
- pollution

Social Issues – Poverty, Inequality and Unemployment

Although the post-apartheid era has seen some national socioeconomic gains, South Africa remains a highly unequal society with respect to wealth and income distribution and access to jobs, social services and land ownership. Most blacks are poor, have limited access to education, and suffer high unemployment, with average incomes far smaller than those of the historically privileged white minority.
In townships – the vast, high-density housing settlements where many of the poor live – social and political tension is fuelled by shortages of quality housing, utilities and social services. Other key problems include public corruption, widespread violent crime, and dissatisfaction among the country's black youth, who face particularly high jobless rates.
In order to change the dissatisfying status quo, the government is investing billions of dollars to upgrade infrastructure and improve public services, while facing continuing challenges in meeting popular expectations.

Politics and History

More than three times bigger than Germany, South Africa has a population of approximately 58.5 (2019) million. The country has important metal and mineral deposits as well as gas, diamond and rare earth mines. Further key exports include machinery and equipment. Altogether there are 11 official languages, of which English, Afrikaans, Zulu and Xosa are the most widely spoken. Nearly 80% of the population is Christian (with Protestants as the largest group). The literacy rate is 95 % (2021, age over 15). Life expectancy at birth is roughly 60 years for males and 63 years for females – relatively low for a developed country. The high HIV adult infection rate of more than 19 % (2018) is one of the reasons.
The COVID-19 pandemic 2020 and 2021 has struck South Africa heavily with a rising unemployment rate and a collapse of the important area of tourism. Infection rates were strong but then went down in spring 2021.
The Cape region was formerly a Bantu tribal area. In 1488 the Portuguese seafarer Bartolomeo Diaz became the first European to set foot on South African soil, and in the second half of the 17th century German and Dutch (Boer) settlement started, combined with a first wave of expulsion or enslavement of indigenous peoples. However, in the late 18th century the Zulu tribe developed territorial power. After occupation by the British in 1806, the Cape region became a British crown colony in 1814, causing aggravation among the Boer population, especially because of the racial equality aspired to by the British. This initiated the "Great Trek", in which Dutch settlers moved up-country in order to find independence and uninhabited grazing land. Instead they came into collision with the Zulu, resulting in a number of battles.

By 1856 the Boers had sufficiently established their control of the Transvaal territories to found the first Transvaal Republic. Annexation of these territories by the British in 1877 triggered the first Anglo-Boer War – or "War of Independence" as it was called by the Boers, who eventually prevailed. In 1880–81 the second Transvaal Republic under President Paul Kruger was proclaimed, and this remained independent until the end of the Second Boer War in 1902. South Africa received dominion status in 1910. In the following decades the first racial discrimination laws were passed, and in 1931 South Africa was given complete independence within the British Commonwealth. After World War II the apartheid system was installed. In 1961 it became a republic.

In the later 20th century increasing international pressure and national opposition initiated a process of dismantling apartheid on the basis of negotiations. The African National Congress (legitimized by President F.W. de Klerk), Archbishop Desmond Tutu, and the later president Nelson Mandela, known to the people a "Madiba" were essential players in the struggle for freedom and equality. In 1997 the new constitution of South Africa came into force, Thabo Mbeki succeeded Mandela, and in 2003 the Truth and Reconciliation Committee handed over its final report to president Mbeki. He was followed by Jacob Zuma, who stepped down in 2018 after many years office and numerous accusations of corruption. The current president is Cyril Ramaphosa.

Present Challenges

Today's national governance challenges include health issues, corruption, crime and increasing labour unrest. The government has admitted that corruption is a problem, and Zuma has taken strong public stances against it. There have been reports, however, that prosecutions of suspected corrupt officials have been selective and that cases reported in the press are not always officially investigated.
South African rates of violent crime are high, and criminals often aggravate crimes like robbery by violent assault, rape or murder. Explanations for such brutality vary. Women's rights activists and others have long denounced the lack of stronger public and state responses to sexual violence. According to many media reports police misconduct incidents, ranging from serious human rights abuses – including torture and targeted killings – to high-level corruption, and lesser misconduct such as roadside bribery, are increasing, which does not help reinstate trust in law enforcement.

Economy

South Africa's economy is the largest on the continent. Although only about 10% of the country is arable, and agriculture contributes less than 3% of GDP (gross domestic product), wine, wool, maize, sugar and fruit is mainly what South Africa is famous for. The industrial sector is more significant (approx. 30% of GDP). The largest share of GDP, namely 67.5 %, is contributed by services. There are well-developed tourism, banking, energy, transport and communications sectors.
The biggest economic domestic challenges include a poorly educated workforce and problems caused by the corona pandemic.[5]

Sindiwe Magona, *Mother to Mother* (gA)

first published 1998, South Africa

Characters

Mandisa – the narrator
Mxolisi – Mandisa's son (1st child)
Lunga – Mandisa's son (2nd child)
Siziwe – Mandisa's daughter (3rd child)
Dwadwa – Siziwe's father, Mandisa's 3rd husband
Lungile – Lunga's father, Mandisa's 2nd partner
China – Mxolisi's father, Mandisa's 1st husband
Mama – Mandisa's mother
Makhulu – maternal grandmother
Amy Biehl – an American student murdered in Guguletu

5 Source: CIA World Factbook 2021

Background

Amy Biehl, a young Fulbright scholar who came to South Africa to assist in the preparations for the first democratic elections, was killed on August 25, 1993 by a mob of rioting students as she drove through the all-black township of Guguletu.

Synopsis and discussion

The story is told through the voice of Mandisa. After it is revealed that her son Mxolisi is guilty of stabbing Amy Biehl, Mandisa writes to Amy's mother, hoping to strike a common chord of grief. For in her lament – above all about the circumstances in which her family lives – Mandisa also sees herself as a victim. Without excusing her son's actions, she sees Amy's mother as a "sister-mother". By describing the background to her own and her family's life, she hopes to explain her son's action: how it was triggered by the relentless apartheid policy of the government. In her eyes there are always two sets of victims when a homicide occurs. The killer, in a different sense, is a victim, too.

The book takes the form of a long letter to Amy's mother, interspersed with an account of the events of the day of Amy's death (as recollected by Mandisa), and with memories from Mandisa's life. It works on at least three levels: the direct address directed to Amy's mother, the description of the day of the murder, and the history of a typical young woman and her family in South Africa under apartheid and post-apartheid.

Mandisa refers to her happy early childhood and tells us that she became a mother at the age of 15, which destroyed her dreams of a well-educated future. She then became a housemaid. One day things became even worse. The Group Areas Act passed by the South African government organized neighbourhoods according to race. Moving blacks to poor and arid ghettos with inadequate housing, a bad school system and insufficient social infrastructure was dehumanizing and fuelled the hatred in the communities towards the white elite.

Her son's introduction to racial violence was when he watched the killing of two older boys he knew. This shaped his view of the world and his view of good and bad. His mental picture was consolidated by the observation that school rebellions and looting were considered a rightful weapon in the fight for freedom and met with admiration within the black community. Consistently with this, Mxolisi later, at the age of 20, became a leader of the student revolutionary movement.

Black children and adolescents often grew up without much contact with their parents, who worked as day labourers in the white neighbourhoods. This increased school dropout rates and youth-related problems in the black communities. Law enforcement did not respond to black on black crime. And this was also true after the end of apartheid, when Amy Biehl was murdered. For it was only then that the police made any real effort to hunt down the killers. This made it clear that the system placed greater value on the life of a white woman than on black citizens. While some community members called Mandisa the mother of a murderer, others labelled her a freedom fighter – a divergent interpretation which shows both the difficulty of moral judgment and the complexity of the racial situation in South Africa.

Style

Magona's prose is full of figurative language. She uses metaphors and metonyms (cf. stylistic devices, p. 116) to describe crowds and their impact on an individual's free will, and in this way opens another perspective on how Mxolisi was influenced to kill Amy Biehl. It becomes an example of the use of violence in freedom movements. The author's metaphorical usage of "whirlwind" to depict the effect of forced removals can be found throughout the novel.
The author does not baulk at unpleasant topics. The rawness with which she describes Mandisa's feelings towards Mxolisi's conception – Mandisa inwardly loathes her child because he symbolizes the end of her dreams – touches the core of motherhood. In the same way she carefully creates Mxolisi's irreducible reality, which opens an unexpected, and at first sight unintelligible, perspective on a delinquent.
As far as form is concerned, Magona borrows from the idea of the epistolary novel[5] in order to underline the authenticity of the narrator's voice.

Main topics for discussion

- day-to-day hardships under apartheid
- dissolution of neighbourhoods and communities caused by the apartheid regime
- artificial racial hierarchy of apartheid
- racial and economic privileges
- ethnic and cultural diversity
- accountability and justice
- values of "justice" vs. "reconciliation"
- immaculate conception as a symbolic Christian reference

Reference to present day South Africa

When Nelson Mandela led the country through a cleansing phase of "truth and reconciliation" to abolish apartheid, South Africa began a peaceful transition period. What was overlooked was the young generation of black people who were, despite being given fresh hope, unable to participate in the country's new economic prosperity. Because of a lack of education, these men and women had to struggle as unskilled workers. Becoming aware of their situation, they responded violently to societal challenges. This is one key aspect of the novel.

Social study topics

- township life
- the multilingual reality of South Africa
- anti-apartheid related school boycotts
- the role of the police during apartheid
- the role of violence in both maintaining and fighting against apartheid
- acts of reconsiliation and healing
- apartheid in South Africa

5 An epistolary novel is a novel written as a series of personal documents such as letters, diary entries etc.

Migration and the World of Work

Human migration means that people move from one place to another. They do this temporarily or permanently. In the history of mankind, migration has been an evolutionary necessity, as in the hunter and gatherer societies, where people were nomadic and were always looking for better places to find food, to hunt and find shelter. In history, freedom of mind, as well as better work opportunities, have been driving factors of migration, as in 19th century immigration to the US.

Today, in a more or less fixed system of states with state borders, migration is still a huge factor in the development of a society, but in increasingly wide sections of society – especially in right-wing and nationalist political groupings – it is also seen very critically (cf. the reference to Enoch Powell's "rivers of blood" speech in *East is East*). In addition to the post-WW II migration to the UK from its former colonies, there has in the past two decades, after Poland and nine other countries joined the EU in 2004, been a huge influx of people from Eastern Europe. People from the new EU member states have been more willing to do non-skilled and low-paid jobs than their British counterparts. This has caused a political debate in Britain and can be seen as one of the many reasons for some people to favour Brexit. As this world is one with large economic differences, i.e. the so-called North-South divide, migration will remain one of the problems of our times, with societies that are better off facing huge numbers of refugees from poorer countries until a certain equality is reached.

In the US, migration has been the driving factor of the nation's creation. However, migration is seen differently when it comes to countries of origin. The southern border of the US has been for a long time the subject of fierce political debate, as a lot of immigrants from Mexico and other Latin American countries cross this border, many of them illegally. The discussion about the so-called "dreamers" (sons and daughters of illegal immigrants to the US – the term probably originates in the abbreviation of the name of a piece of 2001 legislation) was fuelled by former President Donald Trump.

Andrea Levy, "Loose Change" (gA, eA)

A note on the author

Andrea Levy (1956–2019) is of Jamaican descent. As a novelist she explored themes around British Jamaicans and questions of racial, cultural and national identity. Levy's roots included her Jewish (Jamaican) and Scottish grandfathers. Her Jamaican father came to London in 1948, where he was joined by her mother a year later. Levy grew up in a family of four children in a council estate in north London and had a typical working-class background. After finishing school she studied textile design and weaving. Her fiction has been honoured with literary prizes. Her best-known novels are *Small Island* (2004) and *The Long Song* (2010).

Synopsis

Andrea Levy published her short story "Loose Change" in 2005. The story illustrates the fate of an Uzbek refugee, Laylor, who has recently arrived in London. Its message is that being generous does not depend on your own wealth but that many people shy away from helping others because they do not want to become involved.
While it is pouring with rain outside, the unnamed first-person narrator hurriedly steps into the National Portrait Gallery in Central London looking for loose change she could use for the tampon machine in the ladies' toilet. Even though she does not usually talk to strangers, she speaks loudly into the room and gets the attention of another woman who offers her some change.
Back in the gallery, the narrator looks for this other person, Laylor, who starts to talk to her about some of the works of art. They differ about the meaning of the paintings they look at. The narrator then offers to buy the other woman a coffee in the gallery café. Sitting opposite her, the narrator gradually notices Laylor's different attitude, language and background and realizes that she is in a decidedly precarious situation. It turns out that she sleeps in a square with her brother. Even though Laylor never asks for anything either for herself or for her brother (who appears briefly), the narrator feels obliged to offer help and kindness to Laylor, even in a small act. By that point, her unwillingness to talk to strangers has been overcome by growing interest. Laylor's miserable situation dawns on the narrator, who struggles inwardly over the advantages and disadvantages of helping a refugee, connecting Laylor's story to her own family history when they first came to the UK (her grandmother is of Caribbean descent). The narrator is torn between empathy and prejudice against homeless people and refugees.
The narrator, a single mother, has a spare bedroom in the small house or flat she shares with her son; so she could, in fact, do something for the Uzbek woman. In her mind she rehearses the comfort and friendship she could – and actually resolves to – offer. Yet in the end she sees Laylor as a potential intruder into her otherwise quiet life and walks out of the café, leaving the situation and Laylor behind.

Analysis

The story unfolds in the limited perspective of the first-person narrator, a middle-aged woman, who shares her views of the situation and her growing apprehension of Laylor's true character with the reader. The setting and characters are described solely through the narrator's eyes. The woman in need seems the stronger of the two characters, because she offers kindness (loose change) and her story whereas the narrator passes judgment on her before finally leaving the café. The reader gets no idea of Laylor's thoughts. The story expresses the narrator's reflections on social behaviour and on what would happen if she helped the Uzbek woman. Despite knowing that help is necessary for people who have just arrived and are homeless in another country, and despite her own family history – her grandmother had been shown just that kindness – she runs away from the responsibility.

Topics

- migration in Europe – displacement
- giving a chance to refugees and homeless people
- class and social conditions
- the making of identity

Shereen Pandit, "She Shall Not Be Moved" (gA, eA)

A note on the author

The British author Shareen Pandit is a political activist and lawyer of Muslim South African descent. Born in Cape Town, Pandit has always been active in fighting for the rights of the black community. Some of her stories and poems actively condemn discrimination against the black population. This brought her into conflict with the South African government of the time, and in 1987 she fled to London with her husband. She lives in London with her daughter.

Published in 2005, the short story "She shall not be moved" presents an everyday example of racism on a London bus. The scene is told in a very biased way by a narrator whose identity is difficult to grasp. However, the reader can deduce that she must be a woman, and the girl at her side must be her daughter, because at one point she talks about Mariam's dad, with whom she evidently lives. She mentions events like having been forced to leave her country, so she is probably not British by origin.

Synopsis

The unnamed first-person narrator reflects on a scene she and her small daughter Mariam have been involved in when travelling by bus to Mariam's dance class.
As the narrator squeezes onto the bus with her daughter, the bus driver is calling to a woman with a pram to move on. However, this mother cannot use the pram space, as he two middle-aged white working-class women sitting there obviously do not intend to move. The narrator identifies the woman with the pram as probably being Somali and carries on talking about her in that way, also describing her as a "haughty queen". The "Somali woman" seems proudly unmoved by the situation; she does not react to any of the bystanders even when the black bus driver comes up to her and yells at her rather than asking the two white women to make room.
The narrator feels guilty about not standing up against the two white women or against the bus driver, and then tries to sympathize and talk with the "Somali woman". The situation ends when the Somali woman gets off the bus saying in a voice of granite that the bus driver is a slave but she herself is not.
The narrator reflects that the situation must have been erupting before she even got on the bus. She feels the Somali woman's words cut into her. The day finishes with her taking her daughter to a bagel shop after dance class as if to make up for not getting involved and to make the daughter forget the episode. But Mariam still looks

at her in a reproachful, disappointed way. Her attempt at education and her words about getting involved have failed miserably in this situation. She did not follow her own code of moral conduct.

Analysis

The first-person narrator of "She shall not be moved" retells the situation on the bus, limiting the reader to her own perspective. This, however, includes an awareness of her problem with herself and specifically with her desire to educate her daughter in moral courage, as she fails to stand up against the wrongs she sees quite clearly. This awareness overlaps with her description of the journey.
As a narrator she is unreliable and biased. She comments on every action and has her own way of describing and assigning meaning: the white women are like characters from the TV series *Eastenders,* the woman with a pram seems Somali to her from her style of clothes and her height. Only on a close reading does the reader realize that the narrator is probably afraid of getting involved, and that she is in "this miserable country" because she got into trouble "back home". She constantly mentions what she should do but never does, despite her daughter's expectant looks.
The narrator seems politically active and says she would normally stand up against wrong-doing and that principles like human rights have to be defended. In the story, her comments on her bad conscience about not speaking up for the Somali woman constantly break into the description of the situation on the bus. She tries to make her daughter forget the episode but realizes that she herself cannot. She had to leave her country of origin, but now, in a new country, her courage seems to have left her. Like so many immigrants, she just wants to lead a quiet life.

Topics

- everyday racism
- the making of identity
- class and social conditions
- postcolonial experience
- political activism
- displacement: questions of belonging and identity

Individual and Society

The following chapter will focus on the various facets of identity – both ethnic/cultural and personal identity. How does identity affect a person's and his/her position in society?

Central issues to be tackled are:

- the different roles an individual might assume and the potential conflicts between those roles;
- the connection between one's biologically determined sex and the largely socially defined gender of a person;
- minorities and outsiders.

Keywords:

Individual: The term derives from the Latin "indivisible" and commonly refers to an individual subject, i.e. a person, who can be distinguished from his or her surroundings. As such, the individual has to position himself or herself vis-à-vis the society in which they are living. The relationship between the individual and his or her society can be difficult if the former comes into conflict with the latter's norms and values.

Society: This term refers to a collective of individuals united e.g. by a shared territory, history, or ways of living and thinking. In order to be effective and not to fall prey to anarchy, societies are organized according to a set of rules and regulations which can even overrule the interests of the individual for the sake of the community.

Roles and Role Conflicts

- While the individual was traditionally believed to be a unified "whole", the concept of the different roles of a person underlines the fact that one does not just have **one** single identity, but actually has to fulfil a number of different roles in different situations and contexts.
- A social role consists of a certain pattern of behaviour, of rights but also of obligations. Social roles are performed in **interaction** with other persons. Roles are mostly to be seen in relation to others (child – parent; teacher – student).
- Whether one's behaviour is in line with one's particular role can be judged by society's **expectations** of that role.
- If an individual shows forms of behaviour that are considered **inappropriate** for the social role in question, he or she may have to face various forms of **punishment** (ranging from being made aware of one's improper behaviour to actual punishment); if the behaviour in question is deemed **appropriate**, there will, in return, be **rewards** from society.
- A role (e.g. doctor, teacher, bus driver) can be **achieved** by or (e.g. child) **ascribed** to an individual.

- In certain situations, a person can be faced with a **conflict** between contrasting roles which he or she should take on at the same time. Thus, if a mother happens to be her own child's teacher, she would be expected to be simultaneously strict towards the child in her role as teacher and loving in her role as mother.

Gender Identity and sexual diversity

- A central component of an individual's identities is his or her **gender**.
- Unlike the biologically determined **sex** (male/female), **gender** and **gender role** (masculine/feminine) are often perceived as being social constructs.
- Accordingly, a society holds a set of certain stereotypical ideas about how a "real" woman and a "real" man should behave, what they should look like, but also what they are capable of.
- Traditionally, men are thought of as masculine, strong, rational and powerful, while women are considered to be feminine, weak, emotional and submissive.
- These assumed characteristics have also been used as a "justification" for men's dominant role in society.
- With the advent of the Feminist Movement in the 1960s, however, the validity of conventional gender roles was called into question.
- However, the media especially still present largely conservative images of "typical" men and "typical" women, thereby keeping these concepts alive.
- If a person does not conform to the gender role associated by his or her society with his or her sex, he or she may have to face resentment. Even in the comparatively tolerant societies of the West, particularly "masculine" women and "feminine" men are not universally accepted.

Gender Diversity

The aim of gender diversity is to represent people of different genders in a fair way. This concerns mostly men and women and their ratio in companies, politics or other fields of life. Traditionally, men have dominated many areas of public life such as politics, engineering, science, medicine or computing. Gender diversity has been widely discussed, but progress towards having less male and more female company directors – and indeed bosses in many walks of life – has been slow.
However, after the feminist and post-feminist debates of the past decades, discussions about gender have recently become more open, including transgender or non-binary people. This has meant that more people have had the courage to come out with their particular sexuality or their gender identity.

Outsiders

- If an individual deliberately or unintentionally fails to conform to the rules of the society in which he or she lives, they can easily become socially stigmatized **outsiders**.
- When a larger group of people rejects the conventional norms of mainstream culture, this might lead to the formation of a **counterculture** which openly prop-agates a set of values significantly different from these of the society in which they live.
- Such countercultures are often associated with younger generations that rebel against their parents' way of life.
- Famous countercultural movements include the "Beat Generation" of the 1950s, the "hippies" of the 1960s, the "punks" of the 1970s and 1980s, and the "hip hop" scene, which developed from the 1970s onwards, which all included such forms of artistic expression as music, graffiti and dance.
- There are numerous ways of expressing one's dissatisfaction with mainstream culture, e.g. through the use of taboo language (as employed by writers of the Beat Generation), through the open violation of generally accepted moral standards (as in the form of "free love" practised by the hippies), through one's appearance (clothing and hairstyle of the punks), or by aligning oneself with strata of society that are far removed from the mainstream (e.g. hip hop culture).
- Often aspects of countercultures are eventually commercialized and assimilated by mainstream culture, thereby losing their originally rebellious impetus.

Minorities in the US

Since its birth in 1776, the United States of America has been a nation of immigrants. Especially during the 19th and early 20th century, millions of people (at first mostly from Europe, later also from other continents) were allowed to enter the country, since the young nation was in need of settlers and workers. The US has therefore always been an ethnically and culturally mixed nation, which has led to discussions about how this society might deal with its diversity and how it can be defined.

Keywords:

Multicultural society: a society where various ethnic groups and their cultural heritage are accepted in their own right
Salad bowl: the various ethnicities living in the United States adding their own traditions, cultural values, etc. to those of the American people; the various heritages do not merge into one, but stay distinct ("unity in diversity")
Melting pot: the various ethnic groups do not retain their cultural heritage but amalgamate into one new nation. The term first appeared in an essay by Jean de Crèvecoeur entitled "Letters from an American farmer" in 1782.
The term "salad bowl" is now considered to be more politically correct.

One main group which did not enter the United States voluntarily but was deported to the US is the group of thousands of slaves from Africa who were shipped to the British colony and later to the newly founded nation. The descendants of these slaves form the second largest minority in the US (in recent years the number of Hispanic immigrants has exceeded the coloured population). Their history is one of discrimination and deprivation, which will be summarized briefly below.

African-American history

- 1619: first documented ship of African slaves bound for Jamestown, Virginia
- 17th-19th century: the **Atlantic slave trade**; by 1860 an estimated 3.5 million enslaved Africans lived in the US; another 500,000 lived freely in the (northern) states or territories
- 1861-65: American Civil War; caused by the separationist movement of eleven slave states which refused to end slavery; the North fought to prevent secession of these states and eventually won
- **Emancipation Proclamation** 1863: during the Civil War, President Abraham Lincoln declared that all slaves in the secession states (South) were free
- **Jim Crow Era**: after the Civil War, slavery was illegal, however, many former slave states passed laws which discriminated against blacks, prevented them from purchasing land and having the right to vote, and segregated blacks from whites in almost all areas of public life
- racial segregation remained into the 20th century; this system of separation and discrimination was met with increasing resistance and led to the formation of the Civil Rights Movement between 1954 and 1968.

The Situation of Blacks during Reconstruction

The former slaves formally gained freedom after the North won the Civil War, but they were far from having equal rights. Especially in the South, repressive laws and regulations prevented them from purchasing land, participating in elections, etc. (see Jim Crow Era above). This led to a number of developments:

- Many former slaves left for the industrialized cities of the North, in which all-black ghettos developed.
- Freemen who stayed in the South often continued to work as sharecroppers for former slave masters. Unable to buy land, they remained dependent on white landowners and still lived in great poverty.
- Discrimination and racism continued (not only) in the South in an institutionalized form of racial segregation and state legislature. Both in the North and the South, blacks began to put up resistance against all forms of discrimination.

The Civil Rights Movement

- 1909: African-Americans founded the National Association for the Advancement of Colored People (NAACP); the aim was to call attention to discrimination in the South and the cities of the North

- 1954: landmark decision of the Supreme Court in the case of Brown vs. Board of Education, which declared the racial segregation of schools to be unconstitutional
- 1955: Rosa Parks, an NAACP member, refused to give up her seat in a bus for a white person in Montgomery, Alabama and was consequently arrested; led by Martin Luther King, thousands of blacks in Montgomery boycotted public transportation (Montgomery Bus Boycott) ' in 1956, the Supreme Court declared racial segregation on buses to be unconstitutional
- 1950s and 60s: protests continued on various issues, many of them led by the Southern Christian Leadership Conference (SCLC) formed by Martin L. King; following the example of Mahatma Gandhi, they organized peaceful protests and acts of civil disobedience to stop segregation in other areas of public life
- 1963: March on Washington; an estimated 250,000–300,000 people (about 80% black) marched to the Capitol in Washington D.C. to demonstrate peacefully for jobs, freedom and an end to racial discrimination
- during this march, the most famous leader of the movement, the Reverend Martin Luther King gave his famous speech "I have a dream", which moved millions of people and brought widespread attention to the the Civil Rights Movement; King later received the Nobel Peace Prize in 1964 and was assassinated in 1968
- forced by the public to take action, the government passed laws to stop racial discrimination and segregation: the Civil Rights Act of 1964 and the Voting Act of 1965
- racial discrimination, however, did not end immediately and still exists covertly and overtly; blacks in the US still have a higher risk of unemployment, poverty and imprisonment in comparison with the white majority population
- systemic racism towards black people today has created new campaigns against violence like the movement "black lives matter" in June 2013 (cf. below)
- shortly before and after former President Trump's inauguration, a lot of new movements were started. There wete huge demonstrations for human rights and other issues, including women's rights, immigration reform, healthcare reform, racial equality and freedom of religion. Thousands of women wore pink woollen hats in their march on Washington to accuse Trump, among other things, of using sexist and racist language.
- the #NeverAgain movement was created by surviving students of Stoneman Douglas High School in Parkland, Florida, after 17 of their classmates were shot in a massacre in mid-February 2018.

Black Lives Matter

Black Lives Matter is a socially motivated movement internationally known for its spectacular "die-in" actions and street demonstrations. It is a decentralized network of activists without a formal hierarchy which started its actions and protest marches in order to take a stand against racially motivated police brutality towards black people and a series of deaths in police custody.
BLM appeared on the scene in 2013 and entered public awareness in 2016 when the movement became more active in protest against Donald Trump's racist utterances.

In May 2020 it gained global attention in denouncing George Floyd's death in Minneapolis (Minnesota), caused by excessive police violence in arresting him. According to BLM, Floyd died from suffocation. The offender was found guilty of murder in court in April 2021. On the whole, legal proceedings have been instigated against four police officers concerned in this case. All four have been dismissed from the police service. The protest marches related to Floyd's death led to lootings and rampage which ended up with curfews and deployment of the National Guard. The police violence shown there brought Amnesty International into the arena, criticizing violations of human rights.
Sometimes, BLM is criticized from within its own ranks as supporting racial bias and deepening the divide between black and white people, as well as sidelining black women's experiences. So, "Say Her Name" has been created to focus attention on female victims of police violence.

Black empowerment – Amanda Gorman:

Since the inauguration of U.S. President Joe Biden in January 2021, the young poet and activist Amanda S. C. Gorman (*1998) has become globally known. Her poem, "The Hill We Climb", evokes a moment of unity and a new era for her country. However, her acclaimed work has focused on issues of oppression, feminism, race, and marginalization, as well as the African diaspora. She was the first person to be named National Youth Poet Laureate and made the cover of *TIME Magazine's* February 2021 issue.
But even a well-known person like Gorman experiences everyday racism: in March 2021, Gorman said she was racially profiled by a security guard near her home after which she tweeted: "He left, no apology. This is the reality of black girls: One day you're called an icon, the next day, a threat." And then she tweeted that he was probably right. "I AM A THREAT: a threat to injustice, to inequality, to ignorance. Anyone who speaks the truth and walks with hope is an obvious and fatal danger to the powers that be. A threat and proud." (You can find her on Twitter: @TheAmandaGorman)

Jhumpa Lahiri, "The Third and Final Continent" (eA)

A note on the author and the text

Nilanjana Sudeshna Lahiri (born 1967), called Jhumpa in her kindergarten, was born in London to Bengali immigrants, but moved to the U.S. at the age of three. Her father had got a job at the library of the University of Rhode Island in South Kingston. However, her parents remained committed to their East Indian culture and determined to rear their children with experience of and pride in their cultural heritage. Lahiri studied literature and published her first anthology of short stories in 1999.

In her stories and three novels she focuses on the lives of Indian Americans but claims that she is largely talking about her own experience seeking her own roots and trying to build a sense of belonging. In 2001, she married a Greek-American and in 2011 she moved with her family to Italy. Since 2015 she has published in Italian.

(cf. https://www.indiatimes.com/lifestyle/jhumpa-lahiri-biography-377135.html)

Synopsis

Jhumpa Lahiri's short story "The Third and Final Continent" – from her early collection *The Interpreter of Maladies* (1999) – has, like most of her fiction, a strongly autobiographical element. The career of the central character reflects that of her father, and the sense of uprootedness expresses the feelings that made her leave the U.S.

The narrator takes us back to his beginnings in London in 1964, where he had come to study at the London School of Economics, and where he shared a dismal apartment house with other poor Bengali immigrants. At the age of 36, he gets a job offer as a librarian at M.I.T. and his marriage is arranged back in Calcutta. After a week in India, he flies out to the U.S. Despite having a job, his budget is still very tight.

He arrives at Boston on the day the first Americans landed on the moon. His first accommodation is at the YMCA; it is notoriously small and loud, and cooking is forbidden. Originally, he wants to stay there for six weeks till his wife arrives, but the noise from outside is unbearable, so he follows up an advert in the *Boston Globe* for a room to be 'rented to boys from Harvard or Tech' (MIT).

The owner, Mrs. Croft, an extremely old lady dressed in a long black skirt, is seated at a piano. She starts to talk about the American flag on the moon and wants him to answer "splendid". He is satisfied with the room, and she produces the key, warning him about "no lady visitors". This makes him think of his wife Mala, and of their marriage, which he regards as a duty he had to fulfil.

The narrator moves in with Mrs. Croft, who seems not to have moved from her piano bench, and who orders him every night when he comes home to sit down beside her and engage in the same conversation about the American flag on the moon and to answer "splendid". This becomes a daily routine. He meets Mrs. Croft's daughter, Helen, who tells him he is the first boarder her mother has called a gentleman; he learns that Mrs. Croft is 103 years old and that the piano had been her source of income after she was widowed. He draws parallels to his own mother and starts to worry about his landlady and to imagine her past life.

After six weeks, his wife arrives and they move into a furnished apartment. He is disappointed at Mrs. Croft's unemotional reaction to his leaving her house, but Mala now makes the apartment their home. It is strange for him to have someone at his side, and he tries to anticipate his wife's needs and to get used to having a home that smells of cooked rice and soap. Still, they talk little.

One evening, the narrator suggests they should go out. Mala dresses in a beautiful sari and makes up her hair elegantly. They find themselves near Mrs. Croft's house, where Helen answers the door and he learns that the old woman has broken her hip.

When Mrs. Croft tells him that she called the police and he responds "Splendid!", Mala laughs. Mrs. Croft announces that Mala is a perfect lady. And now the narrator laughs, too, quietly but noticed by his wife. Their is first real intimacy.
From that moment on, things change between them and they start to share the experience of the new city. The narrator calls this time a sort of honeymoon. Months later, Mala consoles him when the narrator learns that Mrs. Croft has died. She is the first person he mourns in America.
The story moves into the present. The narrator and Mala have been married for decades now and can barely remember a time when they didn't know each other. Their son is at Harvard. They still live in Boston and have integrated into American society.

Analysis

The first-person narrator talks about the different cultures he has faced: outwardly, he has adapted to wherever he lives, but inwardly he remained rooted in his original Bengali culture for a long time. He does a good job as a librarian and moves on to higher levels as time goes by. Overall, the reader is left with a positive impression of his immigrant experience in America.
The narrator explains his distance to Bengali traditions food and clothing, and he initially remains a stranger to his wife after she arrives, finding it awkward to eat with his hands or to speak Bengali. Only during the visit with Mala to his former landlady, Mrs. Croft, does his attitude to his wife change slowly: for the first time he realizes how difficult it must be for Mala in this totally strange country and remembers his first weeks in London. Their contrasting expectations and feelings are bridged over only slowly, but in the process the two become a married couple adjusting to life in a different country and enjoying new circumstances together. This makes the story one of successful immigration to the U.S.
After the death of his own mother, the aged widow Mrs. Croft, deeply rooted in another century and different mental and cultural traditions, seems like a foster mother to him. Unintentionally, she provokes a change in the couple's understanding of each other and facilitates their integration. The narrator is able to truly mourn her, which he had not done with his own mother, as he was then only fulfilling the duties of a son.
Lahiri's message is that life is unpredictable, with extraordinary turns of event bringing great sorrow and love. Her story addresses the wide Indian diaspora, especially in the West.

Topics

- the American Dream
- immigration
- the individual and society
- the making of identity

Qaisra Shahraz, "The Escape" (eA)

A note on the author

The widely acclaimed, award-winning British Pakistani novelist Qaisra Sharaz (born 1958) is also active as a screen writer and journalist. She has lived in Manchester ever since she was nine years old and has worked as a college inspector, an international teacher trainer and an education consultant, among other things. One of her central focuses is the question of race, cultural divisions and diversity, and the question of gender. A short story touching on all these topics – the question of clothing, female modesty, multiple identities and cultural clashes – is "A Pair of Jeans" (1988).

Synopsis

The story "The Escape", from 2009, features seventy-three-year-old Samir celebrating the Muslim festival Eid ul Fitr, when he looks back on his life and the changes he and the area he lives in have gone through, and his memory of a trip he made to Pakistan, where he understood what "home" meant to him.

Samir now lives alone in his large family home, a detached house in a suburb of Manchester, but only uses his master bedroom, as his wife has recently died and his children have all left the house. He does not really feel at home there any more, as too much of what was known to him has changed.

The story begins with Samir praying in a mosque where he does not feel a sense of belonging either, because of different – younger – generations praying there now and because of the different cultural backgrounds the community comes from. In his now multi-ethnic area, a mix of Pakistani, Bengali, Asian and Somali shops and mosques have sprung up where formerly there where only Catholic schools and churches and some small shops that he remembers with nostalgia.

His son Maqbool brings him home and later picks him up for the first Eid family gathering at his eldest daughter's house. Samir reflects that they used to celebrate this feast at his own house, which was filled with chatter and joy and delicious smells.

On this first Eid ul Fitr without his wife, Samir announces, to his children's surprise, that he will be going "home to Pakistan" for a few months to be with his family there and revisit some of the places of his childhood.

But, on returning to Pakistan, he realises he's no longer sure where his real home is. Samir takes his brother's family in Lahore by surprise, too. They greet him with hospitality but are unsure what his true intentions are. Only the young children's reactions are natural; everyone else reacts awkwardly.

Samir travels to his home village and visits his parents' grave, where he takes in the experience of Pakistani life around him and reflects on his past and his possible future life. He remembers how, over 40 years earlier, he had come to London with a friend, felt uneasy there, and moved on up North. He recalls the different stages of assimilating to the British workforce and of taking care to settle in good surrounding (a detached house in a good area) and to ensure the education and career of his children. Back in the village, he visits a widow and her teenage daughters who were supported

by his late wife. He is touched and embarrassed by their humility and their behaviour. He is overwhelmed by the grief for his late wife and re-establishes the sponsorship and offers to pay for the daughters' college education. On leaving the widow's home, he walks back through the village, noticing no one of his own age-group nor anyone he recognizes.
Back in Lahore, he tells the family that he will be going "home" to England. His brother does not understand Samir's concept of home but is relieved that the guest is leaving. During the flight back, Samir meets another Pakistani man of his age and they start to talk about home, the homeland and homecoming, and escaping back to the UK "to a new home".
Once back, Samir decides to leave his house to his children, moves into an elderly people's home and rewrites his will in order to settle the financial support for the widow in the village. A week after arriving there, his new friend Ibrahim moves in three doors from him and pure joy returns to Samir's life as he shows him around the house. The escape is over and both decide they have the right to enjoy their lives as "the new English babus" who, having worked enough, can now enjoy their remaining years in a home of their own choice.

Analysis

The short story is told from Samir's point of view by a third-person narrator. The question of belonging is central: torn between his memories of his old life, his upbringing in Pakistan and his present circumstances, Samir is shown to have multiple identities: he has a growing sense of loss and confusion especially after his wife's recent death. The question of where the elderly first-generation migrants belong is a poignant one. What is their "homeland"? Is it the place of their birth or where they have spent most of their lives? The story answers this question inasmuch as, towards the end of the story, Samir finds out that his home is in Manchester – a place changed noticably since he arrived there, but richer for all its cultural variety – despite the fact that he maintains emotional links with his country of birth. This is shown by the gestures, tone of voice and facial expressions that Samir notices, but also by the distance and the lack of understanding he encounters. But he can only begin to understand what "home" means to him after he has made his escape to Pakistan. Back in England, he can escape a lonely life in his family home by making a move to a new home, with new friends, not cut off from his family, but independent.

Topics

- post-colonial experience
- migration
- the making of identity
- questions of belonging
- age and memories
- the generation gap

Glossary – Identity

alienation	Entfremdung (z. B. von der Ursprungskultur)
assimilation	Anpassung (Aufgabe der urspr. Kultur)
to adapt to sth.	sich an etwas anpassen
to blend in	sich einfügen, integrieren
to integrate	integrieren
immigrant, to immigrate, immigration	Einwanderer, einwandern, Einwanderung
colonialism, colonizer, colonized	Kolonialismus, der Besiedler, kolonisiert
citizenship	Nationalität, Staatsangehörigkeit
naturalization [BE]	Einbürgerung
to receive/to be granted citizenship	die Staatsbürgerschaft erhalten
fugitive, asylum seeker	Flüchtling, Asylsuchender
ethnic minority, ethnicity	ethnische Minderheit, Volkszugehörigkeit
indigenous	einheimisch
integration	Integration
imperialism, imperialistic	Imperialismus, imperialistisch
loss of identity	Verlust der Identität
cultural clash	kultureller Zusammenprall (Konflikt)
melting pot vs. salad bowl	„Schmelztiegel" vs. „Salatschüssel" (unterschiedliche Konzepte, die die Vielfalt der Kulturen in den USA beschreiben sollen)
mutual understanding	gegenseitiges/beiderseitiges Verständnis
open-minded vs. narrow-minded	aufgeschlossen vs. engstirnig
pluralistic society	pluralistische (vielseitige) Gesellschaft
covert/overt discrimination	versteckte/offene Diskriminierung
(racial) segregation	(Rassen)trennung
deprivation	Aberkennung, Entzug (z. B. von Rechten), Benachteiligung
oppression, to be oppressed by s. o.	Unterdrückung, von jmd. unterdrückt werden
racial equality	Gleichwertigkeit verschiedener Rassen
civil rights	Bürgerrechte
civil disobedience	ziviler Ungehorsam
boycott	Ablehnung etwas zu kaufen, zu benutzen, um z. B. eine Institution zu schwächen

Globalization

Effects on the World of Work and on Personal Lives

Keyword:
Globalization: a worldwide development involving the integration of financial, economic and communications systems; often seen as an unstoppable process, affecting people all around the globe, no matter whether they live in industrialized or developing countries, in big cities or rural villages. Transfer of goods, capital, and services, as well as communications, made life easier, but not everyone profits from the development; smaller economies may suffer.
The world is said to be getting smaller, i.e. it has become a **"global village"**. The term was coined by Marshall McLuhan, a Canadian philosopher and media specialist.

Economic Challenges

As today's customers wish to buy products at the best cost/performance ratio, the global market has become very **competitive**, with the following (and related) consequences:

- More and more jobs are outsourced or offshored to cut down production costs, thereby severely damaging local labour markets.
- When jobs are outsourced to low-wage countries, the workers often work in so-called "sweatshops" for long hours at a stretch, earning only minimum wages and under working conditions that are often inhumane.
- While "global players" consider efficiency, speed, flexibility and profit most important, employees are increasingly unable to defend their rights.
- Critics like the Canadian journalist Naomi Klein accuse multinational companies of exploiting the poor and indirectly supporting child labour by only having their own profit in mind.
- People in developing countries often live under poor conditions, without a decent education or access to new means of communication. Therefore they cannot reap the benefits of globalization.
- In order to reduce the number of sweatshops, fair trade is becoming increasingly important. Its aim is to ensure that workers and small-scale producers in poor countries are paid a fair price for their work and products.
- Despite these attempts, a growing number of experts and laypeople alike fear that the gap between the rich and the poor is widening.

Aspects of the "Global Village"

- The development of aeroplanes, fast ships and trains has made fast transportation of goods and people from one part of the world to another possible.

- New means of communication, especially the Internet, have made collaboration between business partners and private individuals easier.
- Multinational companies have branches all over the world, and cost-effectiveness is a decisive factor when new production sites are set up.

Effects on the way of life

Anyone can experience the effects of globalization, e. g. when
- travelling (and meeting people from one's own town halfway round the globe)
- keeping in touch with friends or business partners in distant countries with the help of new means of communication, which are faster than ever before
- buying new goods that come from or were processed very far away
- calling a service "hotline" of a company that uses a call-center in India.

Globalization is not always regarded as a positive process:
- Some people fear that individual cultures will finally blend into a single global culture, thereby losing their cultural identity and the benefits of diversity.
- Despite or because of a globalized world, millions of people in developing countries still suffer from malnutrition or die of incurable diseases.
- Others work under cruel working conditions, producing goods that will be shipped to and sold in industrialized countries at a low price.
- One of the latest financial crises, starting in the USA in 2008, has shown that national crises will ultimately affect other nations as well, as businesses are linked and global trade is now the rule.
- Due to increased mobility, diseases like H1N1 ("swine flu") or the corona virus (cf. p. 62) can easily spread all around the globe, developing into a pandemic.
- The refugee crisis in Europe (coming to its crisis in 2015) can partly be seen as connected with globalization: people from all over the world want to participate in growing economic wealth. Many people from poor countries want to find a better future and leave their homes – just like people have always done over the centuries (e. g. emigration to America in the last two centuries). At the same time, civil and other wars force people to emigrate. As more and more countries close their borders, problems in many regions are growing. Among these problems are huge refugee camps, and people drowning and starving during dangerous journeys.
- Terrorism has become an ongoing global threat which has led to a growing feeling of insecurity in many societies. In some countries (e. g. Israel) terrorist attacks have been a virtually permanent feature of life, going back six or seven decades. In most Western, as well as Middle Eastern countries, what we know as Islamist terrorism (Al Qaeda, the "Islamic State") began with the "9/11" attacks on the World Trade Center in New York and the Pentagon in Washington on September 11, 2001. This lead to military reactions from the USA and its allies. Since then, the world has seen a large number of terrorist attacks connected with Islamist ideology (e. g. in France, England, Nigeria, Berlin in Germany) or with the ideology of white supremacy (e. g. in Christchurch in New Zealand or Utøya in Norway).

INFO Anti-globalization

Many ecological and political movements around the world criticize the levelling and disadvantageous effects of globalization. This has led to the formation of NGOs and alliances opposing the rule of capitalism over the economy of this increasingly smaller world. In opposition to the G8 summit, these organizations formed the **World Social Forum**.

Global competition

The increasingly global working world demands new skills and abilities of each individual. Since not only multinational companies but also smaller firms are outsourcing parts of their production, making use of cheap and well-educated workforces abroad, people in the industrialized countries will experience more competition when looking for work, as well as later on the job. This requires both white collar and blue-collar workers in the west

- to acquire skills and competencies that are either very specialized or carried out with special qualities no one else can offer
- to become more flexible; one must be able to adapt to changes on the job and learn new ways of working quickly
- to continue learning throughout one's whole life; it is no longer sufficient to learn a job and expect to stay in it for the remainder of one's career
- to be familiar and keep up with new forms of (computer) technology and communications, since these are constantly changing and improving
- to be able to compete with workers from all around the world who can offer the same or similar skills and abilities for maybe lower wages.

Globalization and the Corona Pandemic

At the beginning of 2020, a highly-infectious and often lethal pandemic caused by the COVID-19 corona virus started to spread rapidly across the world. Governments worldwide faced a situation threatening health and lives as never before. Harsh measures, including travel bans and stay-at-home-orders which sometimes stretched over several weeks, were imposed to keep the disease at bay, temporarily infringing fundamental rights like freedom of assembly and movement. All kinds of public services and shops were put under lockdown; night-time curfews were even decreed to prevent people from leaving their homes.

Interestingly, not all countries reacted to the virus in the same way. Sweden, for instance, did not impose any lockdown at the beginning of the pandemic and was therefore watched curiously. How would the virus spread and what damage would it do there? The strategy ended, in fact, in a higher death toll than in other countries which had imposed restrictions on movement and assembly at the peak of the disease.

Now, in spring 2021, the fight against COVID-19 has been in full swing for over a year.

As there was initially no vaccine to cope with the virus, the pandemic had the world under control until the first vaccines were developed and administered a year after the original outbreak. The vaccination programme has unfortunately developed into a problem in its own right, with manufacture, distribution and administration obstacles arising on international as well as national and local levels.
The spread of the pandemic can be seen as a negative effect of globalization: it has definitely been fostered by long-distance travelling from one continent to another.
In economic terms, the epidemic has severely damaged global trade and caused heavy financial losses. Even famous, financially strong brands have suffered, because customers have had to stay at home. Online orders have flourished, but can hardly cushion the drastic losses to local businesses. Moreover, distortions in global supply and demand – as for FFP2 masks – have demonstrated the vulnerability of global trade to unscrupulous business practices.
The various lockdowns have hit social and cultural life in particular very hard, closing entire entertainment branches like theatres, cinemas, and concerts, along with museums and art galleries, as well as restaurants, hotels and bars. The restrictions on even informal group and family meetings have made people very lonely. Elderly people and people living on their own, who have not been allowed to receive visits or to visit other people, have suffered greatly from this situation.
School – and with it family – life has also been massively affected. Teachers and students have had to adjust to digital schooling without any personal presence, and families to the new discipline of home schooling. Similar conditions have been imposed on university staff and students. The natural needs of children and young people to grow up together have been disrupted, and the changing requirements imposed by governments, sometimes relaxing and then reinstating lockdowns, have done nothing to alleviate matters.
The COVID-19 health crisis will only be overcome when herd immunity is established among the different populations of the world, after a certain level of vaccination has been achieved. But, this goal can only be reached by acting in solidarity, with vaccines distributed fairly to all countries – a real test of globalization.

Global Responsibilities

The UN

- October 24, 1945: A group of 51 countries founded the United Nations (UN) as a replacement for/successor to the League of Nations.
- The UN headquarters is located in New York City and the current Secretary General is António Guterres.
- The UN has 193 member states (2021).
- It defends human rights and fundamental freedoms

Five of the six **main organs** of the UN (General Assembly, Security Council, Economic and Social Council, Trusteeship Council and Secretariat) are located in New York City, while the International Court of Justice is in The Hague (the Netherlands). There are **various programs** and funds affiliated to the UN. Two of the best known are UNICEF (United Nations Children's Fund) and the UNHCR (Office of the United Nations High Commissioner for Refugees). The latter deals with the needs of refugees and displaced persons in post-conflict countries, e. g. Djibouti.

Aims of the UN

- to preserve international peace and security
- to promote friendly relations between member countries
- to support international cooperation with regard to economic, social and cultural as well as humanitarian issues.
- Apart from **peacekeeping** and **peacemaking** operations, peacebuilding has become more and more important.
- Here the UN and its affiliated organizations work to equip national groups with the necessary skills in conflict management, to ensure lasting peace.
- Currently (April 2021) the UN is involved in 12 peacekeeping operations, e. g. in Haiti, Mali and South Sudan.
- **Humanitarian aid** is also of major importance, e. g. providing relief for people affected by either man-made or natural disasters, and helping refugees and displaced persons.
- Other main concerns of the UN are **international law and development** (e. g. sustainable development, agriculture, international trade).

Global political changes

International peacekeeping is one of the aims of the UN:
- Once peace has been established in a country or region, peacekeepers are sent to the country or region in question to oversee the peace process.
- This can be done by overseeing elections, providing reconstruction aid and supervising the withdrawal of combatants.
- Very often, UN peacekeepers are soldiers, but they can be police officers or other civilian personnel.

- The UN Security Council authorizes peacekeeping missions, which are then carried out by the international community.
- Many of these missions are organized and led by the UN itself. There is no UN army. While the troops acting as peacekeepers are under the control of the UN, they still belong to the armed forces of their country of origin. The UN itself is controlled by the Security Council and the UN Secretariat. This reduces the risk of one peacekeeping party only following its own interests.
- Regional organizations (e. g. NATO) can be authorized by the UN to lead peacekeeping missions. These regional organizations can also organize peacekeeping missions of their own.

Migration – a global challenge

- Migration has been a worldwide phenomenon since the beginning of human history.
- People have had a number of reasons for leaving their places of origin: poverty and the dream of a better life elsewhere, climatic reasons, wars and civil wars or religious persecution, to name only the most important.[5]
- One has to distinguish between migrants and refugees:
- **Migrants** leave their countries of origin for a limited period of time or permanently, usually for economic reasons. They might have job offers in a different country, or they might have heard of good opportunities. Examples of this are emigration from European countries to the USA in the 19th century, immigrants from Poland to the Ruhr district also during the 19th century, migrant workers inside Europe today, for example to help on farms, as carers for elderly people, or to work in hospitals, and people from Africa trying to find better living conditions in Europe.
- **Refugees** usually flee their homes in order to get away from persecution or wars. Examples of this at present are the Muslim Rohingya from Myanmar, Venezuelans to other South American and Central American countries, or Syrian or Afghan people to Europe. An important example from the past are the Jews from Germany and other countries who had to flee from the Nazis.
- The International Migration Report of the UN from 2019 states that most migrants worldwide go to countries in Asia, followed by Europe and North America. The countries with the most migrants are the USA, followed by Saudi Arabia and Germany. These migrants for the most part seek – and find – employment in the countries of destination. They are not refugees, but quite a large number of them are illegal immigrants. According to the UN, there were 272 million migrants in 2019.
- The UNHCR (United Nations refugee agency) states in its statistical report for 2020 that the world is now witnessing the highest levels of displacement on record. 79.5 million people around the world have been forced to leave their homes. Among them are nearly 26 million refugees, over half of whom are under the age of 18.

5 Information based on:
https://www.un.org/en/development/desa/population/migration/publications/migrationreport/docs/MigrationReport2019_Highlights.pdf
https://www.unhcr.org/figures-at-a-glance.html
https://refugeesmigrants.un.org/refugees-compact
https://www.refugeesinternational.org/reports-overview

45.7 million are internal refugees, i.e. they flee from one part of the country to another (Nigeria is one example). There are 4.2 million asylum seekers worldwide. However, 73 % of refugees stay in neighbouring countries: Syrian refugees mainly flee to Turkey, Jordan and other countries close by. More than half the refugees worldwide come at present from Syria, Afghanistan and South Sudan.
- In 2020 Turkey hosted the largest refugee population worldwide, with 3.6 million refugees and asylum seekers, followed by Colombia (1.8 million), Pakistan (1.4 million) and Uganda (1.4 million). Most refugees come from Syria (6.6 million), Venezuela (3.7 million), Afghanistan (2.7 million), South Sudan (2.2. million) and Myanmar (1.1 million).
- There are also millions of stateless people who have been denied nationality and access to basic rights such as education, healthcare, employment and freedom of movement.
- About 1 percent of the world's population have fled their homes.
- Nearly 1 person is forcibly displaced every two seconds as a result of conflict or persecution.
- The fact that most refugees seek help in neighbouring, not always wealthy countries can cause major problems there: the population of these countries has to share access to education, healthcare and jobs with the refugees. Compared to rich countries like Germany, countries like Jordan or the Lebanon find it far more difficult to cope with the situation. Colombia is another example of these conflicts: it is a country which is only just beginning to overcome the effects of a civil war. Recently it has also been the destination of over 1 million refugees from Venezuela.
- On the other hand, migration always also means enrichment: the destination country will, with time, integrate the new arrivals. Their culture, beliefs and customs will become part of the country, thus leading to a more diverse culture in general.
- Many migrants and refugees want to return to their home countries if the situation allows them to. Seasonal migrants, for example, usually leave their families behind and return when their work has finished for the year. Many refugees want to return to their old home after the end of a war, others would like to stay in their new home and build a new life there.

The EU

- Currently 28 states belong to the European Union (EU). The newest members are Bulgaria and Romania, which both joined the EU on January 1, 2007, and Croatia which became a member on July 1, 2013.
- After World War II there was a desire for a united Europe in order to prevent extreme forms of nationalism. The European Coal and Steel Community, the European Economic Community (EEC) and the European Atomic Energy Community (Euratom) were merged into the European Community (EC) in 1967.
- The EU as we know it came into existence in 1993, when the Maastricht Treaty, which among other things initiated the euro as a common currency, was ratified.
- The individual member states came to be regarded as one single global player.

- At present the EU faces the challenge of maintaining its unity – and indeed remaining a union at all – in the face and the aftermath of the refugee crisis. The countries of the EU have very different attitudes to solving the refugee problem.
- In December 2019 the United Kingdom (UK) left the EU, a decision taken by referendum in June 2016. There are numerous consequences for companies, employees and people from other EU countries working in the UK. Many companies have already withdrawn their head offices and/or large facilities from the country.

Aims of the EU

- to promote prosperity and social progress with European citizenship for its peoples while still keeping their diversity alive
- to promote friendly relations between member countries
- to guarantee freedom and justice for the peoples of Europe
- to represent the member states internationally with a single voice, tackling the various challenges of globalization, as well as respecting human rights.

When it comes to defence, the individual member countries are sovereign. However, there is military cooperation in peacekeeping missions.

The three main groups, which make up the EU are
- the Council of Ministers
- the European Parliament
- the European Commission.

Although the EU has no official capital, the official seat of the European Commission and the Council of the European Union, and the second seat of the European Parliament are in Brussels, Belgium.

Global Ecological Challenges

Environmental pollution has been growing rapidly and globally. The following factors in particular create global problems:
- **waste gases** from factories
- Over the last decades the number of **vehicles** on the roads has steadily increased. Cars are no longer found only in industrialized countries.
- The number of people travelling by plane is also greater than ever, due to the fact that plane tickets have become affordable for a larger number of people. Short-haul **flights** have become particularly popular.
- **Food miles:** Whereas some years ago many people bought fruit and vegetables locally and ate seasonal products, they now want to eat strawberries and cherries in December. So more goods are transported by plane. Ecologically conscious customers ask themselves whether it is better to buy local products than food (even fair trade products) that has been flown across continents.
- Everyone leaves a **carbon footprint** (emission of greenhouse gases from factories, cars, trains, planes, etc) either directly or indirectly.

- **Greenhouse gases** cause chemical damage to the atmosphere (e.g. hole in the ozone layer) as well as global warming.
- Lots of pupils from all over Europe have left their schools on (some) Fridays and joined the movement *Fridays for Future* started by the Swedish teenager Greta Thunberg in a protest against climate change.

Global warming and its consequences

After years of heated discussion among scientists and (especially) politicians worldwide, it is now considered common knowledge in most nations around the globe that the world's climate is changing. This change manifests itself most dramatically in the fact that the global average temperature is rising, and this has many side effects. The first documentary *An Inconvenient Truth and its follow-up* lay out the scientific facts on global warming in detail.

Causes of global warming

- Fossil fuel emissions, so-called greenhouse gases, form a layer in the earth's atmosphere which traps the sun's heat and thereby causes the temperature on the ground to rise; this is called "global warming".
- The quantity of greenhouse gases produced worldwide is rising, because
  - more cars, planes and industrial complexes are being built and used;
  - forests are burnt to make way for agriculture, people, roads etc.;
  - growth in the number of cattle is increasing the emission of methane.
- The global rise in temperature is causing the polar ice caps to melt, diminishing their efficiency as a cooling device and mirror to reflect sunbeams, and thus speeding up the heating process in the atmosphere.

Effects and consequences

There are many consequences of climate change. Some may seem rather insignificant at first but turn out to be disastrous in the long run. Although these effects are often spoken of as taking place in the future, many of them are already happening. Thus the present tense is used here:

- Rising global temperatures are causing more water to evaporate both on land and in the oceans, changing historical patterns of rainfall and drought; many people are unable to adapt to these irregular weather phenomena.
- Oceanic warming is causing hurricanes to become more frequent and violent, as the warm water enhances evaporation and (indirectly) wind speed.
- Changes in temperature also cause natural habitats to change. Plants and animals have to adapt, and if they cannot do so they will die out. Biodiversity is therefore endangered, limiting the natural resources on which we subsist.
- Diseases are spreading more quickly because parasites like mosquitoes and their animal hosts are affecting populations in previously safe areas.
- If the polar ice caps were to melt completely, a process which is already under way, a large part of the earth's landmass would be flooded, leaving millions homeless.

- If enough polar ice melts, the North Atlantic current (Gulf Stream), which guarantees Europe's warm climate, might stop. In a worst-case scenario, Europe might experience another ice age.
- In other areas, desertification will continue to increase, a phenomenon which is already taking place.
- All these developments will dramatically reduce the area of land on which human existence is possible and will therefore lead to worldwide migration that the countries affected will be unable to deal with.

The effects are threatening the entire planet and the way we live today. Because of this, scientists, politicians and citizens worldwide have a duty to seek ways of reducing greenhouse gases in order to slow down climate change. Each individual can participate in reducing greenhouse gas emissions by using better insulation in houses, saving electricity, recycling waste, using public transportation instead of a private car, flying only when absolutely necessary, etc.
The key to saving the environment is "thinking global and acting local". More information on climate change can be found on the website of Al Gore, who made the movie "An Inconvenient Truth" www.algore.com.

INFO

International efforts to stop climate change – the Kyoto Protocol and the Paris Agreement

The international political elite came together in Japan in December 1997 and issued a common declaration, the **Kyoto Protocol**, which came into effect on February 16, 2005. The protocol aimed to reduce the emission of greenhouse gases by an annual 5.2% by 2012, taking 1990 levels as a basis.
Ever since then, numerous other summits have taken place in order to reduce and slow global warming. In Paris in 2015 a global agreement on the slowing of climate change (the **Paris Agreement**) was reached and adopted by 195 countries. Among the decisions made was the resolution to limit the long-term increase of global average temperature to well below 2°C above pre-industrial levels. The agreement came into effect on November 4, 2016, as enough countries had ratified it. In June 2017 the USA withdrew its consent to the agreement.
One of the first actions of the new U.S. President, Joe Biden, was to announce that the USA was to rejoin the Paris Agreement on Climate Change: it did so on 19 February, 2021. With the USA being part of the Paris Agreement again, two-thirds of the countries producing half of global carbon pollution have committed to carbon neutrality. This agreement, the first legally binding global climate change agreement, has been ratified by 191 countries (April 2021).

Political efforts to reduce greenhouse gas emissions are still faced with various difficulties and conflicts of interests. So each climate summit only achieves small steps to stop or slow down climate change. Scientists and independent organizations alike argue that these small steps might not be enough to prevent the consequences of global warming. The main goal remains to cut greenhouse gas emissions, especially those caused by the burning of fossil fuels.

Fridays for Future

- In August 2018, Greta Thunberg, a then 16-year-old Swedish climate change activist, started protesting outside the Swedish parliament in Stockholm in order to raise awareness of the dangers of climate change.
- According to Thunberg, politicians are not taking enough action against climate change, which is putting our planet's future at risk. Thunberg's solitary school strikes soon caught the attention of the media in countries all over the world.
- Up to May 2019, an estimated 1.4 million teenagers and young adults worldwide have followed her example by going on strike from school every Friday and protesting against climate change. This movement is known as "Fridays for Future". Since the beginning of COVID-19, it has been more difficult to demonstrate for new climate change policies, but the movement has tried to find other ways of protesting.
- Greta Thunberg has delivered several public speeches in which she has put pressure on politicians and world leaders to combat climate change more swiftly and resolutely. She spoke at various important global meetings, e.g. the United Nations Climate Change Conference in Katowice, Poland in December 2018 and at the World Economic Forum in Davos, Switzerland in January 2019.
- The speed of the reaction and the immense sums of money provided by governments during the corona crisis seem to prove Fridays for Future's point: Immediate global action is possible, but the governments all over the world do not seem to regard an effective fight against global warming as a top priority.

Alternatives to Using Fossil Fuels

Recent discussions on fossil fuels and their effect on the atmosphere have supported the development of technology to make use of renewable sources of energy such as wind, water and solar power. In many European countries, national programmes to subsidize these technologies have been established. The US is also aiming to support these alternative energies more substantially, but this has not been achieved by recent administrations. The Fukushima disaster in spring 2011 led the German government to withdraw from using nuclear energy in future. Other parties urge that nuclear power should be used instead of fossil fuels (which are still the most important sources of energy). However, the use of nuclear energy has always been discussed controversially.

Natural alternative energy sources

In general, the use of wind, water and solar power seems far less risky and also less expensive in the long run. The challenge engineers have to face is to make these technologies more efficient and find ways to store the energy produced. One main hindrance is posed by companies investing more money in fossil fuel exploration and exploitation and in expanding nuclear power facilities. Since these technologies are well established, their exploitation yields enormous profits, whereas investment in new ecologically-friendly sources of energy is costly, but could create many jobs.

Non-renewable and/versus renewable energy

- Since the Industrial Revolution, western societies have been in constantly growing need of energy resources to power industrial production and satisfy communal and household requirements for fuel and electricity.
- This increasing demand for energy has led to various developments:
  - The exploitation of natural resources such as oil, gas and coal has led to the destruction of natural habitats on land and in the oceans.
  - The use of nuclear power plants had created a seemingly safe, cheap and climate-friendly source of power. This has changed since the disaster in Fukushima.
  - New inventions have succeeded in making use of renewable energies such as wind, water and solar power.
- The most immediate result of the use of fossil fuels since the Industrial Revolution is the amount of carbon dioxide and other pollutants emitted into the atmosphere.

Environmental sustainability

It will prove difficult to sustain usable natural resources. Industrialization, together with a continuously growing world population, has led to a massive exploitation of limited resources. Thus the sustainability of resources and natural habitats is one of the most important global ecological challenges.

Global goals

In 2015, world leaders agreed on 17 goals for a better world by 2030. These goals seek to end poverty, fight inequality and stop climate change. It is now up to all of us, governments, businesses, civil society, and the general public to work together to build a better future for everyone. (cf. https://www.globalgoals.org/):

1. no poverty
2. zero hunger
3. good health and well-being
4. quality education
5. gender equality
6. clean water and sanitation
7. affordable and clean energy
8. decent work and economic growth
9. industry, innovation and infrastructure
10. reduced inequalities
11. sustainable cities and communities

12. responsible consumption and production
13. climate action
14. life below water
15. life on land
16. peace, justice and strong institutions
17. partnerships for these goals

English as a Global Language

The general importance of English in the globalized world of international trade and politics, science, popular culture and travel is still unrivalled. No matter where you are in the world, a command of English will always help.
Worldwide, 1.348 million people speak English as a native speaker or as a second language, followed by Mandarin, the main language in China (1.120 million), Hindi (600 million) and Spanish (543 million)[5].
Especially in the countries of the former British Empire, English is not just a language universally understood and spoken, it is very often still an official language. In India, for example, more than 3,000 newspapers are published in English, but English is spoken by only about five per cent of the population. There are 1,652 languages and dialects in India, which makes English as a working *lingua franca* even more important. All in all, English is the official language in 59 countries today.
It has been estimated that about a billion people worldwide speak English as a second language[6]. According to the EU statistical service, 96% of all students at lower secondary level in the EU study English as a second language[7]. International organizations like NATO or OECD use English exclusively, as do many internationally operating enterprises like Airbus Industries and even Volkswagen in their Shanghai branch.
According to Bill Bryson[8], English differs from other languages in three outstanding respects that make it attractive even to speakers of other mother tongues. First, its rich vocabulary is wider than that of other languages. The latest edition of the *Oxford English Dictionary* lists 615,000 words; 200,000 words are commonly used in English, compared to 184,000 in German and just 100,000 in French. What adds to the wide range of words is the large number of synonyms. The best known collection of synonyms and antonyms, *Roget's Thesaurus*, has over 100,000 entries. There is an almost endless list of words that can be used both as noun and verb.

English as a *Lingua Franca*

A *lingua franca* is a language that can be used by speakers who do not have any knowledge of each other's mother tongue. It is therefore also referred to as a "contact" or "link" language. English used in this context bridges the linguistic gap for non-native speakers of English who do not share a common first language and thus serves as

5 Figures for 2020: https://www.statista.com/statistics/266808/the-most-spoken-languages-worldwide/
6 figures according to the British Council: https://www.thoughtco.com/how-many-people-learn-english-globally-1210367
7 https://ec.europa.eu/eurostat/documents/2995521/5177306/3-25092014-AP-EN.PDF.pdf/568bd6e0-0184-444e-b965-ffc801c7df99
8 Bill Bryson: Mother Tongue. The Story of the English Language (London 1990).

a means of intercultural communication. Since this happens worldwide, English has been called a "global *lingua franca*".
The result of this extensive use of English is that it is shaped not only by its native speakers but also by those who use it as a foreign language.
Researchers[9] have found that although speakers of English as a *lingua franca* do not always adhere to the rules of grammar and pronunciation, communication is not necessarily inhibited by this. What seems more important in this respect is language awareness, along with a command of communication strategies. Nevertheless, the more closely a person's grammar approximates to Standard English, the more readily they will be understood.

Varieties of English

American English

- American English is relatively homogeneous compared to British English. About 80% of the population speak with the same accent.
- The USA contains four speech groups: Northern, Midland, Southern and New England. Midland is subdivided into North and South Midland.
- Regional variation due to geographical and historical factors: colonists on the East Coast were in touch with people from England via trade; therefore similarities with British English (e.g. the pronunciation of "Tuesday", "news"; the absence of [r] in "horse", "car").
- Social prestige is linked to pronunciation, e.g. the sound of [r] is carefully produced by upper-middle-class speakers when they want to indicate their social standing.
- There has been some rivalry between England and America as to the question whose language is more correct. On becoming independent, Americans emphasized the differences between British and American English, thus creating some sort of language nationalism.
- Immigrants often try to conceal their origins by overemphasizing vowel sounds, e.g. in "coffee". This is called hypercorrection.
- The phenomenon of t-dropping is widely practised. That means that [t] is not pronounced in the middle of a word, e.g. in "winter" or "Internet".
- [o] in "clock" is realized like the [a] in British English "car". A British native speaker could therefore mistake the American "clock" for the word "clerk".
- The way Americans speak is often referred to as "the American twang". This most commonly refers to "General American", which is a generalized Midwestern accent used by many TV and radio hosts. (cf. p. 76 for AAVE/Black Vernacular).

9 Cf. Barbara Seidlhofer: *English as a lingua franca*, in: ELT Journal Volume 59/4 October 2005; doi:10.1093/elt/cci064, p. 339 f. Oxford University Press.

British English

- In the Middle English period Oxford, Cambridge and London shared the same kind of English. Because of the prestige attached to it, London English became the basis for Standard English as early as the time of Chaucer's Middle English. This became the national language.
- One variety of English spoken in London is called Cockney. In the sixteenth century this was not associated with the language of the East End working-class, as it is today, but it was the language spoken by all Londoners outside the Court. It was only in the eighteenth century that Cockney became regarded as coarse or low English. One of the reasons for this development is that the City became the centre of commerce and trade, thereby making the old inhabitants move east to Wapping, Shoreditch and Bermondsey.
- Characteristics of Cockney include h-dropping, which means that the [h] at the beginning of a word is not pronounced, and the "glottal stop", which is the result of not pronouncing the [t] in words like "butter" or "bottle". Furthermore, the [g] in word endings is often omitted, for example in "eatin'".
- Standard English as spoken by a mere two to five per cent of the British population has also been labelled "Received Pronunciation" or simply "RP". It was until recently spoken by British middle-class people, especially in the South, and it was used by most TV and radio news presenters.

Australian English

- Like American English, Australian English is fairly uniform in pronunciation.
- Three different social accents can be distinguished: "Cultivated" (similar to British English; 10% of speakers), "Broad" (working-class accent; 10%) and "General" (80%). On the whole, there is not much regional variety in accent.
- Girls and women tend to speak General or Cultivated Australian, whereas boys and men prefer General or Broad Australian.
- Using a rising tone at the end of a statement, which has become popular with girls and women (not only in Australia), is called "rising inflection".
- Words from the Aboriginals: "billabong", "didgeridoo", "boomerang", "koala", "kangaroo".
- Usage is influenced by America: "cookies", "station wagon", "teller", "mail", "labor", "dollar".
- Australian English has been influenced by large numbers of immigrants, so-called "New Australians" from Turkey, Greece, Italy, Sri Lanka, etc.

New Zealand English

- It is very similar to Australian English, although New Zealanders tend to believe their way of speaking is more sophisticated and try to be as close to British English as possible.

Canadian English

- Beginnings of Canadian English: in the wake of the American Revolution Loyalists (supporters of the English) fled in large numbers to Ontario, providing the basis for "General Canadian" as an urban middle-class variety of English.
- Along the Atlantic coast there were many English-speaking settlements.

English in India

- Approximately 70 million people use English in India. About 25 million use English regularly, thus making it an important language of official life.
- English is spoken mainly by the educated ruling classes.
- Many national daily papers are in English (e.g. *The Times of India*).
- All-India Radio broadcasts in English all over India.
- English was used in the fields of government, education and imperial rule.
- In 1857 English-speaking universities were established in Bombay, Calcutta and Madras.
- English had also become the language of prestige as well as the language of nationalist opposition (not Hindi, as might be expected).
- A large number of Indian words have been integrated into English, e.g. "curry", "bungalow" or "veranda", especially by English administrators in the nineteenth century.

Pidgin

A pidgin is an artificial, auxiliary language without any native speakers. It is used by people with different mother tongues who need a common means of communication. Pidgin English was the traders' and slaves' *lingua franca*. The word "pidgin" is derived from the way the Chinese pronounced the word "business". There are French, English and Portuguese pidgins.
There was a sailors' *lingua franca*, Sabir, a Mediterranean language dating from the time of the Crusades. Europeans involved in trade with Africa needed a different means of communication.

Creole

- If a pidgin is used as a first language, it is called a creole. This process happens gradually and it takes several generations.
- When slaves from many different African tribes with different languages were transported to America by slave ships, they needed a common language. Therefore, they spoke pidgin English, which was accessible to all of them.
- Examples are the Caribbean creole of Barbados, which is based on English, or Haitian creole, which is based on French. The creole of Papua New Guinea (Tok Pisin) has a written as well as a spoken form.

African American Vernacular English (AAVE)

- formerly called Black English, AAVE has absorbed aspects of African pidgin and Caribbean creole, and has a long and distinctive tradition. It has a set of rules, although whites have often misunderstood and misjudged Black English as inferior because certain grammatical structures of English are simplified or do not occur. Nowadays, however, it is considered to be another variety of English. It is also called "Black Vernacular".
- The verb "to be" is often left out. There is no present-tense inflection: "He angry when he come".
- On the one hand, Black English is representative of a disadvantaged past, on the other hand, it is also a means of self-expression.
- Contributions from the African world to everyday English are words and expressions like "voodoo", "banana" or "high five".
- Black Vernacular probably originated even before the slave trade began.
- Due to music and popular films and series, it has achieved wide public attention. Outside the academic community AAVE is commonly called Ebonics. Some features of AAVE are apparently unique to this variety, but the structure is often similar to other English varieties spoken in the US and Caribbean. The number of speakers of AAVE is extremely difficult to establish.
  (for more information cf. https://www.youtube.com/watch?v=aQrtB7cZDrA or https://www.youtube.com/watch?v=0rQ94hYGJZA or https://www.youtube.com/watch?v=pkzVOXKXfQk)

South African English (SAE)

English was first brought to the Cape area by British settlers, fortune seekers and missionaries in the late 18th and early 19th century. The minority of about 3 million first-language SAE-speakers is outnumbered by second- and third-language speakers, because English is seen both as the language of communication and aspiration, as well as a 'colonist' language. For many black parents English is an instrument for their children's advancement. SAE is dominant in public life, for reasons of practicality and cost-efficiency, even though official documents are also translated into the other ten official languages.

In the Soweto uprising in 1976, the question of a teaching language in black schools was crucial: the students opted for English, as they did not want to study in Afrikaans, the language of their white oppressors. So English has always been seen as opposing Afrikaans with the black population preferring to use English and the language of their own cultural origin whereas many white people have kept to Afrikaans.

Strong influences on SAE vocabulary and pronunciation mainly come from the surrounding African languages as well as from Afrikaans or unclear sources. Due to SAE having different native tongues, the pronunciation tends to vary a lot. In general, pronunciation is closest to NZE (New Zealand English), tending to become more levelled through teaching in urban schools and through modern communications media.

Glossary – Globalization

anti-globalist	Globalisierungsgegner/-kritiker
backwardness	Rückständigkeit
company philosophy	Geschäfts-/Firmenphilosophie
competition; to be competitive	Konkurrenz(kampf)/Wettbewerb; konkurrenzfähig sein
corporate identity	Firmenimage
crop diseases	Krankheiten von Pflanzen/Saatgut
debt relief	Schuldenerlass, Entschuldung
desertification	die Desertifikation/Wüstenbildung, das Vordringen der Wüste
developing countries	Entwicklungsländer
development aid	Entwicklungshilfe
driving forces of globalization	die Antriebskräfte der Globalisierung
drought	Dürren, Dürreperioden
earth's atmosphere	die Erdatmosphäre
economic growth	Wirtschaftswachstum
economic prosperity	ökonomischer Wohlstand
emerging markets	Schwellenländer
environmental commitment	Umwelteinsatz
environmental damage	Umweltzerstörung
environmentally friendly	umweltfreundlich
expansion of capitalism	Ausbreitung des Kapitalismus
fair trade	fairer Handel
floods	Hochwasser, Überschwemmungen
global interconnection	globale Querverbindungen
global marketplace	globaler Marktplatz
global player	Weltfirma
global super power	eine globale Supermacht
global warming	Erderwärmung
"going global"	umgangssprachlicher Ausdruck, der ursprünglich für die globale Expansion von Firmen verwendet wurde
greenhouse gases	Treibhausgase
human rights	Menschenrechte
increase profit margins	die Gewinnspanne erhöhen

Industrial Age	das Industriezeitalter
industrial nations	Industrieländer/-nationen
international stock markets	internationale Börsenmärkte
labour laws/ market	Arbeitsgesetze/ Arbeitsmarkt
lingua franca	eine Sprache, die von Personen mit unterschiedlichen Muttersprachen benutzt wird
low-wage countries	Niedriglohnländer
mass tourism	Massentourismus
micro-credits	Kleinkredite
NGO (non-governmental organization)	Nichtregierungsorganisation
outsourcing	Produktionsverlagerung
political turmoil	politischer Aufruhr, politische Turbulenzen
pollution	Verschmutzung
population overshoot, overpopulation, excess of population	Überbevölkerung
poverty	Armut
greenhouse gas emissions	den Ausstoß von Treibhausgasen
cost of production	Produktionskosten
rise in global temperature	ein weltweiter Temperaturanstieg
robotized production	computergesteuerte Produktion/Fertigung
shareholder	Aktionär
supremacy	Vormachtsstellung, Überlegenheit
sustainability	Nachhaltigkeit, Zukunftsfähigkeit
sweatshop	ausbeuterischer Betrieb
trade	Handel
trademark policy	Markenpolitik
undernutrition, malnutrition	Unterernährung; Mangelernährung
unemployment	Arbeitslosigkeit
workforce	Arbeiterschaft
working conditions	Arbeitsbedingungen

Science and Technology

The dawn of science in the modern sense of drawing factual conclusions from empirical, experimental or statistical data can be dated back to ancient Greece, when scholars aimed to explain the world on the basis of observation and elaboration. During the Renaissance, science experienced a rebirth, and in the wake of the Industrial Revolution it evolved to become what it is today: the basis of our modern way of life.

Gaining background knowledge:

The emergence of today's technology-oriented societies can only be fully understood by studying the Industrial Revolution. The full extent of the changes the Industrial Revolution brought cannot be presented in this context. Various informative sites can be found online.

Chances and Risks

Scientific research aims to explore and explain the world around us and improve the means by which we cope with it. Technology, in turn, is the practical outcome of this research, resulting in the tools and machines we use to make our lives (seemingly) easier. Each new technology, however, harbours risks as well as opportunities and creates new kinds of dependencies unknown before. One simple example will suffice to prove this point:

- at the end of the 19th century the first automobiles were produced; eventually they would replace horse-drawn vehicles and other means of individual transport;
- in contrast to older technologies, cars need fossil fuel;
- demand for cars increased during the 20th century, production became cheaper, and today almost every household in western societies owns at least one car.

The increasing use of cars has had various consequences:

- more demand for fossil fuels: increased drilling for oil on land and at sea;
- demand for larger roads: expansion of highways, parking lots etc.;
- consequences: growing destruction of natural habitats and resources;
- increasing mobility: the former luxury of owning a car has become a must; some jobs cannot be done without a car, one is expected to own a car; public transport systems aim to meet general mobility needs;
- cars produce exhaust fumes: the amount of carbon dioxide and other climate-changing fumes released into the atmosphere has increased dramatically;
- once limited to the so-called developed countries, cars are now in increasing demand in developing countries such as India and China;
- this development will further increase the amount of atmospheric pollution and have an effect on the global climate.
- recently a lot of research has been done in the field of hybrid and electric mobility.

Of course, the invention of the car has improved our lives in numerous ways by making transport and mobility easier and cheaper. The example of the car represents a simple model of how you should view technological developments: always consider their positive as well as negative potential. One such ambivalent area of current scientific research is genetic engineering.

Genetic engineering

Genetic engineering is being applied in different areas, such as reprogenetics, prenatal diagnostics, human and animal cloning and agriculture.

- after the discovery of DNA, scientists have succeeded in analysing animal and human DNA sequences, and seek to establish how genes determine our bodily functions, appearance etc., searching for causes of inherited diseases
- positive effect: knowing about genetic reasons for certain defects can save people's lives, once cures and treatments have been developed
- ambivalent effects: genetic engineering (influencing animal or human DNA by implanting or changing specific genetic material) can be used to improve plants/animals/even humans to be less prone to diseases, parasites, etc.; genetically modified foodstuffs can be grown more intensively (in developing countries starvation might be combated more efficiently), but it is largely unknown whether modified corn or other plants might also cause changes to our DNA or metabolism
- possible negative effects: the downside is a wide range of unknown effects of manipulating natural genetic material: natural plant variants can be contaminated with the new genetic material and become extinct; cloning and manipulating animal DNA might lead to similar effects; natural selection processes might be interfered with, thus man might actually change evolutionary development; the eradication of unwanted DNA in humans might lead to the development of a new caste system of improved and unimproved humans; the latter might eventually no longer be able to find jobs or insurances willing to take them; disabled people will be excluded even more from society; natural evolutionary processes might be halted and/or altered completely

The effects of genetic engineering on our everyday lives might turn out to be more far-reaching and irreversible than we can imagine today. Consequently, there is an ongoing debate on whether everything that can be done should be done. Because new developments emerge so quickly, laws and regulations are often slow to follow, which is also a result of the complexity of these innovations. As a result, many inventions have already been achieved before ethical questions and possible negative effects can be considered. Science is often ahead of people's ability to use the new technology sensibly.

Keyword:

Cloning: by definition the process of making an identical copy of an organism or cell[1]
Cloning human beings has long been ousted internationally. However, continuous research was put into it and the first clones of a species close to a human being, two monkeys, were reportedly born in China in 2018.

1 https://www.collinsdictionary.com/dictionary/english/cloning

Visions of the Future

Humankind has always dreamed about the future and has created the world it wanted to live in. People have always aimed at new challenges and tried out new ideas. In literature, these ways have been formulated in utopias and dystopias, positive and negative visions of the future. Technological innovation has fuelled the creation of dystopian visions of societies, often in the form of a science fiction novel, prominent examples are Huxley's *Brave New World*, Orwell's *1984* or Ishiguro's *Never Let Me Go*. However, broadly dystopian ideas are also present in popular fiction like *The Hunger Games* by the American novelist Suzanne Collins.
However, some social movements are still actively seeking new and positive ways of living with each other, sharing space, goods and work-skills in community projects and living. In the aging societies of the West, this is proving very important. Increasingly, ideas like urban gardening might also change the city space to create a more liveable environment.

Mary Shelley, *Frankenstein* (eA)

A note on the author and the work

Mary Wollstonecraft Shelley (1797–1851) was the daughter of one of the first feminist activists, Mary Wollstonecraft, and the political philosopher William Godwin. Her father gave her a wide-ranging but somewhat informal education, and at the age of 17 Mary eloped with the married poet Percy Bysshe Shelley to France, accompanied by her stepsister Claire. On her return to England, Mary was pregnant, but her daughter, born prematurely, died.
In summer 1816 the couple set out on a trip to Switzerland, with Claire and with two of Shelley's friends. They stayed near Lake Geneva. In 1818, they moved on to Italy. Two other children died, and only the couple's fourth child, a boy, survived. In 1822, Percy Shelley drowned in a storm off the Italian coast. Mary returned to England. She remained true to her mother's ideas of feminism and to her father's political philosophy, and always showed an open-minded attitude despite the hardships and setbacks she endured. The final decade of her life was full of writing and editing but also marked by illness. She died at the age of fifty-three.
Mary Shelley started writing the story of Frankenstein and his unorthodox scientific experiment during a stay in Switzerland in the cold, wet summer of 1816. As a way of countering boredom, the party – Mary, Percy Shelley, and two friends, one of them the poet Lord Byron – started a competition for the best horror story. Mary Shelley's figure, the scientist Victor Frankenstein, creates life out of stolen body parts. Then, terrified at what he has created, he leaves his "creature" alone to cope with its destiny. The being, which has no name and receives no moral education from its creator, turns violent and is finally hunted down by its creator. Mary's story won the competition. A striking piece of early science fiction, Frankenstein is a fine example of a dystopian Gothic novel. As such, it reproduces themes from the Romantic literature popular at the time.

The story addresses the potential of science to destroy rather than to support and sustain human beings. It was written at a time of rapid scientific progress and industrialization. The novel asks the question: What happens if humans decide to play God? This question remains a poignant one today with advances in genetic engineering, artificial intelligence and nuclear science as well as robotics threatening traditional values and beliefs.
The full title oft he novel is *Frankenstein; or, The Modern Prometheus*[1]. The story was first published anonymously in London in 1818, a second edition 1821 showed the author's name; the 1831 edition was revised. Ever since the first publication of the novel, the name "Frankenstein" has often been used to refer to the 'monster' rather than its creator.

Plot and structure

Frame story by Captain Robert Walton

The novel has a frame story in the form of letters by Captain Robert Walton to his sister in which Walton tells her about an expedition to the North Pole, where he rescued Victor Frankenstein. Half frozen from having been out on the ice, Frankenstein sees that Walton shares the obsession that has almost destroyed him. He tells him the story of the creature he had pursued, who had been seen earlier by Walton's sailors.

Victor's story

Having grown up in Italy, Victor Frankenstein studies chemistry in Ingolstadt, Germany, and is fascinated by the idea of alchemy. He is a fervent student and particularly interested in giving life to non-living matter. He collects body parts from local cemeteries and assembles a seemingly well-chosen human body, forming a creature some 2.4m in height. When the creature wakes, Victor discovers that it is ugly, has watery eyes, a deathly skin colour and visible muscles and blood vessels.
On his return from meeting his friend, Henry Clerval, the creature has disappeared. Victor falls seriously ill and only recovers because Henry nurses him. Four months later, Victor's father informs him of the murder of his brother William in Geneva. Near the scene of crime, Victor observes the creature and suspects that it is responsible for the deed. But he sees no way of telling the truth and William's nanny, Justine, is accused of the crime and hanged. Victor flees to the mountains. While he is hiking near Mont Blanc, the creature approaches him to talk about the past and future.

The creature's story

After his creation by Frankenstein, the creature turns to the wilderness. Noticing that people run away from him, he hides from them. But, living in the woods near a poor family's cottage, he develops positive feelings for them and secretly helps them. He learns their language and even teaches himself how to read from books he discovers in the forest. One day, he sees his reflection in the water and realizes how hideous he

1 Original title, today often shortened. In Greek mythology, Prometheus is the Titan god of fire, capable of creating humans from clay, among other gifts.

is and why humans have reacted to him with horror. He stays near the family, hoping to become friends with them, and enters their house when only the blind father is present. When the rest of the family returns, the son attacks him and he flees, enraged. Giving up hope of ever being accepted by human beings, he decides to find his creator in Geneva. He believes that Frankenstein will help him.
On his way, the creature saves a child from drowning, only to be shot at by the child's father, who misunderstands his harmless intentions. This event marks a turning point, in that it makes the creature swear revenge against humans in general. On arriving in Geneva, the creature talks to Frankenstein and demands that he create a female companion for him, because, he argues, he has the same right to happiness as any other being in the world. He promises to disappear into the wilderness with his mate if Victor agrees. Otherwise, he will kill his remaining family and ruin Victor personally.

Frankenstein's story continued

Frankenstein reluctantly agrees to the creation of a second being and on the Orkney Islands starts to work on a female. But, fearing that she might be even more evil than his first creation, and that together they might breed a new race, he destroys the unfinished creation at a moment when his first creature is looking though the window. Falling asleep in his boat, Frankenstein is blown to Ireland, where he is arrested for the murder of Clerval, who had been strangled by the creature. He has a mental breakdown, is put into prison, proven innocent of the crime and released. His father and he return to Geneva, where he plans to marry and to kill the creature, who, however, strangles his future bride, Elisabeth, almost under Victor's eyes. To revenge these deeds, Victor chases the creature through Europe and Russia into the arctic region of the North Pole. However, the creature always stays a step ahead. Victor collapses, and the creature escapes again. Victor is driven towards Walton's ship and rescued.

Captain Walton's conclusion

The winter is fierce and Captain Walton's ship is trapped in pack ice. Once it is freed, he decides to turn south. Frankenstein vows to go off by himself, despite his weak condition: he is determined that the creature must die, but before he can fulfil his pledge, he dies. In his last words, he makes Walton promise to kill the monster for him. The creature is seen on board the ship mourning over Victor's body: the death of his creator has not brought him peace, he says, and his crimes have made him more miserable than Frankenstein ever was. He tells Walton that he will kill himself so that no one need ever know of his existence. Walton watches the creature disappear for good, drifting away on an ice floe. It is never seen again.

Reception and analysis

Creators must assume responsibility for their creation. This message has not always been stressed in interpretations of the story or in the numerous adaptations and films based on it. Of these, the 1931 film version with Boris Karloff as the monster stands out. From the early days of film, the element of horror has attracted filmmakers: the development of a creature without ethical principles or any kind of moral notion has been a focal point of the story's reception. No pity has been shown for 'the fiend', only pity for the creator pursued by such a demon. While Frankenstein is said to play God, his creature is compared to Adam, the first man, or to Milton's Satan in *Paradise Lost*. The novel was well received and immediately turned into a popular play, which prompted Mary Shelley to revise and republish it. Her final revision is the popular edition of 1831. The novel has since seen many editions and many different – including feminist and psychoanalytical – readings.

Shelley also invokes supernatural elements, especially in association with the creation and life of Frankenstein's monster. The setting is isolated and eerie. The scenes of action (e.g. the Alps or the Arctic) reflect Romantic interests in the wild and undiscovered elements of nature. The deep exploration of human emotions is also new to literature, as is the attraction shown for figures that break traditional social boundaries. Following their lofty ideals and their own curiosity, they are driven into dangerous situations. Thus, at a time when the ideas of the Enlightenment and the ideal of scientific knowledge are becoming popular, the author warns against the obsessive pursuit of scientific knowledge. This was also a time when rationalism and order in the arts was being contested by thinkers like Percy Shelley, who stress individual experience over objective principles.

The novel contains a lot of symbolism, including darkness (standing for emptiness and despair), light (representing hope and learning) and fire, which both creates and destroys. Electricity, a discovery of the 1800s, promises new scientific possibilities. Galvanism is seen in the same way but, in her preface to the 1831 edition, Mary Shelley warns that scientific experiments can be taken too far.

This conflict has endured till the present day, when Shelley's *Frankenstein* has been invoked to criticize scientific breakthroughs, with cloned animals rejected as "Frankensteinian" and genetically modified crops called "Frankenfoods" (a word coined in the early 2000s).

The Media

Keyword:

The Media: a collective term that denotes means of mass communication, particularly referring to newspapers, radio, TV, and the Internet. Communication through these media is characterized by the fact that it is public, reaches a broad audience, is not bound to a particular place and time, and that it is largely unilateral, i.e. the audience does not normally interact with the sender of the messages it has received.

In the following chapter diverse aspects of the media will be presented. The central issues are:

- various forms of the the media and their prime functions
- the concept of "media literacy"
- the role of the media in contemporary society
- advertising as an example of a text that makes an appeal to the reader.

Newspapers

- printed publications that appear regularly (most commonly daily or weekly) and that are issued in an inexpensive form, affordable for a broad audience
- normally cover a wide range of up-to-date topics from politics, economics, and sport to culture and entertainment, also featuring a certain amount of advertising
- the first newspapers were published in the early 17th century
- due to the growing availability of information on the Internet, however, the number of printed newspapers has been steadily decreasing
- one can distinguish between the so-called **quality press**, i.e. newspapers in which well-researched information is offered at a high level of credibility (e.g. *The Times* and *The Guardian*) and the **tabloids** (Am. **yellow press**), in which sensational stories are combined with eye-catching headlines and images (e.g. *The Sun* and *The Daily Mirror*)

Radio

- invented in the late 19th century, originally referred to as "the wireless"
- from the 1920s onwards, more and more radio stations started broadcasting and radios became affordable for an ever growing audience
- "Golden Age" of radio: between the 1930s and the mid-1950s, when radio programmes included not only music, news, and advertisements, but also shows and radio plays
- with the advent of television, the popularity of radio started to decline

TV

- first introduced to the general public in the late 1930s
- did not become widely available and popular until after World War II
- originally based on a limited number of state-owned broadcasting stations
- the number of private channels, funded either by advertising or by subscriptions, has increased in the last few decades
- most recently, internet television has enjoyed a growing audience

Advertising

- Advertising is a vital financial aspect of all forms of the media.
- It is a form of communication that makes an appeal to the reader or viewer and as such tries to persuade her or him to carry out an action (to buy the advertised product or to use the advertised service).
- With the advent of the "new media" (primarily the Internet), new advertising opportunities opened up for companies. Nowadays, online advertising – e.g. in the form of pop-ups, banners, and advergames (free online games that advertise a certain product) – is a growing market, whereas the rate of advertising in the traditional media has been steadily declining.
- One way of describing the effects which a particular ad might have on the receiver is the **"AIDA"** principle: the ad should first catch her or his **A**ttention, then arouse his or her **I**nterest, create a **D**esire for the advertised product or service and finally lead to **A**ction, i.e. the purchase of that particular product.

- Advertising is often criticized for promoting ideal images of people, thereby putting consumers under psychological pressure by making them feel inadequate.

The Internet

- term derives from the longer "interconnected networks"
- it is a system of computer networks interconnected to each other which enables users to publicize and access information on a global scale
- originally developed to allow some American universities to exchange data quickly
- was made accessible to a broad public and commercialized in the 1990s
- by 2021 the number of internet users worldwide had risen to 4.66 billion, i. e. 59.5 %, more than half the global population (source: www.statista.com)
- in many areas mobile phones are used to log in online
- **advantages**
  - makes it possible to communicate with people over long distances in real time, thereby turning the world into a **"Global Village"**
  - easy access to almost every kind of information imaginable
- **disadvantages**
  - due to the fact that anybody can put basically anything on the Internet, the **degree of credibility** of the information available is **not always clear**
  - the rate of **criminal activities** on the internet (from the violation of privacy to internet fraud) has been steadily rising
  - some countries try to suppress information that collides with their own ideologies, employing **censorship** (e. g. China)

The mass media fulfil a number of **functions**. Originally one of the prime functions was the transmission of **information** to the broadest possible audience, which made the media a vital means of **education**. Public **entertainment** has been equally **important**. With the advent and ever-growing popularity of online social networks such as *Facebook, Instagram* and *Twitter* creating and maintaining **social contacts** independently of time and place has also become a crucial function.

Keyword:

Media literacy: this term refers to the ability of a recipient to analyze and evaluate the messages he or she receives through the media. Thus one is expected to question the information one is given, e. g. by asking who is the actual creator/sender of the message, what is their aim in sending this message, how does the message try to catch my attention, what is the point of view presented in the message? Ultimately, media literacy is also vital in producing one's own messages.

The Influence of the Media on Society and Personal Life

- Being **the prime source of information**, the media can influence a whole society's opinion about certain topics.

- With the help of more or less open forms of **censorship** public opinion can be controlled; this was most famously fictionalized by George Orwell in his novel *1984*, in which a totalitarian regime represses its people by – amongst other means – **controlling** and **manipulating** the **information** communicated through the media.
- It is still being debated whether **images of violence** presented on **TV** and in **computer games** are actually responsible for the growth in adolescent violence.
- In consumer societies **advertisements** determine to a high degree what is considered to be a desirable lifestyle. This can be seen as a form of **indoctrination** and **social control**.

INFO "Fake news"

"Fake news" refers to false stories appearing as genuine news items on the internet or other media. It is usually created to influence political opinion, or as a joke or provocation. Recently, fake news has been used to manipulate public opinion and even, it seems, to affect election results.

Background knowledge – Social Network Services (SNS)

Social network services enable users to build or maintain social relations and networks via the internet. Users can create individual profiles and share their whole lives virtually with others by posting texts and photos or emojis (small digital icons). When Facebook was launched in 2004, it soon turned into the most popular SNS of all, with over a billion users by 2013. The founding of *Facebook* is described in the partly fictional book *The Accidental Billionaires* by Ben Mezrich (2009). *Facebook's* figures have been dwindling, however, and there is growing competition in the field. Recently, social network services have come under attack, accused of saving users' data without their consent.

Facebook uses the data provided by its users and links them with other information in order to create ads tailored to a certain audience. The more specific the targeted group, the more money *Facebook* can charge from the advertising companies. Internally, *Facebook* can give advertisers the type of audience they want to reach without even selling their data. In a recent scandal, a British company gathered data on tens of millions of users with an app that looked like a research tool.

Young people have increasingly been using other online services like *Instagram*, *Twitter* or *Snapchat*. *Instagram* is a networking service for sharing photos on various social media. *Twitter* is an online social networking service for sending and reading very short messages ("tweets"). Since former President Trump's arrival on the scene, "tweets" have even been used to make politics.

The Digital Revolution

While the Industrial Revolution changed the way people worked and lived together, the so-called Digital Revolution has converted the whole analogue world into a digital one. This process started soon after WW II and increasingly accelerated from the moment when data storage facilities became smaller and smaller, when chips, and then wireless technologies, were introduced.
The year 2002 is generally seen as a turning point, because from then on more data has been stored in a digital than in an analogue way. The invention and spread of the internet has made this process possible. Today, more than half the world's population is continuously online, thanks to the usage of computers and smartphones. This interconnectivity means that everyone who is connected to the internet has the world's information at their fingertips and can communicate worldwide.
The notion of privacy will have to be closely monitored, as more and more people give personal data to a few big companies such as Apple, Google or Amazon. Physically tracking or locating a person has become easy, as smartphones continuously show their position. Wireless technologies have made these developments possible.
Digitization has entered all areas of life: communications, homes, banking, work, and industry. The Internet of Things (IoT) – as found in a smart home – means that objects and machines are online and have hardware with sensors that interconnect them and communicate autonomously – i. e. without human interference. The IoT is not without hazards, so far as privacy, data storage and security are concerned. In fact, cyber security is an increasingly important issue. People have made themselves dependent on the exchange and storage of data, and hacking into data systems, whether personal, corporate, or governmental, has become a real threat to modern society. You will find more information online.

Glossary – Science and Technology

genetic engineering	Gentechnik, -manipulation
fossil fuels	fossile (endliche) Brennstoffe (z. B. Öl)
renewable energy non-renewable energy	regenerative (erneuerbare) Energien nicht erneuerbare Energien (Öl, Kohle, Gas)
carbon dioxide (CO_2)	Kohlendioxid
methane	Methan
(exhaust) fumes	Abgase
to contaminate	etw. vergiften, verseuchen
fuel rod	Brennstab (im Kernkraftwerk)
half-life	Halbwertzeit (die Zeit, die es dauert, bis ein radioaktives Material die Hälfte seiner Strahlkraft einbüßt; bis zu mehreren Mio. Jahren)
power station, power plant	Kraftwerk
global warming	globale Erwärmung

climate change	Klimawandel
to have an adverse effect	eine nachteilige Wirkung auf etwas haben
to emit, emission	ausstoßen/emittieren, Ausstoß/Abstrahlung
water supply	Wasserversorgung
drought	Dürreperiode
flooding	Überflutung
soil	Boden, Erde
landfill	Mülldeponie
deforestation	Waldrodung
oil spillage/spill/pollution	Ölverschmutzung/-pest
incineration	Verbrennung
to evaporate, evaporation	verdunsten, Verdunstung
precipitation	Niederschlag
greenhouse effect	Treibhauseffekt
(radioactive, chemical, ...) waste	(radioaktiver, chemischer, ...) Abfall
to reprocess something	etwas wiederaufbereiten
raw materials, natural resources	Rohstoffe, natürliche Rohstoffe
energy-efficient	Energie sparend
subsidize	subventionieren
biodegradable	biologisch abbaubar

Glossary – The Media

prime function	Hauptfunktion
public	öffentlich/Öffentlichkeit
unilateral	einseitig
advent	Aufkommen
spread	Ausbreitung
access	Zugang/Zugriff
credibility	Glaubwürdigkeit
censorship	(politische) Zensur
Internet fraud	Internetbetrug
literacy	Lese- und Schreibfähigkeit
indoctrination	Indoktrination/ideologische Beeinflussung
inclination	Bereitschaft

William Shakespeare (erhöhtes Anforderungsniveau)

The World that Made Him: The Elizabethan Age

Keyword:

The Elizabethan Age: named after Queen Elizabeth I, born 1533, crowned 1558, died 1603 (reign of 45 years)

Politics and economics

- England emerged as a world power
- international trade → the rise of capitalism
- strongest naval force (defeat of the Spanish Armada in 1588)
- internal problems: constant clash between Catholics and Protestants: firm establishment of a Protestant Church with Elizabeth as head of the Church of England
- exploration of the New World
  - Sir Francis Drake
  - Sir Walter Raleigh

Culture

Keyword:

The Golden Age: term used for the Renaissance in Britain at the time of Elizabeth I

- freedom of spirit → imagination
- Greek and Roman thought
- domestic study of the Bible, widely read and heard
- opened new worlds of history and poetry, stimulated English culture
- cultural flowering: theatre, music, poetry, art, architecture
- Writers: William Shakespeare, Christopher Marlowe, Edmund Spenser
- Architect: Inigo Jones (introduced Italianate architecture to England)
- Composers: Thomas Tallis, William Byrd

The era was dominated by contrast: life for ordinary people could be hard, but economic growth also meant better conditions for many.
negative aspects:

- harsh criminal laws
- whipping and hanging for minor offences
- illiteracy

- short life-expectancy
- no rights for women

positive aspects:

- public provision for the poor (possible because of economic growth)
- few beggars

The Elizabethan World Picture

The Great Chain of Being

- vertical chain, hierarchically ordered → universal order
- every single speck of creation a link in the chain → almost infinite chain
- place in the chain determined by the relative proportion of spirit and matter
- the more spirit the higher the place in the chain

Hierarchy of the chain

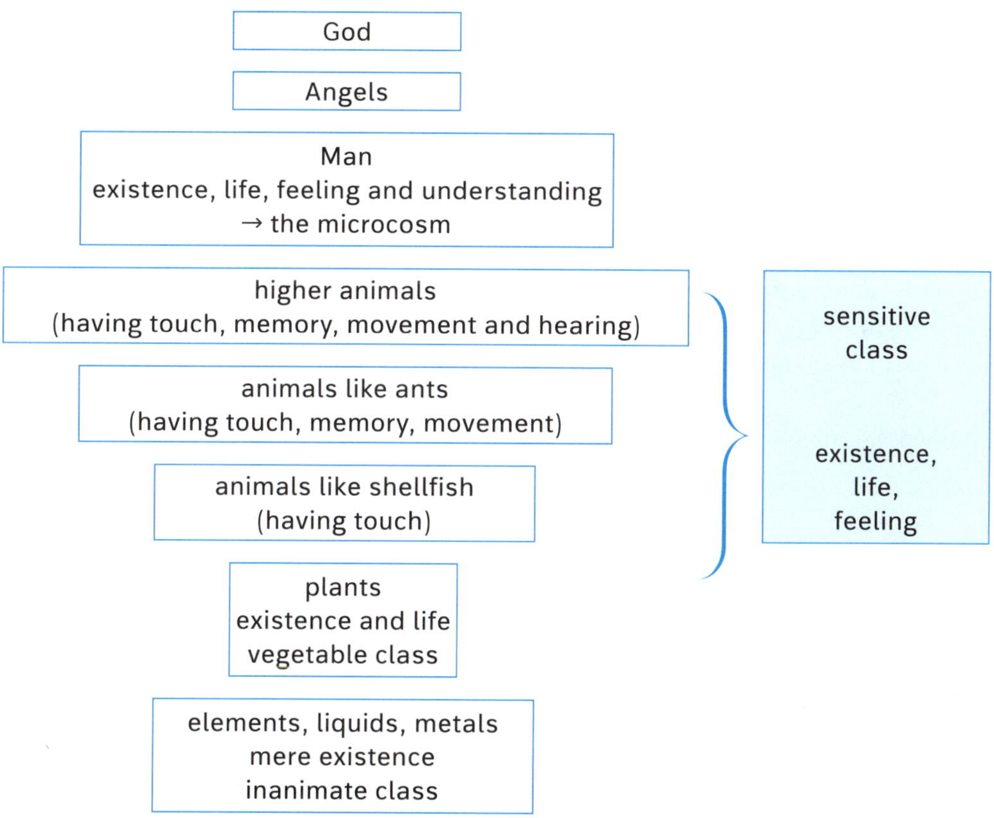

The hierarchical order also applies within the classes:

- Water is nobler than earth.
- Gold is nobler than silver.

- The oak is nobler than the bramble.
- The lion is nobler than the dog.

The corresponding planes

Different segments of the chain are reflected in other segments. This means there is universal interdependence, i. e. there are correspondences.

Corresponding planes

- divine and angelic
- man or microcosm
- universe or macrocosm
- lower creation
- commonwealth or body politic

The planes were connected by an immense network of correspondences.

> **Keyword:**
>
> **Correspondences:** They existed everywhere. When things were properly ordered, reason ruled the emotions, just as a king ruled his subjects, the parent ruled the child, and the sun governed the planets. But when disorder was present in one realm, it was correspondingly reflected in other realms.[1]

Examples of correspondences

macrocosm/microcosm	storms and earthquakes in the macrocosm ↔ passions of human beings
macrocosm/body politic	hierarchy of sun/moon/rainbow ↔ hierarchy of king/princes/governors
body politic/microcosm	debates between king and council ↔ commotions in a person's mind

Elizabethan thinking in terms of correspondences led to the abundance of images in Elizabethan literature.

Elements and humours

As the human being was seen as a microcosm (literally, a "little world"), it reflected the structure of the world as a whole, the macrocosm. The world was composed of four "elements" (earth, water, air, fire), the qualities of which were based on the notions of hot and cold, dry and moist.
Correspondingly, the human body was composed of four substances called "humours"

5 Quelle: http://academic.brooklyn.cuny.edu/english/melani/cs6/ren.html

with characteristics corresponding to the four elements. Imbalance or "disorder" among the humours, i. e. when they did not exist in proper proportion to each other, caused illness.

element	humour	common quality
earth	melancholy	cold and dry
water	phlegm	cold and moist
air	blood	hot and moist
fire	choler	hot and dry

Elizabethan Theatre

Theatres in Elizabethan London were venues of mass entertainment.

Theatres

- were situated outside the city
- staged performances every day
- presented plays, dances and music
- were also used for bear baiting, which was the cruel killing of bears
- were attended by people from all social ranks.

- All performances took place during the day.
- There was no lighting or special sound effects.
- Women's roles were played by men.
- The audience could smoke, eat, and drink.

Note: Imagination depended totally on the language used in the play.

Common complaints about the theatre

- disorderly
- corrupts young people
- led to evil and immoral ("ungodly") character and behaviour
- stage stories were morally uncontrolled and primitive, not religiously inspiring
- led to lewdness
- kept people away from work and prayer
- attracted criminals

Elizabethan Poetry

Sonnets

Keyword:
Sonnet form: originally from Italy, 14th century
Sonnets were made popular by Francesco Petrarca (in English: Petrarch)
The fashion of sonnet writing spread to France and England.

Important Elizabethan sonnet writers
- Thomas Wyatt (introduced sonnets to England, translations from Petrarch)
- Sir Philipp Sidney
- Edmund Spenser
- John Donne
- William Shakespeare

The Italian (Petrarchan) sonnet

	rhyme scheme	
octave/octet	a, b, b, a	quatrain
	a, b, b, a	quatrain
turn		
sestet	c, d, e	*tercet*
	c, d, e	*tercet*

Characteristics of the sonnet
- addressed to a beloved person
- 14 lines
- clearly defined rhyme scheme (the most common is given above)
- divided into an octet and a sestet
- turn after the octave

The turn after the octave is a shift in thought or feeling, often indicated by “but” or “yet”.
Variations in the rhyme scheme within the conventional structure are justified by the function they serve.

The English (Shakespearean) sonnet

	rhyme scheme	
octave	a, b, a, b	quatrain
	c, d, c, d	quatrain

sestet	e, f, e, f	quatrain
turn		
	g, g	*couplet*

The turn in the English sonnet occurs after the third quatrain. The couplet is a conclusion or a summary. However, the traditional turn can still be after the octave. A sonnet may also be structured in terms of the three quatrains. Ideally there should be "three turns of the screw" in the three quatrains, before the point is driven home in the couplet.

Shakespeare's sonnets

- Shakespeare wrote 154 sonnets.
- Sonnets 1 to 126 are addressed to a young man.
- Sonnets 127 to 154 are addressed to a "dark lady".

Main themes: love, beauty, transience, old age, death

The **basic metre** is iambic pentameter, but Shakespeare does not use it slavishly. Metre is used functionally, e. g.
- regular metre: harmony, peace, tranquillity, balance, stability, etc.
- irregular metre: disharmony, confusion, parody

Shakespeare's Plays

The Universal Appeal

By 1592 William Shakespeare had managed to establish his reputation as a playwright in London. Due to his success, other writers envied him enormously.
A remarkable feature of Shakespeare's time is the complete lack of what we know today as copyright regulations. Authors could not protect their work from being adapted freely or even copied as a whole. Shakespeare himself was engaged in this process of "play-doctoring", modifying existing plays for his acting company. As a consequence, his authorship of a number of plays has been questioned.
From about 1595, however, Shakespeare no longer cooperated with other authors and became the respected playwright with the reputation he has had until today. The fascination of his plays has not been lost over the more than four centuries since their first appearance. It can at least partly be attributed to the universal appeal of the topics he deals with. Love, happiness, envy, jealousy, treachery, humour – all of these profoundly human emotions and forms of behaviour enter easily into every spectator's heart.
Unfortunately the dating of the plays, and therefore the order in which they were written, is difficult to determine. Shakespeare did not issue a printed collection of his dramatic works, since no copyright existed. *Richard II*, however, appeared in six printed editions from 1597 to 1623, and *Romeo and Juliet* had five printed editions in

the same time span. If all the plays had been printed and published in Shakespeare's lifetime, they would have been used by countless actors and authors. As a result, only an approximate order can be suggested. Shakespeare's opus can be broadly divided into four periods:

Period 1 (1590–1595)

The first period is clearly the one that least shows Shakespeare's literary genius. The style and imagery of the plays are rather simple. Although he does use rhyme, there is also a lot of prose. It is a time of experimentation with the genre.

Period 2 (1595–1600)

During this period, which is marked by improved characterization and style, Shakespeare wrote some of his best comedies and history plays, among which are *Henry IV and Henry V*. He also wrote his sonnets during this period.

Period 3 (1600–1608)

Many scholars consider this to be the most important period. Shakespeare wrote great tragedies like *Hamlet* and so-called problem plays, also known as "bitter comedies".

Period 4 (1608–1613)

In this period Shakespeare wrote his romances, which deal with the topic of losing and regaining happiness. The plots are rather melodramatic, but they also display an idyllic atmosphere. Shakespeare's last play was *The Tempest*.

Shakespeare's Dramatic Works

Period	Comedies	Tragedies	History plays
1590–1595	*The Comedy of Errors* *The Taming of the Shrew* *Two Gentlemen of Verona* *Love's Labour's Lost*	*Titus Andronicus*	*Henry VI*
1595–1600	*A Midsummer Night's Dream* *The Merchant of Venice* *The Merry Wives of Windsor* *Much Ado About Nothing* *As You Like It* *Twelfth Night*	*Romeo and Juliet*	*King John* *Richard II* *Henry IV* *Henry V*

1600–1608	*Troilus and Cressida* *Measure for Measure* *All's Well That Ends Well*	*Julius Caesar* *Hamlet* *Othello* *Timon of Athens* *King Lear* *Macbeth* *Antony and Cleopa-tra* *Coriolanus*	
1608–1613	*Pericles* *Cymbeline* *A Winter's Tale* *The Tempest*		*Henry VIII*

Quelle: Rotter/Bendl: *Your Companion to English Literary Texts.* Manz (München 1991), S. 182 ff.

Shakespeare's Language

The language Shakespeare used is not easy to understand because it differs from the English spoken today. Some words have changed their meaning since the Elizabethan Age, others have been dropped altogether, and certain grammatical peculiarities need to be explained. We must also keep in mind that the lines Shakespeare makes his characters speak were intended to be performed on stage. In order to achieve a combined dramatic and artistic effect, he frequently employed blank verse, which is a fixed rhythmical pattern of iambic pentameters, as in this example from *Macbeth:*

Tomórrow ánd tomórrow ánd tomórrow

Especially for the less serious or comic characters, however, Shakespeare used prose, whereas verse is spoken by the noble ones.
Shakespeare's impact on the English language has been immense. He coined more than 500 neologisms (new words), and his works are still appreciated worldwide as examples of true linguistic genius. It should be kept in mind, though, that Shakespeare never intended his plays to be read as books; they were to be performed on stage. This is where the beauty of their language is most evident.
The table lists some examples of characteristic vocabulary and grammar used in Shakespeare's plays:

Shakespeare	**modern English**
Thou	You (used for children, subordinates, ordinary people and friends. Juliet in *Romeo and Juliet*, however, addresses Romeo as "you".)
Ye, you	You (plural); form showing respect
Thee	You (object form)

Thy	Your (determiner)
Thine	Your (determiner) before vowels
Mine	My (determiner) before vowels
Doth	Does
Hath	Has
Thou canst	You can
Thou wilt	You will
I have writ	I have written
I would	I wish
You know not	You don't know
Why call you...?	Why do you call...?
The guests are come.	The guests have come.

Richard III (eA)

Shakespeare is believed to have written this historical play around 1592-1593, which makes it one of his earlier works. Originally titled *The Tragedy of King Richard* the Third, it forms the conclusion of Shakespeare's first (historical) tetralogy, which also comprises Henry VI, Parts 1-3.
The play is set at the end of the "Wars of the Roses" (1455-1485), in which the House of Lancaster (whose emblem was the red rose) and the House of York (whose emblem was the white rose), both of them descended directly from King Edward III (1327-1377), fought a bitter feud over the throne of England. Shakespeare's Richard (of the House of York) is not the originator of this feud, but a product and energetic pursuer of it and the murderous evil it entails. The play shows his rise, fall, and fatal end as an unscrupulous seeker after power, who will directly or indirectly kill anyone – brothers, cousins, nephews, kings and princes, adversaries and supporters, men and women – who stands in his way to the throne. Matching the Tudor version of history, Shakespeare's plot shows Richard's progress to kingship and his defeat at the Battle of Bosworth Field (1485) by Henry Tudor, Earl of Richmond, who followed him on the English throne as Henry VII. At Bosworth the House of Lancaster finally prevails over the House of York, and Henry's marriage to Elizabeth of York ends the feud, bringing the two warring dynasties together. The play in five acts follows the traditional Aristotelian form of dramatic exposition, rising action, climax, falling action, and denouement. In Act I Shakespeare employs eloquent curses, whose dramatic function gives the play a grim, even mystic atmosphere. Mostly uttered by the women characters (especially Queen Margaret, widow of the murdered Henry VI), these curses predict disaster for Richard and his supporters. Given that they on the whole come true, the curses also tempt the audience to believe that the play's events follow some kind of divine providence and justice in which good will finally triumph over evil. A sign of this is Richard's dream on the eve of the Battle of Bosworth in which the ghosts of his victims return to haunt him, causing him to doubt the ultimate value of his crimes.

The play's monologues function as literary means to portray the characters' thoughts and intentions directly to the audience, making it easier for them to catch the ideas and motives of the different figures and thus aiding the play's exposition. For instance, the audience soon learns about Richard's ambitions from the play's famous opening soliloquy. Further stylistic and rhetorical means employed in the play are puns, irony, metaphors, repetition, foreshadowing, imagery, hyperboles, symbolism, oxymorons and parallelisms. All these language devices give the play additional aesthetic force.
Shakespeare's view of Richard of York's behaviour and ambitions corresponds to the perception of history, and specifically of the crimes committed by the House of York, propagated during the Elizabethan Age. Queen Elizabeth I (1558–1603) was the granddaughter of the Lancastrian Henry VII, who inaugurated the Tudor dynasty. Today scholars point out that Shakespeare, as a playwright of the Tudor Age and a subject of Queen Elizabeth I, intentionally drafted a distorted image of Richard III. By creating a sinister, murderous and cynical character with the physical disfigurement of a hunchback with a limp and a crippled arm, Shakespeare burned Richard's alleged viciousness deeply into his audiences' minds. Consequently, the last Plantagenet ruler was for several centuries considered a wicked, crazed and vengeful person – a perception long shared even by historians. In his slanted interpretation of history, Shakespeare was a man of his time. His play also served the Elizabethan view that an evil spirit was matched by an ugly body and vice versa – an assumption with which modern audiences, with our different awareness of disability, may well be uncomfortable. Richard of York was never portrayed by contemporaries as having any physical deformity. Moreover, no written source provides evidence of bodily impediments. The question has had a modern sequel, as Richard's remains were discovered and excavated in 2012 and reburied, after scientific examination, in Leicester Cathedral in 2015. Today, it is undeniable that he suffered from scoliosis (a lateral curvature of the spine) but there was no hint in his bones of any other abnormality.
This leaves the question of the many murders in the play. Shakespeare evidently accepts it as fact that several murders were prompted or even committed by Richard himself. Looking at the mysterious disappearance of the two "Princes in the Tower" – Richard's child nephews, Edward V (King of England for 11 weeks in 1483) and his younger brother – there is no direct evidence that Richard ordered their murder in order to become king himself. And his brother George, Duke of Clarence, had already been sentenced to death for high treason by parliament in 1478.
Shakespeare's *Richard III* highlights the dramatic course of a convinced and ruthless villain rather than a tragic hero – his Richard already shows the depth of his "fall" in his opening speech. The impact of the play lies in the way the author lays bare before us the horror and fascination of a character who gains his ends with brilliant rhetoric, manipulation, and deceit. But he is up against adversaries, above all in the persons of the former queens, Margaret and Elizabeth, and his mother, the Duchess of York, who see through him from the start and are rhetorically – especially in Margaret's curse scene (Act I sc. iii) and the three women's scene (Act IV, sc. iv) – virtually his equals. Thus there is in the end a dramatic balance of power between the force of their righteous insights, and the furious (good or evil?) curses these evoke, and the force of evil that Richard represents.

This echoes the political balance brought about by Richmond's victory at Bosworth and enacted in the play's final speech when he, as King Henry VII, promises to "unite the white rose and the red" and bring peace to a long-troubled land (Act V, sc. v).

Modern Adaptations

Shakespeare's works have often reached the cinema or TV screen. One has to differentiate here between straight versions and modern adaptations. Concerning storyline, characters and setting, a straight version keeps closely to the original work by taking over the metric verse scheme – with Shakespeare for the most part blank (i. e. unrhymed) verse in iambic pentameters – and generally also the historical costumes and stage set. Moreover, the characters keep their original names.
An adaptation – generally also in some way or other a modernization of the play – is typically based on the original, but may show a very different presentation of the storyline, characters and setting. It may be put in a contemporary setting, or an historical setting later than Shakespeare's time – e. g. the 19th century setting of *Midsummer Night's Dream* in Michael Hoffmann's 1999 film, or Mankiewicz's 1953 *Julius Caesar* with its references to recent European fascism. The characters can be transplanted into different social or ethnic groups (as in the musical *Kiss Me Kate*, or in Baz Luhrmann's 1996 Californian *Romeo & Juliet* starring Leonardo DiCaprio), but the storyline is often followed closely.
Such modernizations aim at developing a market for a potential audience that might be attracted by the ease/lightness of a musical version or an animated cartoon film like *The Lion King* – an adaptation of Shakespeare's *Hamlet*. This film clearly aims at a younger audience.
In such modern presentations the original poetic language, with its distinct metric scheme, is either not adopted at all, or – to make it different from other modern adaptations – the director sets the original language in a modern setting, as in Baz Luhrmann's *Romeo & Juliet* (cf. also p. 10).
New film versions of historical plays, like Kenneth Branagh's *Henry V*, seek to attract younger audiences and spell-bind their audiences with traditional plays with Shakespeare's original language in settings with which they are familiar. By presenting modern versions and adaptations in the theatre or on film, directors can attract people who enjoy watching modern plays and films but have no interest in history.

Richard III (film, eA)

Ian McKellen (plays Richard III) and Richard Loncraine (director) wrote the screenplay for this 1995 film. They present a comparable historical era to that of the bloody Wars of the Roses, setting the action in the 1930s, a time when fascism and dictatorships were on the rise all over Europe. The period, which culminated in the Second World War, is close enough to today's audiences to get them involved without making people identify the film's action with present-day events.
The film shifts the emphasis of Shakespeare's play, looking forward rather than back.

Hence it removes some characters completely, like Queen Margaret (wife of the murdered King Henry VI), who represented the past in the original play. Key aspects of her role (e. g. the curse scene) are transferred to Richard's mother, the Duchess of York. On the other hand, Richmond's role is widened and the young Elizabeth – future wife of Richmond (later King Henry VII) – is brought to life.
Costumes, furniture and architecture are transposed to 1930s Britain, with familiar London landmarks used in new and surprising places, underlining the fictitious nature of the "historical" action. Consistently with this transposition, Shakespeare's language is "translated", omitting archaic words and dropping old-fashioned grammatical forms like "thee" and "thou". The original 16th century vocabulary is transformed into modern English to ease its understanding and acceptance by today's audiences. Blank verse is retained in the film, at least with Richard and other key figures like Clarence. For McKellen, the rhyme scheme of blank verse emphasizes important words, enhancing the impact of the speeches. Moreover, Shakespeare's rhythms are familiar to the English ear and as such do not hamper the audiences' understanding.
The plot of the play – as with virtually all modern film versions of Shakespeare – has been reduced. But vital aspects like the nightmare scene and important monologues are retained in the modern setting. The setting itself is suitably extravagant, with noble houses, flamboyant cars and costly wardrobe, the latter displayed especially by the women. The male characters frequently wear uniforms that remind the spectator of the Nazi era in Germany. The proclamation scene explicitly alludes to that era, with Richard III holding a speech in a setting that looks like the Nazi party rally grounds in Nuremberg. The flags, banners and SS-like uniforms clearly refer to that era, and the weapons and equipment (trains, aircraft, tanks, guns etc.) presented in the final battle scenes underscore this impression.
An important role in Shakespeare's play is taken by Richard's soliloquies. In the film the same function (to inform the audience about his thoughts and plans) and effect (to reveal his ambition and deception) is taken by Richard's direct addresses to the camera, looking the audience close-up in the eye. The final scene of his downfall is performed in slow motion, with Richard falling backwards into a sea of flames.
Important scenes are accompanied with music intensifying the action: in the coronation scene with an anthem and in the proclamation scene with a military march. An interesting piece was chosen for the closing credits: the pop song "I'm Sitting on Top of the World", sung by Al Jolson. Is this intended to propitiate audiences? Its cheerful mood completely contrasts with the bloodthirsty action of the film. Written in the USA (c. 1928) to cheer people up during the Great Depression, it at first seems out of place but on closer inspection it has parallels with Richard's character and era. He, too, feels "on top of the world" – albeit more as a dictator than a lover. Or is the intention rather ironic mockery at the tyrant's fall?
The action of the film is bracketed by two scenes of military violence – an acknowledgement of audience (and box-office) expectations and a rhetorical device rounding off the thread of brutality that runs through the storyline.

Methoden der Textarbeit

Anforderungen von Aufgaben mit Textbezug

Alle im Abitur gestellten Aufgaben sind textbasiert. Sie können auch Bildmaterialien sowie audio-visuelle Materialien umfassen, auf die sprachlich reagiert werden muss. Zu den typischen Aufgabenformaten, die bei fiktionalen sowie nicht-fiktionalen Textvorlagen im freischriftlichen Teil gestellt werden, zählen die Zusammenfassung, die Analyse und der Kommentar bzw. kreative Aufgaben, die unterschiedlich ausgeprägt sein können (vgl. Hinweise zu den Operatoren, S. 103). Neben diesen freischriftlichen Aufgaben werden auch neue Aufgabentypen zur Mediation vorkommen, die im Einleitungskapitel bereits thematisiert wurden. An dieser Stelle erhalten Sie Hinweise zu den üblichen schriftlichen Aufgaben, die weiterhin Teil der Abiturprüfung sind.

Aufgabenarten und Anforderungsbereiche

Aufgabenart	Anforderungsbereich
u. a. *summary* Operatoren: *describe, outline, state, summarize*	***I – comprehension, orientation, context*** – Wiedergabe der zentralen Aussagen eines Textes – ggf. auch Einordnung des Textes in einen bekannten Kontext, aber üblicherweise ist die Aufgabe rein auf Basis des Ausgangstextes zu beantworten
u. a. *analysis* Operatoren: *analyse, examine, compare, explain, contrast*	***II – analysis*** – Anwendung von Fachmethoden: textanalytische Verfahren, exakte Arbeit am sprachlichen Detail, Belegen und Zitieren, problemlösende Argumentation – gezielte Anwendung von Kenntnissen und Wissen – z. B. soziokulturelles Wissen oder Wissen über Sprache
u. a. *comment* Operatoren: *comment, discuss, justify, evaluate* ——— u. a. *write* Operatoren: *write, imagine, continue, find*	***III – comment, evaluation, re-creation of text, creativity*** für die analytisch-interpretierende Aufgabenstellung: – Bewertung der Textvorlage auf Basis der vorher gewonnenen Erkenntnisse, Einordnung des Textes in einen größeren Zusammenhang – persönliche Stellungnahme, eigene Meinung für die produktionsorientierte/kreative Aufgabenstellung: – Umsetzung, Bewertung, Reflexion der Problematik des Ausgangstextes bzw. der Analyse in einem kreativen Kontext: z. B. Perspektivwechsel (Sicht einer Figur) – Füllen von Leerstellen (Weitererzählen, neues Ende) – Textsortenwechsel (Brief an Protagonisten, Leserbrief, Brief an *agony aunt*, Tagebucheintrag, Dialog usw.)

Die Bedeutung der Operatoren[1]

Für die Formulierung der Aufgaben gibt es klare Vorgaben. Verben für die Arbeitsanweisungen (= Operatoren) müssen in ihrer exakten Bedeutung verstanden werden. Eine ungefähre Ahnung, was gefordert ist, reicht keinesfalls aus. Die folgende Operatorenübersicht ist der Website des Ministeriums entnommen. Die mittlere Spalte definiert die genaue Wortbedeutung der Anweisung, die dritte Spalte gibt jeweils ein Beispiel für eine mögliche Aufgabenstellung.

Operatoren	Definitionen	Beispiele
	(schwerpunktmäßig) Anforderungsbereich I	
describe	give a detailed account of something	Describe the soldier's appearance. Describe the situation ...
outline	give the main features or the general principles of a text/ topic omitting minor details	Outline the author's views on love, marriage and divorce and point out how ...
state	specify clearly	State briefly the main developments in the family described in the text.
summarize, write a summary	give a concise account of the main points	Summarize the information given in the text about the hazards of cloning.
	(schwerpunktmäßig) Anforderungsbereich II	
analyse, examine	describe and explore in detail certain aspects and/or features of the text and how they are presented	Analyse the views on class held by the two protagonists. Examine the author's use of language ... Examine how the author characterizes ...
compare	show similarities and differences	Compare the attitude of the two characters towards war.
explain	show causes and effects in a given context	Explain the protagonist's obsession with money. Explain XYZ's attitude towards ...
contrast	emphasize the differences between two or more things	Contrast the author's idea of human aggression with the theories of aggression you have read about.

1 Quelle: https://www.nibis.de/uploads/1gohrgs/operatoren_2021/EN_2021Abi_Operatoren.pdf

(schwerpunktmäßig) Anforderungsbereich III		
comment	state clearly your opinion on the topic in question and support your views with evidence	Comment on the suggestion made in the text that a "lack of women in the armed forces demonstrates a weakness in the role of women in society".
discuss	investigate by giving reasons for and against	Discuss the implications of globalization as presented in this text.
justify	present reasons for decisions, positions or conclusions	You are the head boy/head girl of your school. Justify a decision taken by the pupils' council when you meet with your headmaster.
assess/ evaluate	consider in a balanced way points for and against something	Evaluate the author's view of the impact of the American Dream … Assess the importance of standards in education.

Kreative Aufgaben

Der **Anforderungsbereich III umfasst auch kreative Aufgaben**, für die jedoch keine allgemein verbindlichen Operatoren formuliert werden können. Folgende Aufgabenstellungen sind möglich:

- Write a letter, e-mail to a friend/to the editor/of complaint/ of enquiry/…
- Write a dialogue/the dialogue between X and Y/a script (film, play …) based on/ XYZ's diary entry ….
- Write an article (for …)/ a report (for …).
- Continue the story …/ Find a suitable ending …/Imagine you are XYZ. Continue/Tell the story … from her/his point of view …

TIPP zum Punktesammeln

Befassen Sie sich intensiv mit den Operatoren. Nur wenn Sie genau wissen, was in der Aufgabenstellung gefordert ist, können Sie eine gute Lösung schreiben.

Grundlegende Hinweise zu den Aufgaben: *summary, analysis, comment*

Summary

- Inhaltlich soll hier gezeigt werden, dass der **Textinhalt** verstanden wurde.
- Aus diesem Grund ist es entscheidend, sich von der Textvorlage zu lösen und in eigenen Worten die Hauptinhalte wiederzugeben; das heißt auch, dass weder Passagen übernommen noch Zitate integriert werden dürfen.

- Sprachlich ist Folgendes zu beachten: Bei Zusammenfassungen von **fiktionalen Texten** ist durchgehend das **Präsens** zu verwenden (bei Vorzeitigkeit kann vereinzelt das *present perfect*, bei Nachzeitigkeit das *will future* eingesetzt werden, auf keinen Fall aber eine Vergangenheitsform).
- Bei **nicht-fiktionalen Texten** (z. B. Zeitungsartikel) sind die Hauptaussagen des Autors ebenfalls im Präsens wiederzugeben; nur in Einzelfällen ist es zulässig, für Ereignisse, die in der Vergangenheit tatsächlich stattgefunden haben, das *past tense* zu verwenden.
- **Autorenbezug herstellen:** Besonders bei **nicht-fiktionalen Texten** ist es wichtig, immer klarzustellen, wer welche Aussagen trifft (besonders bei Zeitungsartikeln, in denen verschiedene Meinungen wiedergegeben werden).
- Je nach Operator kann eine pointierte oder umfassende Zusammenfassung verlangt werden (vgl. Operatoren, S. 103).

Analysis

- Inhaltlich soll hier gezeigt werden, inwiefern die **Form des Textes** dessen Inhalt, Aussageabsicht oder die Haltung des Autors beeinflusst.
- Hier wird verlangt, dass die sprachliche Form des Textes genauer untersucht wird (z. B. im Hinblick auf Sprachebenen, stilistische Mittel, Erzählhaltung etc.) und dass daraus Rückschlüsse auf den Textinhalt bzw. dessen Wirkung gezogen werden; auch hier wird der Text im Präsens verfasst.
- Für eine sprachliche Analyse genügt es nicht, lediglich Stilmittel zu identifizieren und aufzulisten, es kommt vor allem darauf an, deren Wirkungsabsicht zu erkennen.
- Typische Analyseaspekte sind bei **fiktionalen Texten**: *point of view, character analysis, analysis of atmosphere/setting, analysis of tone,* usw.
- Typische Analyseaspekte bei **nicht-fiktionalen Texten** sind: *the use of language/ structure, the intention or attitude of the author, the intended effect on the audience (i. e. in speeches), the use of language to achieve the text's aim (e. g. to convince, to provoke, to educate, etc.),* usw.
- **Autorenbezug herstellen:** Es ist sinnvoll klarzustellen, welche Aussageabsicht dem Autor oder dem Erzähler oder einer der Figuren zuzuordnen ist und welche Wirkungsabsicht damit verfolgt wird.

Comment *(Evaluation)*

- Inhaltlich soll hier gezeigt werden, dass der Textinhalt reflektiert werden kann.
- Diese (kritische) Auseinandersetzung mit dem Text kann in unterschiedlicher Form gefordert werden:
  - persönlicher *comment*: Hier wird eine persönliche Stellungnahme zum Material verlangt, die fachlich-argumentativ begründet sein muss und in der Regel auch Hintergrundwissen erfordert; das reine Feststellen der eigenen Meinung reicht nicht, sie muss erläutert werden und fundiert sein.
  - argumentativer *comment*: Hier wird in der Regel eine sachlich-distanzierte Gegenüberstellung von Vor- und Nachteilen bzw. Pro- und Kontra-Argumenten verlangt, die in einem abwägenden und schlüssigen Fazit enden müssen.

- *comment* aus der Sicht einer anderen Person: Unter Umständen ist gefordert, dass Sie sich in die Situation einer Figur des Textes oder einer anderen Person versetzen, um aus deren Vorstellung heraus den Inhalt zu kommentieren; hier kann es sinnvoll sein, auch die Sprache/den Ausdruck dieser Figur zu übernehmen, um den Kommentar authentischer wirken zu lassen (insbesondere bei kreativen Aufgaben wird diese Form häufig verlangt).

Hinweise zu kreativen Aufgaben

Typische Formen

- formeller oder persönlicher Brief, E-Mail
- Tagebucheintrag, *blog entry, interior monologue*
- eine Geschichte erzählen (ein Ende für einen Text verfassen, eine Geschichte zu einem Bild erfinden, die Erzählperspektive wechseln, etc.)
- einen Artikel schreiben, einen Leserbrief verfassen
- einen Dialog zwischen zwei Figuren eines fiktionalen Textes entwickeln etc.

wichtige Aspekte für die Bearbeitung

- auf das Material eingehen und dieses einbeziehen: Unabhängig davon, welche Art von kreativer Produktion verlangt wird, sollte der Ausgangstext oder das Ausgangsbild nie aus den Augen verloren werden.
- Der selbst produzierte Text muss den formalen Anforderungen entsprechen (z. B.: Adresszeile, Anrede, ggf. Betreff, Datum, Abschlussformel bei Briefen) und muss als Brief, E-Mail, Zeitungsartikel o. Ä. klar erkennbar sein.
- Sprachlich sollte der Text den Ton der Vorlage bzw. der Figur treffen: Ein Brief aus der Sicht eines Kindes kann nicht in stilistisch gehobenem Englisch verfasst werden, ein Brief an einen Redakteur nicht mit Umgangssprache durchsetzt.
- Hier ist es also entscheidend, dass man das eigene Sprachrepertoire durch ein anderes ersetzen bzw. ergänzen kann, damit der Text glaubwürdig wird.
- Auch hier ist es wichtig, dass der Inhalt nicht zu oberflächlich bleibt (auch ein Tagebucheintrag eines Jugendlichen sollte emotionale Tiefe zeigen und nicht lediglich beschreibend sein).
- Insgesamt sollte der Text so verfasst werden, dass er den Leser überzeugt und authentisch wirkt.

Literarische Texte

Narration

Keyword:

narrative texts: narrative texts can have many forms, among them short story, novel, fairy tale, satire, parable, legend, etc.
The ones that are most relevant for your final exam are the short story and the novel.

When asked to analyse a narrative text, you will have to focus on particular elements that are characteristic of short stories or novels.

Elements of narration

Structure

Plot

INFO Elements of a complete plot

exposition → rising action → climax/turning point → falling action → ending

A **plot** need not necessarily be complete (there may be an open ending).
The **sequence** need not necessarily be chronological.
There may be foreshadowing or flashbacks or there may be reverse narration (umgestelltes Erzählen).
In particular, an excerpt from a longer text, which is the most common sort of text in the final exam, may not contain all the elements of the plot.
Certain **key events** within the action of a story will increase the tension; they will create suspense, rising to a climax or turning point. After that there will be falling tension or relief.

INFO Tension curve

rising tension → climax or turning point → falling tension or relief

Theme

The **theme** of a story is always abstract. Themes can be love, poverty, racism, childhood etc. The **subject matter** of a story is the concrete realization of the theme.

<u>Example</u>

Two stories may have the same theme: racism. The subject matter of one may be the murder of an African American, of the other the bullying of a black schoolgirl.

Character

When asked to characterize a figure from a narrative text, you must be aware of different aspects. There are key questions that can guide you.

<u>Direct characterization</u>

- What does the narrator say about the character?
- What do other characters say about the character?
- What does the character say about himself/herself?

- How objective is what they say? Be aware of words with negative or positive connotations.

Indirect characterization
- How does the character act?
- What does the character say?
- What kind of language does he/she use?

It might help to fill in a table with the following headings:

Character's outward appearance	Character's language	Character's actions	What the character says	Other characters' statements (or actions)
...	...	...	...	...

Narrator/point of view

INFO Narrator

The narrator is either a first-person or a third-person narrator.
The first-person narrator is NOT the author!

limited point of view	**unlimited/omniscient point of view**
first-person narrator	third-person narrator (neutral omniscience, God-like know-ledge of all the facts)
third-person narrator (one character's point of view, "select-ive omniscience")	third-person narrator (several characters' points of view)

Mode of presentation

Panoramic presentation (telling) vs. scenic presentation (showing)

There are two modes of presentation to be found in narratives: the **panoramic** and the **scenic** mode:
The **panoramic** mode is employed when the narrator summarizes several events, whereas **scenic** mode is used when the narrator describes scenes in great detail.

Interior monologue is a particular kind of scenic presentation in which the thoughts and feelings passing through a character's mind are depicted. In **reported thought** the thoughts are presented as reported speech.

This is closely connected with the concepts of *narrated time* and *narrating* (or *acting) time:*

narrated time longer than narrating time	usually summary of events
narrated time identical with narrating time	e.g. direct speech
narrated time shorter than narrating time	e.g. stream of consciousness, interior monologue, detailed description of a scene, comparable to slow motion in a film

INFO Function of mode of presentation and point of view

A neutral, omniscient narrator, who observes the action and the characters from above and who uses a panoramic mode of presentation, is more detached and thus creates a distance between the reader and the action. On the other hand, a narrator who takes a character's point of view creates immediacy and directly involves the reader in what happens.

Setting

The place and time where the action is set is called the setting. It is especially important for *atmosphere* and *symbolism.*

Atmosphere

Atmosphere is created by means of setting, objects, colours, light and darkness, but also by reference to a character's mood or the use of language.

Symbolism

Symbols are part of the setting of the narrative.

INFO Established symbols

These are conventional symbols which have long been used and have a certain, traditional significance that everybody knows. Examples of established symbols: a rose, a cross, the colour white.

INFO Created symbols

Something becomes symbolic within a certain context, because it is closely connected to an event, a situation or a character.

INFO Symbols

Symbols are NOT metaphors!
Symbols are really there, are part of the story. Metaphors or similes are figures of speech.

Examples:
She was a rose, so beautiful. → metaphor
She was like a rose, so beautiful. → simile/comparison
They fell in love when they first met in her father's rose garden. → symbol

Language and style

In order to determine the style of a text, it is necessary to examine aspects such as register, diction (choice of words), tone, and also sentence structure.

Register is the level of language used in a particular situation. It may be formal, neutral, informal, or vulgar. There may be a lot of slang words, even taboo words, or technical terms, or jargon.

The **tone** may be ironic, sarcastic, sad, humorous, serious, playful, angry etc., depending on the emotional attitude it expresses. This depends on the choice of words, level of speech, rhythm, sentence length etc.

Stylistic devices will be considered at length in the chapters on drama and non-fictional texts (p. 116 and 121).

Poetry

Poetry focuses on the **aesthetic function** of language. Poetry appeals to the senses. It is to be enjoyed for its beauty, its cleverness, its wit, its impact.
This is achieved by
- the sound of words,
- the rhythm of the words and phrases,
- the choice of words,
- the structure of the sentences,
- the composition of the poem,
- the visual arrangement of words and lines,
- and, above all, by means of imagery.

In your final exams however, you will be asked not so much to enjoy the poem but to examine its meaning and the effect of the language the speaker uses.

How to proceed

Questions to be asked

- Who is the speaker of the poem?
- Where is the speaker?
- Does the speaker address somebody?
- Does the speaker contemplate something?
- Does the speaker describe something or somebody?
- Does the speaker tell a story?
- Does the speaker explain something?
- Does the speaker argue against or in favour of something?
- What is the speaker‘s attitude? What is he/she saying?
- How is the poem composed? Is it structured by a rhyme scheme, or by the division into stanzas, or by some other device?
- Is there a correspondence between the structure of the poem and the structure of the speaker‘s thoughts?
- What is the significance of the title?
- What words does the speaker use? What do they mean?
- What is the structure of the sentences? Simple? Complex?
- What poetic devices does the speaker use?
- And what is the effect of all this? What is the experience of reading?

In order to understand and describe poetry, you need to be familiar with its most important elements.

Elements of poetry

INFO Speaker and author

The speaker of the poem is NOT the author. Poems may be autobiographical, but you must still refer to the "speaker in the poem".

Poems are composed of **stanzas** and **lines**.
Stanzas may have a certain **rhyme scheme.**

Rhyme

Rhyme schemes

pair rhyme	a a b b
alternate rhyme	a b a b
embracing rhyme	a b b a

Types of rhyme

masculine rhyme (one syllable)	kiss/this
feminine rhyme (two syllables)	dreary/weary
true rhyme	kiss/this, dreary/weary
slant rhyme assonance (same vowel) consonance (same consonant)	 comb/coat hope/heap

Lines may have a certain rhythm. The smallest unit that determines rhythm is the foot, consisting of at least one stressed and one or two unstressed syllables. The pattern of stressed and unstressed syllables is called **metre.**
A sequence of stressed and unstressed syllables is not something artificial. It is the natural rhythm of the English language. It is the poet's skill to choose words in such a way that this pattern constitutes a regular metre.Types of foot:

foot	**stresses**	**example**
iamb/iambic	–/ (da-**dum)**	compare
trochee/trochaic	/ – **(dum**-da)	lovely
spondee/spondaic	// **(dum dum)**	drop dead
anapest/anapestic	– –/ (da-da-**dum)**	lemonade
dactyl/dactylic	/ – – **(dum**-da-da)	whispering

The number of feet or stressed syllables in a line determines its metre. The most common types are shown here:

number of feet	**metre**	**example**
1	monometer	"And find/What wind ..." (John Donne, "Song", ll. 7 – 8)
2	dimeter	"Why dost thou thus ..." (John Donne, "The Sun Rising", l. 2)
3	trimeter	"Go, Soul, the body's guest Upon a thankless errant;" (Sir Walter Raleigh, "The Lie")
4	tetrameter	"Busy old fool, unruly sun ..." (John Donne, "The Sun Rising", l. 1)

5	pentameter	"Love, all alike, no season knows, nor clime ..." (John Donne, "The Sun Rising", l. 9)
6	hexameter	"A needless alexandrine ends the song That, like a wounded snake, drags its slow length along" (Alexander Pope, "An Essay on Criticism", ll. 356 – 357)

INFO Most important metre in English poetry

Iambic pentameter:
"But thy eternal summer shall not fade" (Shakespeare, Sonnet 18).

Lines

end-stop lines	natural pause for the end of a thought at the end of a line	"Shall I compare thee to a summer's day?" (Shakespeare, Sonnet 18)
run-on lines (enjambement)	The meaning requires no pause between the lines.	"When yellow leaves, or none, or few, do hang Upon those boughs which shake against the cold ..." (Shakespeare, Sonnet 73)
caesura	The meaning requires a pause in mid-line.	"Let me not to the marriage of true minds Admit impediments; love is not love ..." (Shakespeare, Sonnet 116)

Imagery

A writer or speaker using language beyond its dictionary meaning makes use of **imagery.** All figurative use of language is imagery. Imagery appeals to all the senses; it is meant to stimulate the reader‘s or listener‘s imagination.

TIPP Watch out!

The word *imagery* is an abstract noun. There is no plural. You can only talk about single *images*.

Important types of imagery are: metaphor, simile/comparison, personification and symbol (cf. p. 109).

Drama

When asked to analyse a dramatic text, you will have to focus on particular elements that are characteristic of plays.

Elements of drama

Structure

Plot

INFO Elements of a dramatic plot

exposition → rising action → climax or crisis → falling action → dénouement or catastrophe

The audience is confronted with the action on stage directly. There is no narrator. Yet one can identify the same elements of plot as are found in narration.
In tragedy, the opponents of the hero gain the upper hand in the falling action, which ends in the catastrophe.
Comedy has a happy ending, in which conflicts are resolved (dénouement).

Stage directions

The dramatic text consists of **two kinds of text:** the more important kind of text is the dialogue spoken by the characters (i. e. dialogue, monologue, and asides).
The stage directions are the second kind of text. They give instructions concerning the stage design, about sounds to be heard, visual effects, the characters and also the way some of the dialogue has to be spoken.
The following visual and acoustic elements will have to be considered in your analysis of stage directions. They will help to characterize a character, create atmosphere or function as symbols. (cf. p. 109)

concerning the actors		**concerning the stage**	
visual	**acoustic**	**visual**	**acoustic**
size	voice	scenery	music
facial expression	intonation	stage design	noise
gestures	language of the play	lighting	sound
costumes	non-verbal noises	properties *(Requisiten)*	

Characters

The audience is confronted with the characters on stage directly and there is no narrator.

A character is presented through action, interaction and dialogue and, of course, his outward appearance on stage (see above).
There are **flat** characters, types that act in a predictable way, and **round** characters, lifelike characters that are fully developed.

Language/Dialogue/Communication

When analysing the language of a play, you have to keep in mind that it works on two levels:

1. The inner system of communication, i. e. the communication among the characters.
2. The outer system of communication between the playwright and the audience.

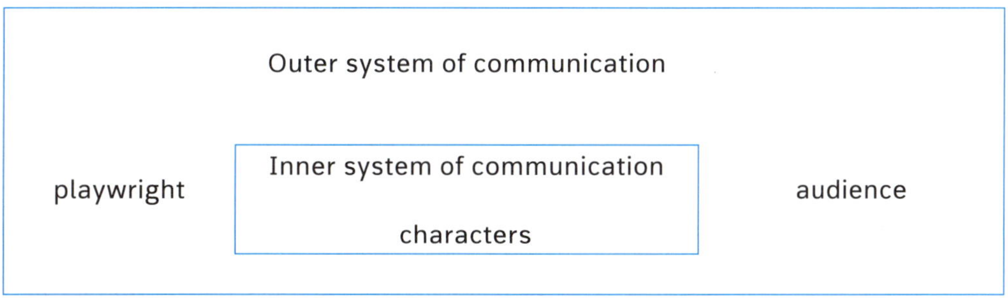

Dramatic irony
Dramatic irony is an important effect that is created by these two levels of communication. If the audience knows more than a character, an utterance will be perceived as ironic when it sharply contrasts with reality.

Example
In Shakespeare's Macbeth, King Duncan praises the peaceful atmosphere at Macbeth's castle, whereas the audience knows that Duncan is going to be murdered.

Comedy
On the level of communication between playwright and audience, dramatic irony, the audience's awareness of facts the characters do not know, may serve a comic effect.

Aside
In an aside, an actor speaks to the audience in order to provide information on his thoughts and feelings or intentions. The other characters on stage supposedly do not hear what he says.

TIPP

As many of Shakespeare's plays are written in verse, you may approach their language in the same way as poetry.

Language and style

Important stylistic devices

device	definition	example
alliteration	repetition of a consonant at the beginning of neighbouring words	From forth the fatal loins of these two foes... (Shakespeare, *Romeo and Juliet*)
allusion	direct or implied reference	Poetry is great. Just think of the most famous writer of sonnets in English.
analogy	A resemblance is established between things that are unlike.	The heart is simply a pump propelling the blood round the body.
anaphora	Neighbouring sentences start with the same word.	We shall not flag or fail. We shall go on to the end. We shall fight in France... (Winston Churchill)
antithesis	contrasting ideas using a parallel syntactic structure	"It's a story that hasn't made me the most conventional candidate. But it is a story that has seared into my genetic make-up the idea that..." (Barack Obama)
assonance	Internal vowel sounds in neighbouring words are repeated.	How now brown cow?
blank verse	poetry without rhyme but with a regular metre: iambic pentameter	"The king has happily received, Macbeth, The news of thy success, and when he reads... (Shakespeare, *Macbeth*)
chiasmus	the reversal of word order in two parts of a sentence	"Fair is foul, and foul is fair" (Shakespeare, *Macbeth*)
climax	an enumeration of arguments that become stronger	Friendship, affection, love.
ellipsis	incomplete sentence	"A good choice!"
enumeration	list of arguments	Macbeth is disloyal, greedy and obedient to his wife.
euphemism	An unpleasant expression is replaced by a more agreeable one.	"Civilizing" Australian Aboriginals meant forcibly removing the children from their families.

hyperbole	exaggeration	I have told you a thousand times.
inversion	reversal of word order	Not only did he like chocolate, he also ate a lot.
metaphor	indirect comparison without "like" or "as"	Love is a red, red rose.
metonymy	figure of speech in which the name of a thing or concept is replaced by a part of it or by s.th. associated with it	"wheels" for "car" / "turf" for "horse-racing"
onomatopoeia	word that imitates the sound that it stands for	Bang! Swoosh! Ding-dong.
paradox	an apparent contradiction	This statement is true and false at the same time.
parallelism	same syntactic structure of two or more sentences	He liked the sea. He liked the sun. He liked holidays in Cornwall.
personification	Inanimate objects or abstract ideas are represented as if they were human beings.	"Too hot the eye of heaven shines" (Shakespeare, sonnet 18)
rhetorical question	a question that does not require an answer	Do you think I'm stupid?
simile	comparison using the words "like" or "as"	Your love is like a red, red rose.
telling name	a name that represents character traits	Doolittle: he is too little or: he does too little (Shaw, *Pygmalion*)

Glossary – Vocabulary for analysing literary texts

the narrator tells of/shows/relates/reveals
the narrator takes xy's point of view
the narrator is omniscient
the story is told in the first person/third person form
the narrator uses/employs/makes use of metaphors, similes, comparisons
a metaphor shows/stands for/suggests
the narrator speaks in an ironic/satirical/detached/matter-of-fact/serious tone
the story deals with/treats of/concentrates on/focuses on ...
atmosphere is created
tension/suspense is created/built up
a poem is written/composed
a poem is read, spoken, recited
the recital of a poem
the poem is by Shakespeare
it is a song by Genesis
the speaker of the poem/the poetic I/the poetic persona
the poem consists of/is composed of/is arranged in stanzas
the comedy ridicules/mocks/satirizes
the exposition sets the action in motion
the action moves towards and culminates in a turning-point
the play has a simple/complex/tight plot
it has a happy/unhappy ending
there are main/major/minor characters
the protagonist is in conflict with an opponent
the antagonist fights the protagonist
the spectator/audience follows the play
the play is performed/produced/staged
scenery is shifted
actors perform/play/enact
an actor enters/makes an entrance
an actor exits/makes his exit

Sach- und Gebrauchstexte

Argumentative Texts: How to Deal with (Political) Speeches

Keyword:

(Political) speeches: aim at convincing *(überzeugen)* the audience of the speaker's position, winning them over to his/her side. Very often, the speaker tries to persuade *(überreden)* the listener by appealing to his/her feelings. In some cases, the orator may even attempt to manipulate *(manipulieren)* his/her audience.
You should always keep in mind that the speaker wants to present his/her opinion/conviction/point of view as positively as possible.

When asked to analyse a political speech, you will have to focus on the topic and characteristic features.

How to proceed

Reading the text

1. Read the (political) speech (or, more likely, an extract from it) as a whole, trying to identify the main topic of the speech (reading for gist).
2. Re-read the (political) speech (the extract) several times, paying special attention to certain characteristic features of such speeches. Mark words or phrases in the text and take notes (intensive reading).

Pay special attention to

- key words and phrases
- references to historical events
- the use of symbols, key words, slogans
- references to famous people
- references to works of literature
- stylistic devices (see below)

Questions to be asked

When it comes to analysing a (political) speech, you should always ask yourself the following questions:
- What is the main topic of the speech?
- What is its political, historical and social context?
- What do I know about the speaker (biography, political orientation)?

Elements of a (political) speech

Structure

(Political) speeches can usually be divided into **an introduction, a main part** and **a conclusion.** These parts serve different purposes:

INFO Introduction to a speech

In the introduction, the orator announces the topic/purpose of the speech and explains its importance. He/She also wants to attract the audience's attention so that they will follow the speech closely and accept his/her opinion.

There are several ways to make listeners interested:

- The speaker can open by telling the audience **something about their personal history/recent experience,** thereby underlining the fact that the topic of the speech is of personal importance to them. By relating a **little story** to the audience, the speaker will also appear more human and less remote.
- Another common way of starting a speech is to **open it with a question** that refers to the main topic and which will be answered later in the speech. By asking the audience a question, the speaker actively involves them, indirectly asking them to think more deeply about the question.
- A speaker may **present visual material to the audience,** e.g. pictures, concrete objects or a short extract from a film. This also helps to attract the audience's attention: listeners will become curious about how the object or visual material is related to the content of the speech.

INFO Main part of a speech

In the main part of the speech the orator needs to keep the audience interested and to make sure that they can follow the train of thought.

Again, there are several ways to do this. The following techniques are particularly effective:

- **using short and simple sentences,** developing the argumentation step by step and ensuring that the audience can follow
- **quoting reliable sources/experts, referring to statistics and providing the audience with facts and necessary background information,** which shows that the speaker is well-informed and has researched the subject
- **pointing out problems, but also providing solutions** to them, thus showing that the speaker is competent
- **including personal experiences** and vivid, concrete events, again aiming for a personal relationship to the audience, **often using personal pronouns like "we", "us", "our".**

Towards the end of a speech the speaker might
- take up a question posed at the beginning of the speech
- appeal once more to both the audience's head and heart
- ask for support, giving the listeners the feeling that their support is of major importance
- develop a vision for the future.

Language and style

There are certain stylistic devices which are often used in (political) speeches. They aim at making the speech more lively and interesting.

Important stylistic devices

analogy	A resemblance is established between things which are unlike.
simile	This is a direct comparison using the words "like" or "as", e.g. *He fought like a lion in the battle.*
metaphor	This is an indirect comparison without using the words "like" or "as", e.g. *He was a lion in the battle.*
alliteration	A consonantal sound is repeated in two or more adjacent words, e.g. *We will win ... "We must understand that ties of trade bind nations in closest intimacy ..."* (Warren G. Harding: Inaugural address, March 4, 1921).
repetition	Repeating certain words or phrases puts emphasis on their meaning, e.g. *"The answer to the slavery question was already embedded within our Constitution – a Constitution that had at its very core the ideal of equal citizenship under the law; a Constitution that promised its people liberty, and justice (...)."* (Barack Obama: *A More Perfect Union)*
parallelism	Two or more parts of a sentence (or two or more sentences) have the same (or similar) syntactic structure. Like repetition, parallelism serves to emphasize the parts of the sentence in question, intensifying the force of the statement and encouraging the audience to think about its meaning, e.g. *"Let us be our sister's keeper. Let us find that common stake we all have in one another, and let our politics reflect that spirit as well."* (Barack Obama: *A More Perfect Union)*
antithesis	Two ideas are opposed to one another, using a parallel syntactic structure to achieve the desired effect, i.e. establishing a contrast, e.g. *"It's a story that hasn't made me the most conventional candidate. But it is a story that has seared into my genetic make-up the idea that this nation is more than the sum of its parts – that out of many, we are truly one."* (Barack Obama: *A More Perfect Union)*

rhetorical question	A rhetorical question is one to which no answer is expected; instead the listener is asked to think about the question and its relevance, e.g. *"How long should this suffering continue?"*
irony	Words or phrases are used to mean something different, often the opposite of their literal meaning. This is often done for rhetorical or humorous effect.

Glossary – Vocabulary for analysing speeches

By telling the listeners something about himself he attempts to establish a personal relationship with his audience.	Er bemüht sich, eine persönliche Beziehung zu seinen Zuhörern aufzubauen, indem er seinem Publikum etwas über seine persönliche Geschichte erzählt.
She attempts to win her listeners over to her side.	Sie versucht, das Publikum auf ihre Seite zu ziehen.
He draws a comparison between … and …	Er zieht einen Vergleich zwischen … und …
He puts emphasis on the meaning of his words by using parallelism/repetition in l. X (line …).	Durch den in Zeile X verwendeten Parallelismus/die in Zeile X verwendete Wiederholung verleiht er seinen Worten Nachdruck.
He refers to well-known historical events such as …	Er bezieht sich auf allgemein bekannte historische Ereignisse wie z. B. …
He wants to call/draw the audience's attention to the fact that …	Er möchte die Aufmerksamkeit des Publikums auf die Tatsache lenken, dass …
His frequent use of rhetorical questions is intended to show that …	Sein häufiger Gebrauch rhetorischer Fragen soll verdeutlichen, dass …
His use of metaphorical language is intended to make his speech more lively and interesting.	Sein metaphorischer Sprachgebrauch soll seine Rede interessanter und lebendiger machen.
In l. X (line …) he directly criticizes his political opponents.	In Zeile … kritisiert er offen seine politischen Gegner.
The frequent use of personal pronouns such as "we", "us" and "our" gives the audience the impression that he does not regard himself as superior to them, but as one of them.	Der häufige Gebrauch der Personalpronomen „wir", „uns" und „unser" soll dem Publikum das Gefühl geben, dass er sich als einer von ihnen und nicht als eine höher gestellte Person sieht.
The speaker appeals to the audience's emotions by …	Der Redner/Die Rednerin spricht die Gefühle des Publikums an, indem er/sie …

The speaker begins by ...	Der Redner/Die Rednerin beginnt mit ...
The speaker makes frequent use of metaphors/similes/symbols/examples to point out/to underline that ...	Der Redner/Die Rednerin macht regen Gebrauch von Metaphern/Vergleichen/Symbolen/Beispielen, um herauszustellen/zu unterstreichen, dass ...
The speaker tries to convince his/her audience of his/her point of view by ...	Der Redner/Die Rednerin versucht sein/ihr Publikum von seinem/ihrem Standpunkt zu überzeugen, indem er/sie ...
The speaker aims to convince/persuade/manipulate the audience.	Es ist das Anliegen des Redners/der Rednerin, das Publikum zu überzeugen/überreden/manipulieren.

Expository Texts: How to Deal with Essays

Keyword:

Essays: There are various kinds.

a) essays which reflect the author's opinion on a certain topic **(comment)**

b) essays in which the author weighs up the pros and cons of a particular subject **(argumentative essay)**

c) essays in which a topic is presented in a clear and logical way and which do not contain the author's opinion **(expository essay)**

How to proceed

First you have to find out which kind of essay you are being asked to analyse.
For details on how to analyze **comments** you can refer to the section on **political speeches** above.
Here we will focus on the **argumentative essay.**

Structure

- In the **introduction** the author expresses the main idea of the essay. Instead of giving a personal opinion, she/he might choose to provide the reader with some background information, or start with a question which will serve as a guideline and be answered in the course of the essay.
- For the **main part** of the essay the author can decide on a dialectical or an enumerative approach.
- In an **enumerative approach** the author will enumerate all the aspects of the topic in a neutral way. A **dialectical approach** can either present all the arguments in favour of a position before focusing on the counterarguments (or vice versa), or it can present the pros and cons alternately. The latter is usually considered more skilful.

- Each **new aspect** is usually presented in a new paragraph. The various **arguments** can be backed with examples from real life, established facts, an expert opinion, or other reliable sources. These pieces of evidence are very important as they enable the author to make his argument convincing and thus to persuade the reader.
- In the **conclusion** the author sums up the arguments, frequently also restating his/her own opinion and referring to what could happen in the future.

Glossary – Vocabulary for analysing essays

The author discusses the pros and cons of …	Der Verfasser/Die Verfasserin diskutiert die Vor- und Nachteile von …
The author gives his/her personal opinion on the problem of …	Der Verfasser/Die Verfasserin äußert seine/ihre eigene Meinung zum Thema …
He/She believes/is convinced/presumes that …	Er/Sie glaubt/ist überzeugt/nimmt an, dass …
She/He wants to persuade the reader …	Sie/Er möchte die Leser überreden …
One can easily follow his train of thought.	Man kann seinen Gedankengang leicht nachvollziehen.
At the end of her essay she draws/comes to the conclusion …	Am Ende ihres Essays kommt sie zu dem Schluss …
His/Her arguments are (not) convincing/well-chosen.	Seine/Ihre Argumente sind (nicht) überzeugend/gut gewählt.
The main topic of the essay is …	Das Thema des Berichts ist …
The tone of this essay is humorous/neutral/ironical/serious.	Der Ton des Berichts ist humorvoll/neutral/ironisch/ernst.
The author uses real examples to convince her readers.	Die Verfasserin verwendet reale Beispiele, um ihre Leser zu überzeugen.
The author's choice of words shows/emphasizes that he is for …/against …	Die Wortwahl des Verfassers zeigt/unterstreicht, dass er für …/gegen … ist.
In the introductory paragraph of her essay she asks a rhetorical question, which serves as a thread.	Im einleitenden Abschnitt ihres Berichts stellt sie den Lesern eine rhetorische Frage, die sich wie ein roter Faden durch den Bericht zieht.
The author uses adjectives with positive/negative connotations to support his/her point of view.	Der Verfasser/Die Verfasserin verwendet Adjektive mit einer positiven/negativen Konnotation, um seinen/ihren Standpunkt zu verdeutlichen.
Her attempt to persuade the readers backfires/works very well.	Ihr Versuch, die Leser zu überreden, misslingt/gelingt.

Narrative Texts: How to Deal with Reports

Keyword:

Report: This is a special kind of newspaper article.
It provides answers to the five "W" questions *(Who? What? Where? When? Why?)*, as well as the *How* question (how something happened). Its aim is to inform its readers and NOT to manipulate or influence them.
A report deals with current events and only contains facts.

Sometimes students have problems when it comes to differentiating between a *report* and an *article,* which can also deal with current events but which is usually a mixture of both fact and opinion.
The style of an **article** is usually more personal and its main aim is to entertain the reader. This is ensured by using many adverbs and adjectives to make the article lively and by addressing its readers directly, often by asking them a hypothetical question, e. g. *How would you feel if you discovered that someone had stolen your brand-new car?*
The main characteristics of a **report** are outlined below.

Elements of a report

Structure

- To arouse the reader's curiosity, reports have **headlines** containing basic information without providing too much detail.
- The basic information is generally provided in the first paragraph, which serves as an **introduction.**
- The **main body** of a report consists of a number of paragraphs, which contain one piece of information each.
- The last paragraph serves as a kind of **conclusion.**

Language and style

- A report is written in a factual style and neither reflects the author's personal opin-ion nor contains any kind of speculation.
- Individual paragraphs are relatively short and consist of short sentences which aim to ensure that the reader understands the information presented.
- Experts – or people who have first-hand experience of the topic in question – are often quoted, but no authorial comment is given on what they say.

Glossary – Vocabulary for analysing reports

The report [title] written by [author] deals with/is about/relates/describes ...	Der Bericht [Titel] von [Verfasser] beschäftigt sich mit/handelt von/berichtet von/ beschreibt ...
The topic(s) of the report is (are) ...	Das Thema/Die Themen des Berichts ist/sind ...
In the introduction the reader learns about/gets to know ...	In der Einleitung erfährt der Leser/die Leserin ...
The report can be divided into ... paragraphs.	Der Bericht kann in ... Absätze gegliedert werden.
The report consists of ... paragraphs.	Der Bericht besteht aus ... Absätzen.
It's the author's aim to inform the reader about ...	Es ist das Anliegen des Autors/der Autorin, den Leser/die Leserin über ... zu informieren.
The 2nd/3rd paragraph contains information on ...	Der zweite/dritte Absatz enthält Informationen über ...
The author quotes an eye-witness/ expert who says that ...	Der Autor/Die Autorin zitiert einen Augenzeugen/Experten, der sagt, dass ...
The author describes how ...	Der Verfasser/Die Verfasserin beschreibt, wie ...
The author does not give his/her personal opinion on the topic/problem/ question but merely relates facts.	Der Verfasser/Die Verfasserin äußert nicht seine/ihre eigene Meinung zum Sachverhalt/Problem/zu der Frage, sondern gibt Fakten wieder.
The factual style of writing shows that it is the author's aim to inform the reader and not to entertain him/her.	Der sachliche Sprachgebrauch verdeutlicht, dass es das Anliegen des Autors/ der Autorin ist, die Leser zu informieren und nicht, sie zu unterhalten.

Visuelle Materialien

Any kind of picture can be considered a type of text: it contains information that can be read and interpreted. This requires knowledge of the language of pictures, which is different for each medium: a cartoon must be approached differently from a photograph, for example. A complete account of every kind of visual material cannot be offered here, but some central aspects will be listed and explained.

INFO A note on visual texts in the Abitur

Pictures have often been used in the Zentralabitur. They generally appear as additional material illustrating a certain text and picking up its issues or introducing new aspects for the student to react to.

Common Types of Pictures Used

- **photographs:** often illustrate an issue or problem; their aesthetic qualities should be considered
- **advertisements:** mostly use photographic material combined with text to promote a certain product; the intention of the ad must be considered and reflected on; political ads also belong to this category
- **cartoons:** reflect an issue from a critical point of view; the cartoonist's intention to criticize a social or political problem plays a central role
- **works of art:** rarely used, but can reflect a society's state of mind and ideals during a certain period (e.g. early American paintings); their aesthetic qualities are essential to an understanding of their message
- **film stills:** a special type of photograph which enables the viewer to analyse the composition of a scene and its meaning/intention
- **films/movies:** for legal reasons these are not likely to be shown in the Abitur, but are used in the classroom for film analysis as well as comprehension tasks and as central study texts
- **statistics:** used to prove or explain a certain issue scientifically

Steps for Approaching Visual Material

Step 1: Describe the picture and its content. Do not begin by analysing or interpreting it, but state clearly and briefly what can be seen in the picture. The central question to be answered is "What type of picture are you dealing with and what can be seen?"
Step 2: Analyse the content and form. The method of analysis depends on the picture. Ask yourself: "What information does the picture convey?" and (except for statistics) "Why was the picture created in this way and not differently?" End by stating what the picture aims to reveal, illustrate, criticize or otherwise convey.

Step 3: Interpret and evaluate the meaning or importance of the picture and the possible intention(s) of its creator. You may ask yourself whether the picture gives a truthful reflection of a certain issue or aspect, whether it distorts or exaggerates reality or whether it is meant to manipulate the viewer.

INFO A note on tasks given to discuss pictures in the Abitur

Many tasks in the Abitur that involve the use of pictures do not specifically ask for an analysis or interpretation, but imply that this must be provided. In most cases, visual materials have been used to illustrate an issue already introduced in a longer text. In such cases, you will be asked to react to the picture and relate it to the text or to a certain general topic discussed in class.

Examples of Types of Picture

Cartoons

When analysing cartoons, pay attention to the following aspects:
context: the circumstances in which it was created: when and in what type of magazine or newspaper it was published (historical, political context), connection to a particular article or reference to a current topic, position of its creator
content: the details of what it shows:

- **target:** who or what is it aimed at, what issue does it discuss/criticize?
- **message:** what point does the cartoon aim to make or what ideas does it propose?
  - Has the cartoonist taken sides? Is he/she biased?
  - Is the cartoon's humour ironic, satirical, aggressive ...?

style: How is this message put across? Consider visual and textual elements.

visual elements	textual elements
Do visual items display incongruities by means of size, contrast, exaggeration, distortion, personification, etc.?	Has the cartoonist used labels/speech bubbles/captions? What words are made up to convey sounds? (onomatopoeia)
What facial features are used to convey expressions?	Does the cartoon use formal or informal language?
Do the images have symbolic meaning?	Does it play with words?
Does it use contrasts to convey certain issues of the main topic?	Does it use technical or specific terms?
Note: Almost every form of humour is based on incongruity. Things that are juxtaposed or compared in a strange way make us laugh.	

Key elements of cartoons

- **visual metaphors:** Cartoons use simplified visual symbols to carry meaning. The viewer can usually quickly decode them without any effort, e.g. when seeing a grey, dissolving shape one can imagine that this represents smoke.
- **caricature** (noun/verb): usually an exaggerated drawing or picture of a well-known person that makes them seem ridiculous but also easy to recognize
- **onomatopoeia** (noun): a word that sounds similar to the thing it describes, for example hiss, bang/pow (adj: onomatopoeic)

Advertisements

When analysing ads, pay attention to the AIDA principle (see below) and ask how the ad achieves the following points:
Attention: ads aim to attract the consumer's attention quickly, for example by showing an appealing, provocative or shocking image or message
Interest: this initial attention must be kept, thus the ad must create a further interest in the product
Desire: once the consumer is interested, the advertisement must spark a desire to buy the product which is advertised
Action: the desire to own or use the product must lead to action by the consumer; he/she must seek ways to buy or access the product

These aspects apply to all ads in general even if they do not directly aim to sell a specific product. Campaign ads in politics aim to "sell" a programme or candidate, whereas campaigns published by organizations such as Greenpeace seek to make viewers change their way of living. One must always consider the context in which an ad tries to affect its audience.

Photographs

When analysing and interpreting photographs, it is important to remember that even if a photograph shows a real environment at a certain time, it is still a fabrication of sorts. All photography is influenced by a) the photographer's choice of perspective, frame and timing and b) the camera itself, which can only show a limited view.
Photographers make choices when taking a picture in order to convey a specific effect or impression of their object. So a photograph must be considered in the same way as a painting – always ask yourself why the photographer chose this specific object, perspective, frame (what can and cannot be seen), moment in time, and rendition (e.g. colour, black and white, sepia).

Modern means of digital photography have also led to increasing manipulation. Thus, even though we still tend to believe that pictures show reality, it can no longer be taken for granted that a photograph shows an aspect of the real world.

Glossary – Vocabulary for analysing visual material

viewer	Betrachter
picture, image	Bild
painting, drawing	Gemälde, Zeichnung
photograph/photo	Fotografie (Vorsicht: nicht Fotograf)
photographer	Fotograf
portrait	Porträt
landscape painting/photograph	Landschaftsgemälde/-fotografie
bird's eye view	Vogelperspektive
worm's eye view	Froschperspektive
incongruity	Widerspruch, Widersprüchlichkeit
background	Hintergrund
foreground	Vordergrund

Basic phrases for a description

In the picture/advertisement one can see ...
In the foreground/middle ground/background ...
The theme/topic/main motif of the advertisement is ...
It's an image of ... (place, person, scene)
The picture shows ... (place, person, scene) close up, from a medium/long distance view
You look at ... (place, person, scene) from ... (above/behind/...)
The picture was taken in/at ... (place)
Above/On top of ... one can read/it says/one can see a short text ...

Basic phrases to express intention/message/aim

The picture/advertisement is aimed at/is meant to attract/is intended to/appeals to/shows a/an (exaggerated, illustrative, provocative, unrealistic, flattering/beautified) depiction/image of ...
It expresses/criticizes/suggests/reveals/claims/manipulates/influences ...

Basic phrases to express stylistic means/how aims are achieved

The photographer/painter/cartoonist achieves his/her aim by presenting ... in an objective/artistic/exaggerated/limited/digitally manipulated way/style.
By using contrasts/incongruities such as .../differences in colour, focus ... the artist/photographer/cartoonist illustrates/emphasizes/shows ...
The perspective/point of view suggests that ...
The motif was chosen deliberately because it illustrates the issue well/evokes emotions/stands for/represents a larger, more complex issue ...

Die sprachliche Leistung im Abitur

Die integrative Sprachbewertung

Mit der **integrativen Sprachbewertung** entfallen sowohl die früher getrennte Bewertung von Ausdrucksvermögen und Sprachrichtigkeit als auch die entsprechenden Fehlerindex-Tabellen.

Nun gibt es nur noch eine Gesamtzensur für die sprachliche Leistung, wobei sich die Bewertung an klar umrissenen Kriterien orientiert. Hierbei hat sich ein grundlegender Wandel vollzogen. Wurden früher insbesondere die fehlerhaften Äußerungen einer Klausur als Bewertungsgrundlage herangezogen, so steht jetzt eine sogenannte **Positiv-Korrektur** im Vordergrund. Zwar werden die Mängel der sprachlichen Leistung nach wie vor rot markiert, jedoch sollen besonders gelungene Teile einer Klausur in grüner Farbe hervorgehoben werden. Beispiele für eine positive, grüne Markierung wären etwa der richtige Gebrauch von Präpositionen, Gerundien oder Konnektoren (zur Satzverknüpfung).

Es wird bewertet, ob und in welchem Umfang die Verstöße gegen die sprachliche Richtigkeit die Kommunikation zwischen dem Schreiber und dem Leser der Klausur beeinträchtigen und ob die Häufigkeit den Gesamteindruck des Textes bestimmt, inwiefern die Fehler störend wirken und ob sie auf eine Nichtbeherrschung grammatikalischer Regeln schließen lassen.

Zur integrativen Leistungsbewertung im sprachlichen Bereich werden folgende Kriterien betrachtet:

Texterstellung

- Ist der Text übersichtlich gegliedert und für den Leser damit leicht zu erfassen?
- Ist der Textumfang angemessen?
- Werden sogenannte *linking words* (Konnektoren) zur Verknüpfung von Satzteilen und Ideen sinnvoll und abwechslungsreich eingesetzt?
- Ist das Ausdrucksvermögen anspruchsvoll und wird evtl. das Risiko von möglichen Fehlern akzeptiert, um einen flüssigen und idiomatisch ansprechenden Text zu produzieren?
- Werden textsortenspezifische Formulierungen verwendet (eine private E-Mail wird anders formuliert als z. B. ein Leserbrief)?
- Werden Zitate sinnvoll integriert (treffend gewählt, nicht zu lang)?

Syntax

- Wird der Satzbau variiert oder werden hauptsächlich gleiche Strukturen verwendet?
- Wird auch komplexerer Satzbau beherrscht oder werden bei den Versuchen, nicht nur einfache Strukturen zu verwenden, viele Fehler gemacht?

Lexik

- Sind sowohl der allgemeine als auch der themenspezifische Wortschatz reichhaltig?
- Wird der Wortschatz treffsicher eingesetzt?

Grammatik

- Ist die Fehlerzahl eher gering und beeinträchtigt sie die Kommunikation eher nicht, oder führt eine Häufung zu einer eingeschränkten Verständlichkeit?
- Deuten die Fehler auf eine Unkenntnis oder Unsicherheit hinsichtlich relevanter grammatikalischer Regeln hin?

Kommunikative Relevanz typischer Fehler

Die folgenden Beispiele zeigen **Fehler, die die Kommunikation beeinträchtigen** und somit zu Abzügen führen. Die Auflistung ist nicht vollständig, sondern vermittelt einen exemplarischen Überblick:

- korrupte Syntax durch Fehlerhäufung
- falsche Bezüge
- uneinheitlicher bzw. falscher Tempusgebrauch (vgl. *summary*)
- falscher Tempusgebrauch bei eindeutigen Signalwörtern (z. B. *last year*)
- fehlende Umschreibung mit *to do* bei Frage und Verneinung
- falsche Präpositionen in *phrasal verbs*
- Germanismen
- falscher Gebrauch von Infinitiv und Gerundium
- *contact clause* im nicht notwendigen Relativsatz
- *that* im nicht notwendigen Relativsatz

Folgende Fehler beeinträchtigen die Kommunikation nicht oder nur in geringem Umfang:

- Rechtschreibfehler, wenn deutlich wird, welches Wort gemeint ist
- falsch gesetztes oder fehlendes Apostroph (**Peters bike; its/it's*)
- fehlerhafte Partizipialkonstruktionen
- Flüchtigkeitsfehler wie gelegentliches Fehlen des *3rd-person singular present -s* oder Plural-s
- ungebräuchliche Präposition bei klarer Aussageabsicht (z. B. **typical for*)
- *Progressive* anstatt *simple* (z. B. **The author is dealing with …*)
- fehlerhafte Zeichensetzung

Operatoren für das Fach Englisch[1]

Die Liste der Operatoren gibt einen Überblick über die wichtigsten Arbeitsanweisungen, die in den Prüfungen vorkommen.

1 Die Operatoren finden sich im *Kerncurriculum für das Gymnasium – gymnasiale Oberstufe (…)* Englisch, S. 44f. (Niedersächsisches Kultusministerium, 2009, Hannover, Schiffgraben 12).
Quelle: https://www.nibis.de/uploads/1gohrgs/operatoren_2021/EN_2021Abi_Operatoren.pdf

Anforderungsbereich I

describe	give a detailed account of
outline	give the main features or general principles of a text; leave out minor details
state	specify clearly
summarize	*give a concise account of the main points*

Anforderungsbereich II

analyse	describe and explore in detail certain aspects of the text and how they are presented
compare	show similarities and differences
contrast	emphasize the differences between two or more things
examine	*cf. analyse*
explain	*show causes and effects in a given context*

Anforderungsbereich III

comment	state clearly your opinion on the topic in question and support your views with evidence
discuss	investigate and give reasons for and against
justify	present reasons for decisions, positions or conclusions
assess/evaluate	*consider in a balanced way points for and/or against something*

Aufgabenarten

Es können auch Aufgaben gestellt werden, die eine **kreative Lösung** erfordern, um dem Anforderungsbereich III zu genügen. Denkbar sind u. a. das Schreiben eines Briefes oder einer E-Mail an einen Freund oder den Herausgeber einer Zeitung, ein Schreiben zur Erlangung von Informationen oder auch ein Beschwerdebrief.
Weiterhin sind Aufgabenstellungen möglich, die das **Verfassen eines Artikels, eines Berichtes, eines Drehbuches, eines Tagebucheintrags oder eines Dialogs** erforderlich machen.
Das Schreiben einer **Fortsetzung** oder eines **alternativen Endes einer Geschichte** ist ebenso eine mögliche Aufgabenstellung wie die **Schilderung einer Begebenheit** aus einer anderen Perspektive, um nur einige mögliche Beispiele zu benennen.

Strukturiertes Vorgehen in der Abiturprüfung

Bei der Bearbeitung der Aufgaben in der Abiturprüfung empfiehlt sich ein systematisches Vorgehen in klar definierten Einzelschritten:
Lesen Sie sich zunächst den Text in Ruhe durch und unterstreichen Sie mit Bleistift Wörter, die Sie nicht kennen und die Sie im Wörterbuch nachschlagen möchten. Konzentrieren Sie sich dabei auf solche Wörter, die bedeutungsrelevant und zentral für Ihr Verständnis des Textes sind. Verlieren Sie keine wertvolle Zeit mit dem Nachschlagen von Füllwörtern. Schlagen Sie dann die wichtigsten Wörter nach und lesen Sie den Text ein zweites Mal – nun zügiger – durch. Wenden Sie sich nun den Aufgaben zu: Lesen Sie zuerst alle Teilaufgaben genau durch. Machen Sie sich nochmals klar, dass die Bearbeitung der *comprehension task* (Anforderungsbereich I) weitgehend am Ausgangstext orientiert erfolgen soll, gegebenenfalls unter Einbindung vorhandenen Hintergrundwissens. Die *analysis* (Anforderungsbereich II) erfordert die detaillierte Betrachtung von Einzelaspekten unter Anwendung Ihrer Kenntnisse aus dem Bereich Zitieren und Argumentieren. In der *evaluation* (Anforderungsbereich III) wird schließlich nach Ihrer persönlichen Einordnung und Bewertung gefragt.

Konzentrieren Sie sich anschließend auf die erste Teilaufgabe und kennzeichnen Sie gezielt unmittelbar relevante Textpassagen mit einem Marker. Machen Sie sich auf einem separaten Blatt stichpunktartige Notizen zur Bearbeitung der ersten Aufgabe und verfahren Sie so mit allen weiteren Teilaufgaben. Strukturieren Sie nun Ihre Stichpunkte durch Nummerieren und prüfen Sie unmittelbar vor dem Ausformulieren noch einmal die Aufgabenstellung, um sich rechtzeitig zu vergewissern, dass Ihre Bearbeitung auf den Kern der Frage abzielt. Nehmen Sie sich genug Zeit für diese Vorarbeiten (etwa ein Drittel der Zeit ist nicht zu viel), da Sie mit gut vorsortierten Inhalten umso schneller schreiben und sich dabei stärker auf die sprachliche Seite im Englischen konzentrieren können.
Es wird als positiv im Sinne der Textkohärenz bewertet, wenn Sie sich bemühen, Ihre Antworten zu den einzelnen Teilaufgaben sprachlich miteinander in Verbindung zu setzen. Betrachten Sie nicht jede Aufgabe als isolierten Einzelaspekt, der jeweils mit einem Satz für Leser ohne Vorwissen eingeleitet wird.

TIPP zum Punktesammeln

Gehen Sie professionell vor und lesen Sie Ihre gesamte Arbeit vor der Abgabe noch einmal gründlich durch. Planen Sie dafür etwa 15 bis 20 Minuten ein. Bei diesem Arbeitsgang werden Ihnen selbst ganz sicher sprachliche Fehler auffallen. Achten Sie besonders auf die Bezüge bei den Pronomina, das *-s* in der 3. Person Singular Präsens, die Zeitenfolge sowie Rechtschreibung und Zeichensetzung.

TIPP zur Zeitplanung

1. Schritt: Text lesen, bedeutungsrelevanten Wortschatz klären	20 Min
2. Schritt: Fragen lesen, Stichpunkte machen und vorsortieren	20 Min
3. Schritt: Fragen unter Verwendung der Gliederung beantworten	80 Min
4. Schritt: Korrekturlesen	15 Min

(Diese zeitlichen Richtlinien gelten für Grundkurse; bei Prüfungen im Leistungskurs verlängern sich die Zeiten entsprechend.)

Wortschatzerschließung

Viele scheinbar unbekannte Wörter lassen sich problemlos ableiten. Hierzu kann man den Kontext oder andere bekannte Wörter aus derselben Wortfamilie zurate ziehen. In manchen Fällen helfen auch fächerübergreifend die Kenntnisse in anderen Fremdsprachen oder der Muttersprache. Insbesondere auf das Lateinische bzw. Französische kann man hier häufig zurückgreifen.

Textgestaltung

Kohärenz, Adressatenorientierung, Leserleitung

Kohärenz

TIPP zum Punktesammeln

Bemühen Sie sich, Ihren Text kohärent, also auch sprachlich zusammenhängend zu gestalten. Schaffen Sie sinnvolle inhaltliche Verknüpfungen zwischen Satzteilen, Sätzen und Sinnabschnitten. Verwenden Sie dazu die sogenannten **Konnektoren,** die als Verbindungsglieder zum besseren Textverständnis beitragen.

Hier ist eine Liste der wichtigsten Konnektoren, geordnet nach Ihrer Funktion im Satz.

Reihung von Argumenten

and	und
first(ly), ... second(ly), ... third(ly), ...	erstens, zweitens, drittens
furthermore, ...	außerdem, darüber hinaus
in addition to ...	zusätzlich zu
moreover, ...	ferner, überdies
not only ... but also	nicht nur ..., sondern auch
as well as	sowie
finally, ...	schließlich

Gegensatz

but	aber, sondern
although	obwohl
however,	jedoch
despite the fact that	trotz der Tatsache, dass
in spite of	trotz
nevertheless, nonetheless,	nichtsdestotrotz
even so,	selbst dann
on the contrary,	im Gegensatz dazu
on the one hand, … on the other hand,	einerseits … andererseits
unlike	anders als
whereas	während/wogegen/indessen
while/whilst	während (dagegen)
yet	dennoch

Bedingung

if	falls, wenn
unless	wenn nicht
otherwise	ansonsten

Folge

because	weil
since	da
so	daher
consequently,	folglich
as a result,	demzufolge
therefore,	daher, deshalb
due to …	infolge
according to …	… zufolge
that is why	deshalb

Vergleich

like	wie
in comparison with	im Vergleich zu
similarly,	ähnlich
equally,	gleichermaßen

Adressatenorientierung

Schneiden Sie Ihren Text genau auf den Adressaten zu und drücken Sie sich präzise aus. Bewegen Sie sich in der Abiturklausur auf einer neutralen Sprachebene, vermeiden Sie also Stilbrüche wie Slangwörter und *spoken English.* Auch *contracted forms (they're, he's got)* sind in einem schriftlichen Text dieser Art nicht angebracht.

Leserleitung: *Writing a paragraph/comment*

Hier soll insbesondere der *argumentative comment* näher betrachtet werden, in dem Argumente für und gegen eine Behauptung erläutert werden. Die Form des *comment,* der eine These stützt bzw. nur antithetisch arbeitet, ist ein Teilbereich eines *argumentative comment.*

TIPP zum Punktesammeln

Entwickeln Sie in Ihrem Text eine für die Leser nachvollziehbare Argumentation.

Ein *comment* folgt einer klaren Struktur: Er beginnt mit einem *topic sentence* zur Einleitung, in dem eine Aussage zum Thema gemacht wird. Anschließend führt er das Argument aus **(These),** geht über zur Darstellung der Gegenargumente **(Antithese),** um mit einer **Schlussfolgerung** bzw. der **Darstellung der eigenen Meinung** abzuschließen. In jedem Teil sollten spezifische Formulierungen zur logischen Verknüpfung eingesetzt werden, um den Lesern die Redeabsicht zu signalisieren.

Eine Sicherheit ausdrücken

The fact is that …	Es ist eine Tatsache, dass …
It cannot be denied that …	Man kann nicht leugnen, dass …
It goes without saying that …	Selbstredend …
Undoubtedly, …	Zweifellos (am Satzanfang) …
I am convinced that …	Ich bin überzeugt davon, dass …
It is indisputable/obvious that … There is no doubt that …	Es ist unbestreitbar/offensichtlich/kein Zweifel, dass …
It is inevitable that …	Es ist unvermeidbar, dass …

Eine Vermutung ausdrücken

Apparently, …	Anscheinend (am Satzanfang) …
They will probably …	Sie werden wahrscheinlich …
It seems highly likely that …	Es scheint äußerst wahrscheinlich, dass …
It may be the case that …	Es kann sein, dass …

Einen Zweifel ausdrücken

It is doubtful whether ...	Es ist zweifelhaft, ob ...
I wonder if ...	Ich frage mich, ob ...
There is no proof/evidence that ...	Es gibt keine Beweise, dass ...

Einen Sachverhalt betonen

In order to stress that ...	Um hervorzuheben, dass ...
to emphasize	betonen
I would like to make it clear that ...	Ich möchte klarstellen, dass ...

Eine Meinung ausdrücken

In my opinion/In my view ...	Meiner Meinung nach ...
My thoughts on the subject are ...	Meine Meinung zu diesem Thema ist ...
Personally, I think that ...	Ich persönlich denke, dass ...
As far as I am concerned, ...	Was mich angeht ...
From my point of view, ...	Aus meiner Sicht ...
I assume ...	Ich vermute ...
I am (not) convinced that ...	Ich bin (nicht) überzeugt davon, dass ...
I can't help thinking that ...	Ich kann nicht umhin zu denken, dass ...
I get the impression that ...	Ich habe den Eindruck, dass ...
I am afraid that ...	Ich fürchte, dass (abschwächend) ...
Honestly, .../To be honest, ...	Ehrlich gesagt ...
I can't judge ...	Ich kann ... nicht beurteilen
I am in no position to say ...	Es steht mir nicht zu, zu sagen ...

Einen Widerspruch einräumen

in contrast to ...	im Gegensatz zu ...
On the contrary, ...	Ganz im Gegenteil (am Satzanfang)
whereas ...	während (dagegen)
I strongly object to ...	Ich spreche mich deutlich gegen ... aus.
One could argue that ... but ...	Man könnte argumentieren, dass ... , aber ...
Although it is true that ... it would be wrong to claim that ...	Obwohl es wahr ist, dass ..., wäre es falsch zu behaupten, dass ...

Zustimmung ausdrücken

Fortunately, ...	Glücklicherweise (am Satzanfang)
I entirely agree with/I share the opinion that ...	Ich stimme vollkommen mit ... überein.

I support his view.	Ich unterstütze seine Meinung.
I share her views.	Ich teile ihre Meinung.
I am of the same opinion (as) ...	Ich bin der gleichen Meinung (wie) ...
I approve of his/her opinion.	Ich bin mit seiner/ihrer Meinung einverstanden.
I take your point about ...	Ich akzeptiere Ihre Meinung über ...
I am in favour of ...	Ich bin für ...
He rightly mentions that ...	Zu Recht betont er, dass ...
I won't object to ...	Ich widerspreche ... nicht.
It cannot be justified that ...	Es gibt keine Rechtfertigung für ...
Nobody would disagree with that statement.	Niemand würde dieser Behauptung widersprechen.
This statement is very convincing.	Diese Aussage ist sehr überzeugend.
I have to admit that the author ...	Ich muss zugeben, dass der Autor/die Autorin ...

Ablehnung ausdrücken

It is only partly true that ...	Es entspricht nur teilweise der Wahrheit, dass ...
I disagree completely with ...	Ich muss widersprechen ...
I see things differently.	Ich sehe den Sachverhalt anders.
I must/have to disagree on this matter.	Ich bin in dieser Angelegenheit anderer Meinung.
One cannot possibly accept that ...	Man kann unmöglich akzeptieren, dass ...
I must object to ...	Ich muss ... widersprechen.
I have to criticize strongly that ...	Ich muss scharf kritisieren, dass ...
I doubt whether ...	Ich bezweifle, dass ...
This statement entirely contradicts ...	Diese Behauptung widerspricht ganz und gar ...
However, ...	Jedoch (am Satzanfang)
It is not as simple as it seems.	Es ist nicht so einfach wie es scheint.
Unlike the author, I think ...	Anders als der Autor/die Autorin glaube ich ...
I cannot share the author's view on ...	Ich kann die Meinung des Autors/der Autorin über ... nicht teilen.

Einen Grund angeben

As/Since ...	Da/Weil ... (am Satzanfang)
In view of the fact that ...	Angesichts der Tatsache, dass ...

The reason for this development lies in ...	Der Grund für diese Entwicklung liegt bei ...
This causes confusion.	Das sorgt für Verwirrung.
That is why .../Therefore/For this reason ...	Aus diesem Grund .../deshalb
Given that ...	In Anbetracht der Tatsache, dass ...
That was caused by ...	Das wurde verursacht durch ...

Eine Folge darstellen

Consequently, ... /As a consequence, ...	Folglich (am Satzanfang)
In view of this statement, ...	In Anbetracht dieser Behauptung ...
in order to	um zu
as a result of	als Folge von

Vergleiche anstellen

to be comparable	vergleichbar sein
compared to/in comparison with	im Vergleich zu
to be different from	sich unterscheiden von
distinguish between (A and B)	(A von B) unterscheiden
to be considerably better than	wesentlich besser sein als
to get more and more difficult	immer schwieriger werden
Nowadays, it is less and less common ...	Heutzutage ist es immer weniger üblich ...
superior/inferior to	überlegen/unterlegen
The former ... the latter	Der erstere ... der letztere ...
They have little in common.	Sie haben wenig gemeinsam.
They are equal in price.	Sie haben den gleichen Preis.

Beispiele anführen

For example/For instance	Zum Beispiel
Let me give you an example.	Lassen Sie mich ein Beispiel anführen.
such as	wie (zum Beispiel)
Look at ...	Sehen wir uns einmal ... an.

Conclusion

To sum up, .../to summarize, ...	Zusammenfassend kann man sagen ...
I come to the conclusion that ...	Ich komme zu dem Schluss, dass ...
In short, ...	kurz gesagt

To put it in a nutshell ...	Um es auf einen Nenner zu bringen ...
I can support the author's view on ...	Ich kann die Ansicht des Autors/der Autorin über ... unterstützen
All in all, I believe that ...	Insgesamt glaube ich ...

Autorenintention

An mehreren Stellen in Ihrer Abiturklausur werden Sie Ihre eigenen Aussagen in Relation zur Autorenmeinung setzen müssen. Dafür empfiehlt es sich, eine Reihe von sprachlichen Ausdrücken parat zu haben, z. B.:

He/She points out/argues that ...	Er/Sie weist darauf hin/argumentiert, dass ...
He implies/claims/states that ...	Er behauptet, dass ...
He/She believes/suggests ...	Er/Sie glaubt/schlägt vor ...
He/She lays emphasis on ...	Er/Sie betont
His/Her idea was to ...	Er/Sie wollte ...
He/She writes with the intention of (+ gerund) ...	Er/Sie schreibt mit der Absicht ...
His/Her aim is to ...	Sein/Ihr Ziel ist es ...
His/Her attitude towards ...	Seine/Ihre Einstellung gegenüber ...
When he/she says/writes ..., he/she means that ...	Wenn er/sie sagt/schreibt ..., meint er/sie ...
According to the author, ...	Dem Autor/Der Autorin zufolge ...

Verweise und Zitate

Um Ihre Aussagen zu belegen, fügen Sie geeignete Zitate aus dem Originaltext in Ihre Antworten ein. Setzen Sie diese in englische Anführungszeichen – diese beginnen oben und enden oben. Da es sich in der Abiturklausur um einen relativ kurzen Ausgangstext handelt, genügt als Quellenangabe die Angabe der Zeilennummer in Klammern direkt hinter dem Zitat.

Beispiel zu Shakespeare, *Romeo and Juliet:*

In his speech Prince Escalus speaks about the Montagues and the Capulets as "enemies to peace" (l. 1) and finishes by even menacing them with "pain of death" (l. 23).

Verwenden Sie nicht das ganze Zitat, können Sie die ausgelassenen Passagen mit eckigen Klammern kennzeichnen. Genauso können Sie ein Bezugswort in eckigen Klammern einfügen, wenn dies aufgrund der Satzkonstruktion notwendig ist.
Die wörtliche Übernahme von Formulierungen aus dem Ausgangstext bzw. einem anderen Text ohne entsprechende Kennzeichnung ist nicht zulässig und wird negativ bewertet.

Da mit Zitaten Aussagen belegt oder gefestigt werden, stehen sie normalerweise nach der entsprechenden Behauptung. Diese sollten Sie zunächst mit eigenen Worten paraphrasieren. Nehmen Sie dabei Ihr einsprachiges Wörterbuch zur Hilfe, um nach Synonymen zu suchen.

Textstruktur und Absätze

Formalia

TIPP zum Punktesammeln

Achten Sie darauf, dass Sie formale Nachlässigkeiten vermeiden. Hier Punkte zu verschenken, ist unnötig.

Zunächst eine generelle Bemerkung: Die Leser Ihrer Englischprüfung werden Ihnen grundsätzlich wohlgesonnen sein und werden Sie gerecht bewerten wollen. Dazu ist es natürlich gerade in einer Fremdsprache eine wichtige Voraussetzung, dass Ihre Handschrift gut lesbar ist, die Buchstaben und die Wortgrenzen deutlich erkennbar sind, damit die Leser nicht raten müssen, ob Sie nun das für den jeweiligen Kontext passende Wort benutzt haben oder nicht. Wenn Sie also wissen, dass Ihre Handschrift schlecht lesbar ist, bemühen Sie sich zu Ihrem eigenen Vorteil darum, besonders groß und deutlich zu schreiben! Reduzieren Sie nachträgliche Ergänzungen auf ein Minimum. Lassen sich diese nicht vermeiden, nummerieren Sie sie fortlaufend und deutlich und listen Sie den eingefügten Text entweder jeweils am Seitenende oder nach Abschluss des Textes in chronologischer Reihenfolge auf.

Rücken Sie zur besseren Lesbarkeit 2 bis 3 Zentimeter ein, wenn Sie einen neuen Absatz beginnen. Erlauben Sie wie gefordert die Hälfte der Seite als Rand für Korrekturzeichen und Bemerkungen der Lehrkraft.

Satzzeichen

Natürlich sollen Sie in der Englischprüfung im Abitur zeigen, dass Sie mit komplexen Satzgefügen umgehen können. Vermeiden Sie allerdings Schwerfälligkeit! Allzu lange Sätze mit vielen Nebensätzen machen Ihren Text schwer lesbar und erhöhen die Wahrscheinlichkeit, dass Sie sich in Ihrer Satzkonstruktion verzetteln. Achten Sie auf sinnvolle Strukturierung durch Satzzeichen; sie helfen dem Leser/der Leserin, Ihren Gedanken zu folgen und sich in Ihrem Text zurechtzufinden. Wechseln Sie ab: Verwenden Sie nicht nur Punkt und Komma, sondern auch Strichpunkt oder Gedankenstrich. Auch durch den Einsatz von Fragen können Sie Ihre Texte ansprechender gestalten.
In den Bewertungskriterien wird Interpunktion nicht aufgeführt und wird in der Schule großzügig gehandhabt. Bedeutungstragende Satzzeichen, z. B. bei *non-defining relative clauses,* werden jedoch verlangt.

Ausdrucksvermögen/Verfügbarkeit sprachlicher Mittel

Klarheit und Präzision

Die Formulierung der Abituraufgaben folgt klar definierten Regeln. So kommen als Arbeitsanweisungen nur bestimmte Verben in Frage, die sogenannten **Operatoren.** Eine Aufstellung der Operatoren, die das Schulministerium auf seiner Website auflistet, finden Sie auf den Seiten 103 und 132 in diesem Buch.
Lesen Sie die Formulierung der Fragen genau und machen Sie sich klar, welche Art der Antwort von Ihnen im konkreten Fall erwartet wird. Der Operator drückt deutlich aus, was von Ihnen verlangt wird.
Nachdem also die Art der Fragestellung aufgrund der Formulierung mittels der Operatoren klar definiert ist, können Sie Ihre Antwort entsprechend ausrichten. Achten Sie beim Verfassen Ihrer Antwort auf Fehlerquellen, die leicht vermieden werden können. Im Folgenden werden einige typische Fehlerquellen genannt und erläutert. Diese Hinweise mögen auf den ersten Blick selbstverständlich erscheinen, doch durch die notwendige Konzentration auf den Inhalt oder das Arbeiten unter Zeitdruck schleichen sich oft unnötige Fehler ein.

Textökonomie

Schreiben Sie nach dem Grundsatz der Textökonomie „Jeder Satz ein Statement." Vermeiden Sie Wiederholungen im Wortschatz und umständliche inhaltliche „Schleifen". Zum einen leidet darunter der Stil und zum anderen wird der Korrektor diese Taktik wahrscheinlich durchschauen.

Vermeiden Sie die Formulierung von Allgemeinplätzen.
(Beispiel: *It is well-known that Europe is suffering from many problems these days.)*
Stellen Sie sicher, dass die sprachlichen Bezüge korrekt sind: Wählen Sie also bewusst die passenden Personal-, Possessiv-, Demonstrativ- und Relativpronomen, um die Leser eindeutig durch den Text zu führen.
Verwenden Sie zusätzlich ***signal words*** *(Firstly, secondly, thirdly, ...)* als Gliederungssignale, um den Text sinnvoll zu strukturieren.
Achten Sie auf die Verwendung der Zeiten! Wenn Sie im ***past tense*** beginnen, müssen Sie diese Zeitebene auch durchgängig beibehalten.
Seien Sie in Alarmbereitschaft bei potenziellen ***false friends.***
Hier ist eine Liste der gängigen Fallen:

deutsch	**englisch**	***false friend***
bekommen	to get	nicht: become
die Kritik	criticism	nicht: critic – der Kritiker
die Politik	politics	nicht: policy – persönliche Strategie –, außer in Begriffen wie „foreign policy" = Außenpolitik
sensibel	sensitive	nicht: sensible – vernünftig

meinen/ glauben	to think	nicht mean – bedeuten (oder Adj. = gemein)
aktuell	current	nicht: actually – in der Tat
also	so	nicht: also – auch
Chef	boss	nicht: chef – der Küchenchef
engagiert	committed	nicht: engaged – verlobt; besetzt
eventuell	possibly	nicht: eventually – schließlich
Handy	mobile phone (AE: cell phone)	nicht: handy – handlich, praktisch
Konfession	denomination	nicht: confession – die Beichte
Konkurrenz	competition	nicht concurrence – Zusammentreffen
konsequent	consistent	nicht: consequently – folglich
mobben	to bully	nicht: mob – das gemeine Volk
prägnant	concise	nicht: pregnant – schwanger
prinzipiell	fundamentally, basically, in/on principle	nicht: principally – hauptsächlich
Prospekt	brochure, leaflet	nicht: prospect(s) – die Zukunftsaussichten
Protokoll	minutes	nicht: protocol – die Etikette (außer bei EDV)
Publikum	audience	nicht: public – die Öffentlichkeit
rentabel	profitable	nicht: rentable – zu mieten
Rückseite	back	nicht: backside – Hinterteil
spenden	to donate	nicht: to spend – ausgeben

Wortschatz

Der in Ihren Texten verwendete Wortschatz sollte sachlich und stilistisch angemessen sein. Demonstrieren Sie, dass Sie über einen differenzierten allgemeinen Wortschatz verfügen, und variieren Sie in Ihrem Ausdruck.

Ausdrucksmöglichkeiten im Wortfeld „sagen“
to say, to tell, to relate, to describe, to let somebody know, to state, to speak, to talk, to answer, to respond, to reply, to inform, to advise, to recommend, to brief, to update somebody, to promise, to lie, to whisper, to shout, to scream, to yell, to report, to repeat, to argue, to converse, to allude to something, to articulate, to suggest, to demand, to insist, to urge, to ask, to question

Achten Sie dabei besonders auf gängige Fehlerquellen. Die Beispiele sollen Sie für die Problematik sensibilisieren, aus Platzgründen werden jeweils nur einige genannt.

Verwendung der richtigen Präposition nach Verben oder Adjektiven

Orientieren Sie sich hier nicht am Deutschen, das kann leicht zu einem falschen Ergebnis führen.

Collocations

Bestimmte Verben und Nomina treten immer in einer **festen Verbindung** auf, einer **Kollokation.** Die Verwendung eines anderen Verbs ist nicht möglich.

Darüber hinaus wird von Ihnen die Verwendung eines angemessenen **thematischen Wortschatzes** erwartet. Prägen Sie sich die Glossare zu den lehrplanrelevanten Themen der vorangegangenen Kapitel ein, um den thematischen Wortschatz bei Bedarf zur Verfügung zu haben (vgl. Kapitel „Basiswissen“, S. 18).
Zu guter Letzt sollten Sie über einen präzisen **fachmethodischen Wortschatz** verfügen. Das Handwerkszeug dazu bekommen Sie im Kapitel „Methoden der Textarbeit“ (S. 102) dieses Buches, wo Sie geeignetes Vokabular zum Thema finden. Sie sollten sich sowohl Vokabular für literarische Texte als auch für Sach- und Gebrauchstexte aneignen.

Differenzierte Satzgestaltung

Neben der Gewandtheit im Wortschatz wird natürlich auch Ihr Können im Bereich Syntax bewertet. Wechseln Sie also je nach Kontext ab zwischen Parataxe und Hypotaxe, d. h. einer Reihung von Hauptsätzen bzw. komplexen Satzgefügen mit Nebensätzen. Verbinden Sie diese entsprechend mit Konnektoren (s. Liste S. 135); erwähnen Sie Bezüge in temporaler, kausaler, konzessiver, konditionaler, resultativer Hinsicht.

Übersicht über die möglichen Konjunktionen

temporal	while, before, after, until
kausal	since, because, as, for
konzessiv	(al)though, while/whilst, whereas
konditional	if, unless
resultativ	so (that)

Integrieren Sie Partizipial-, Gerundial- und Infinitivkonstruktionen sowie Passivkonstruktionen. Wechseln Sie zusätzlich durch Inversion sowie gelegentliche Verwendung von (rhetorischen) Fragen mit anderen Satzformen ab.

Eigenständigkeit (Paraphrase)

In der Abiturklausur werden Ihr Textverständnis und Ihre Ausdrucksfähigkeit bewertet. Ihr Ziel muss es deshalb sein, dem Korrektor ein umfassendes Bild von Ihrer Ausdrucksfähigkeit im Englischen zu geben. Greifen Sie dabei häufig auf längere

Textpassagen des Originaltexts zurück, kann die Eigenständigkeit der Leistung nicht ausreichend bewertet werden. Denken Sie also daran, Zitate nur zum Belegen Ihrer eigenen Thesen zu verwenden.

Sprachliche Richtigkeit (Fehlerschwerpunkte vermeiden)

Orthografie, Grammatik

Orthografie

Rechtschreibfehler passieren leicht als Flüchtigkeitsfehler beim Schreiben. Um dem entgegenzuwirken, sollten Sie sich eine funktionierende Zeitplanung aneignen, die Ihnen genug Spielraum lässt, nach Abschluss der produktiven Phase den Text noch einmal durchzulesen und eventuelle Rechtschreibkorrekturen vorzunehmen. Achten Sie dabei besonders auf Interferenzen mit dem Deutschen.

Grammatik

Wie bereits zu Eingang des Kapitels erwähnt, kann in diesem Rahmen keine umfassende Grammatikwiederholung stattfinden. Gehen Sie also Ihre individuellen Problempunkte selbst an.
Trotzdem können an dieser Stelle einige gängige Fehlerquellen genannt werden, auf die Sie ein besonderes Augenmerk legen sollten:

Verben

Sehen Sie sich vor der Prüfung noch einmal die Liste der unregelmäßigen Verben an und prägen Sie sich die Formen ein, die keinem gängigen Schema folgen, z. B. *lie, lay, catch.*

Denken Sie darüber hinaus auch an *phrasal verbs,* deren Bedeutung zum Teil nicht aus den Bedeutungen der Einzelwörter erschließbar ist, z. B. *turn down* (etwas ablehnen).

Adverbien

position of adverbs in the sentence: Adverbien können im englischen Satz an verschiedenen Stellen stehen, die oft nicht mit dem Deutschen übereinstimmen. Sie können folgende Positionen einnehmen: Satzanfang, vor dem Verb, das sie näher bestimmen (bei zusammengesetzten Verbformen nach dem Hilfsverb), Satzende.

Beispiele:
Unfortunately, the turnout for the country's first free election was very low.
They had counted the votes carefully.
Nevertheless, the bad news weighed heavily on them.
I often wonder what became of him.
My sister also came.
We must also consider the opposite case.

Beispiele für Prüfungsaufgaben

Die Beispielaufgaben sind vom Umfang und vom Schwierigkeitsgrad her teilweise für Leistungskurse, teilweise für Grundkurse konzipiert.
Um den verschiedenen Vorgaben für die beiden Kursarten gerecht zu werden, wurden überwiegend Texte ausgewählt, die den Vorgaben beider Kursarten entsprechen. Von Fall zu Fall werden Aufgabenstellungen ergänzt oder angepasst. Eine gute Möglichkeit, sich auf diesen Teil der Prüfung vorzubereiten, sind die TED talks: www.ted.com.

Aufgaben mit Beispiellösungen

Hörverstehen

Beispielklausur: *Immigration in Britain*

You can listen to the audio file by scanning this QR code:

Quelle: http://www.marketplace.org/2013/08/08/world/britains-immigration-crackdown-sparks-anger
(Download am 08.05.2017)

You will hear a radio programme called *Marketplace* dealing with the topic of immigration in Britain. While listening, tick the right answer (a, b, c, or d). Do not tick more than one answer. You will hear the recording twice. You have 2 minutes to look at the task. You will have 30 seconds to finalize your answers after the second listening.

1. The British government is planning to reduce illegal immigration because
a) illegal immigrants are too expensive. ☐
b) residents living in Britain legally don't get enough jobs. ☐
c) illegal immigrants are known for their drug abuse. ☐
d) British citizens have racial views. ☐

2. The billboard carried by a van in the northeast corner of London
a) made most people who saw it smile. ☐
b) diverted other drivers' attention. ☐
c) caused a lot of anger. ☐
d) was created by illegal immigrants ☐

3. Neemal Patel claims that
a) black people have raided a supermarket. ☐
b) black people were asking for a place to live. ☐
c) the official's behaviour was illegal. ☐
d) some of the black people refused to give their names. ☐

4. Immigration minister Mark Harper says that
a) the billboard campaign must be stopped. ☐
b) the officials acted legally. ☐
c) black people have to be checked. ☐
d) immigration status must be controlled. ☐

5. James Goddard from Ilford complains that
a) the reporter's English is rather poor. ☐
b) only a few people in Ilford speak English. ☐
c) nobody speaks English accurately. ☐
d) in Ilford it is dangerous to walk along the street. ☐

6. According to Goddard, life in Ilford has changed because
a) whites are now a minority. ☐
b) the press only reports about positive aspects of immigration. ☐
c) the media ignore the immigrants. ☐
d) the white people have left the immigrants behind. ☐

7. James Goddard's reaction to the billboard campaign shows that
a) he is in favour of it. ☐
b) he wants to see another campaign like that. ☐
c) he likes the idea of stirring up trouble. ☐
d) he is against campaigns like that. ☐

Lösungen

1. b	5. b
2. c	6. a
3. c	6. a
4. b	

Beispielklausur: *British Asians are Living in Fear*

You can listen to the audio file by scanning this QR code:

Quelle: https://www.bbc.co.uk/sounds/play/p01hn2xg
(Download am 07.04.2021)

You will hear a radio programme dealing with the topic of Asians in Britain. While listening, complete the table below. Write your answers in the boxes. You do not have to write complete sentences. There is one example answer (0). You will hear the recording twice. You have 90 seconds to look at the table. You will have 2 minutes to finalize your answers after the second listening.

0	The Runnymede Trust made a survey and argues that, due to race and religion, 60% of members of ethnic minorities are worried about ... (Give two examples)	a) personal safety b) discrimination in education services (and the workplace)
1	As a means to stop the harassment, one woman says she had to ... (Give two examples)	a) b)
2	Being British, she says, has always been ...	
3	The leader of a Meena women's project says the massive media coverage has led to ... (Give two examples)	
4	The fear of Asians to leave their homes and their immediate area has been creating ...	
5	The Runnymede Trust claims that there have been discussions on whether women should still be wearing ...	
6	A survey has shown that the colour of people's skin has had a negative impact on ... (Give two examples)	a) b)
7	It is feared that a change will only happen in something like ...	

Lösungen

1. a) change her (personal) appearance
   b) stop wearing certain clothes
2. a part of their lives
3. a) a sense of concern
   b) anxiety
4. enclaves
5. the niqab
6. a) their life chances
   b) their security
7. 50 years

Beispielklausur: *Mum's cooking makes jobs*

You can listen to the audio file by scanning this QR code:

Quelle: https://www.bbc.co.uk/sounds/play/p018zgpl
(Download am 07.04.2021)

You will hear a radio programme dealing with the topic of Asians in Britain. While listening, complete the table below. Write your answers in the boxes. You do not have to write complete sentences. There is one example answer (0). You will hear the recording twice. You have 90 seconds to look at the table. You will have 2 minutes to finalize your answers after the second listening.

0	The speaker's mother has always wanted to start a food business but did not do it because of ... (Give two examples)	a) lack of confidence b) lack of formal qualifications (and language barriers)
1	Things started to change when the speaker ... (Give two examples)	a) b)
2	Together with some friends, the idea of home delivery made him ...	
3	In the South Asian community, after the children have left the house, women consider themselves ...	
4	Women of these ethnic minority backgrounds are not usually found in the statistics and do not claim ...	
5	They are so scared that they lack everything, so they do not even start ...	
6	Irene motivated herself to be a part of 'Mummy's Cooking' because she thought she ... (Give two examples)	a) b)
7	How she was going to be perceived was something that she at first ...	

8	That training would be for young people only is what Irene considered ... at first.	

Lösungen

1. a) was studying at university
   b) had to eat bad food there
2. found a company with friends
3. too old
4. unemployment benefit
5. the process of getting benefit
6. a) was a good candidate
   b) could be independent
7. feared
8. a barrier

Kombinierte Aufgabe – Sachtext und Politische Rede

Part 1: Mediation

Aufgabenstellung

Sie nehmen gemeinsam mit einer Schule in England an einem internationalen Projekt zum Thema *Climate Change* teil.
Ihre Aufgabe besteht darin, auf der Grundlage des folgenden Textes einen Artikel für den Internetauftritt des Projektes zu verfassen, in dem Sie die Ergebnisse der Klimatagung in Peru darstellen.
Ihr Text soll etwa 250 Wörter umfassen.

Materialgrundlage

M1 Axel Bojanowski: „Uno-Klimatagung in Lima: Die heimliche Veränderung der Welt", S. 153 (Axel Bojanowski), DER SPIEGEL, 14.12.2014; https://www.spiegel.de/wissenschaft/natur/un-klimatagung-in-lima-ergebnisse-der-uno-konferenz-in-peru-a-1008356.html

Hilfsmittel

Den Prüflingen stehen einsprachige sowie für den schulischen Gebrauch geeignete zweisprachige Wörterbücher der Allgemeinsprache (Deutsch-Englisch/Englisch-Deutsch) zur Verfügung.

M1 Uno-Klimatagung in Lima: Die heimliche Veränderung der Welt

Axel Bojanowski

Am Ende herrscht Entsetzen: Die Uno-Klimatagung in Peru hat sich nicht auf konkrete Schritte zur Minderung der Treibhausgase einigen können. Und doch hat sie die Welt entscheidend verändert.

Lima/Hamburg – Nur noch 362 Tage bleiben. In 362 Tagen will die Gemeinschaft aller Staaten in Paris einen Vertrag schließen, der die erwartete Erwärmung des Klimas bremsen soll. Die entscheidenden Voraussetzungen dafür sollten in der peruanischen Hauptstadt Lima in den vergangenen zwei Wochen geschaffen werden. Doch nun herrscht Entsetzen.

Nach dem Ende der Uno-Klimakonferenz von Lima, die sogar noch um zwei Tage verlängert werden musste, haben manche die Hoffnung aufgegeben: „Wir rasen mit Vollgas in eine vier Grad wärmere Welt", schimpft etwa ein Vertreter der Südseeinsel Tuvalu angesichts des Gipfelbeschlusses.

„Die Lima-Konferenz war eine Verschwendung von Zeit und Energie", sagt Regine Günther vom WWF. „Mit solchen Beschlüssen werden wir den Klimawandel nicht eindämmen", sagte der BUND-Vorsitzende Hubert Weiger. Kaum ein Staat befände sich auf dem Weg in eine klimafreundliche Zukunft. „Lima setzt ein falsches Signal: Alle können die Atmosphäre ungestört weiter aufheizen", kommentiert er.

Die Bundesregierung indes bewertet den „Lima-Aufruf zur Handlung" als solide Basis für den geplanten Weltklimavertrag. „Das waren sehr zähe Verhandlungen. Wir haben nun ein Ergebnis, das alle Möglichkeiten eröffnet, zu einem ambitionierten Klimavertrag zu kommen", sagte Umweltstaatssekretär Jochen Flasbarth am Sonntag in Perus Hauptstadt. […]

Die Staaten werden aufgefordert, in den kommenden Monaten darzulegen, wie viel Treibhausgase sie ab 2020 einsparen wollen.

Sie werden ermuntert, Maßnahmen vorzustellen, die bereits ab 2015 zum Klimaschutz beitragen können.

Klimaschutzmaßnahmen sollen transparent werden, damit geprüft werden kann, ob die CO_2-Einsparungen gerecht verteilt sind.

Die entwickelten Staaten werden gedrängt zu erklären, wie ihre Finanzhilfen beim Klimaschutz für arme Länder anwachsen sollen.

Alle Staaten werden ermuntert, Beiträge zum Klimaschutz zu leisten.

Damit hat die Lima-Konferenz ihr entscheidendes Ziel verfehlt: Eigentlich sollten präzise Umrisse eines Weltklimavertrags für Paris entstehen. Deutlich werden sollte, mit welchen Maßnahmen der Treibhausgasausstoß bis 2030 seinen Höhepunkt erreichen kann.

Stattdessen ist das Lima-Dokument allenfalls eine Einladung, sich konkrete Beiträge zum Klimaschutz zu überlegen. Die schwierigen Entscheidungen wurden nach Paris verschoben. „Der Frage, wie man diese Klimaschutzangebote auf Fairness überprüfen könnte, sind die Regierungen auch in Lima wieder ausgewichen", sagt Jan Kowalzig von Oxfam. […]

Und was geschehen soll, wenn die

Klimaschutzbeiträge der Länder nicht ausreichen, um die globale Erwärmung unter der vereinbarten Grenze von zwei Grad Celsius zu halten, bleibt auch nach Lima unklar. Ist der Kampf gegen die Klimaerwärmung jetzt verloren?

„Alles im grünen Bereich", beruhigt Reimund Schwarze, Klimaökonom vom Helmholtz-Zentrum für Umweltforschung UFZ, ein langjähriger Beobachter der Klimapolitik. Die Ergebnisse von Lima seien auf den ersten Blick zwar dürftig. Aber unterschwellig habe sich Erstaunliches getan. Und tatsächlich: Bei genauerer Betrachtung hat sich in Lima in gewisser Weise die Welt verändert.

Das Lima-Dokument ermöglicht den Industrienationen Unterstützung: Es wird nicht mehr strikt unterschieden zwischen Industrie- und Entwicklungsländern – damit wird nun angedeutet, dass alle Staaten zum Klimaschutz beitragen sollten.

Die Industriestaaten ließen sich aber nicht darauf ein, einen konkreten Plan für das Aufstocken der Zahlungen für Klimaschutzmaßnahmen zu erstellen. Auch eine historische Schuld aufgrund ihrer CO_2-Emissionen seit Beginn der Industrialisierung gegenüber der weniger entwickelten Welt bleibt unerwähnt. [...]

Wirtschaftsmächte wie China oder Indien, die auf Klimakonferenzen weiterhin als Entwicklungsstaaten gelten, gehören mittlerweile zu den größten CO_2-Verursachern. Die „schematische Unterscheidung zwischen Industrie- und Entwicklungsländern" müsse aufhören, hatte Bundesumweltministerin Barbara Hendricks in Lima gefordert.

„In dieser Hinsicht hat sich in Lima tatsächlich Entscheidendes bewegt", meint Klimaökonom Schwarze. Die scharfe Trennung der Welt sei gebröckelt, nicht mehr nur Industrieländer würden sich zum Klimaschutz bekennen. „Die alten Lager sind obsolet geworden", sagt der Experte. Tatsächlich haben die wichtigsten Schwellenländer China, Brasilien, Indien und Indonesien erklärt, erhebliche Anstrengungen gegen die erwartete Klimaerwärmung unternehmen zu wollen.

Die Gruppen jener Länder, die auf einer Zweiteilung der Welt beharrten, gingen erheblich geschwächt aus Lima heraus, betont Schwarze. Die finale Fehde in Lima zwischen den USA und China sieht er als taktisches Manöver: China wolle das Vertrauen der Entwicklungsländer nicht verspielen, deren Anführer es immer war.

Quelle: http://www.spiegel.de/wissenschaft/natur/un-klimatagung-in-lima-ergebnisse-der-uno-konferenz-in-peru-a-1008356.html Zugriff: 14.12.2014

Part 2: Politische Rede

Aufgabenstellung Writing

1. Outline the main points in Kamala Harris's speech.
2. Imagine you are a member of a journalist club in your school. Write an article expressing your own views towards the possibility of change in the USA, referring to Kamala Harris's visions and to information you have gathered during your English lessons.

Materialgrundlage

M2 "Senator and Vice-Presidential Nominee Kamala Harris' 2020 Democratic National Convention (DNC) speech on August 19", 19.02.2020. General Counsel, Austin z. B. hier zu finden: https://www.rev.com/blog/transcripts/kamala-harris-2020-dnc-speech-transcript

M2 Kamala Harris: 2020 Speech at the Democratic National Convention (extract)

Aug 20, 2020

That I am here tonight is a testament to the dedication of generations before me, women and men who believed so fiercely in the promise of equality, liberty, and justice for all. [...]

My mother instilled in my sister Maya and me the values that would chart the course of our lives. She raised us to be proud, strong Black women, and she raised us to know and be proud of our Indian heritage. She taught us to put family first, the family you're born into, and the family you choose. [...]

And even as she taught us to keep our family at the center of our world, she also pushed us to see a world beyond ourselves. She taught us to be conscious and compassionate about the struggles of all people, to believe public service is a noble cause, and the fight for justice is a shared responsibility. [...]

I accept your nomination for Vice President of the United States of America.

I do so committed to the values she taught me, [...] and to a vision passed on through generations of Americans, one that Joe Biden shares. A vision of our nation as a beloved community, where all are welcome, no matter what we look like, no matter where we come from, or who we love. A country where we may not agree on every detail, but we are united by the fundamental belief that every human being is of infinite worth, deserving of compassion, dignity, and respect. A country where we look out for one another, where we rise and fall as one, where we face our challenges and celebrate our triumphs together.

Today, that country feels distant. Donald Trump's failure of leadership has cost lives and livelihoods. [...] And while this virus touches us all, we got to be honest. It is not an equal opportunity offender. Black, Latino, and Indigenous people are suffering and dying disproportionately. And this is not a coincidence.

It is the effect of structural racism, of inequities in education and technology, healthcare and housing, job security and transportation. [...]

So we're at an inflection point. The constant chaos leaves us adrift. The incompetence makes us feel afraid. The callousness makes us feel alone. It's a lot, and here's the thing. We can do better, and deserve so much more. We must elect a president who will bring something different, something better, and do the important work. A president who will bring all of us together, Black, White, Latino, Asian, Indigenous, to achieve the future we collectively want. We must elect Joe Biden. [...]

Right now, we have a president who turns our tragedies into political weapons. Joe will be a president who turns our challenges into purpose. Joe will bring us together to build an economy that doesn't leave anyone behind, where a good paying job is the floor, not the ceiling. [...]

That's the vision that our parents and grandparents fought for. The vision that made my own life possible. The vision that makes the American promise, for all its complexities and imperfections, a promise worth fighting for. So make no mistake, the road ahead is not easy. We may stumble. We may fall short, but I pledge to you that we will act boldly and deal with our challenges honestly. We will speak truths, and we will act with the same faith in you that we ask you to place in us. We believe that our country, all of us, will stand together for a better future. [...]

In this election, we have a chance to change the course of history. We're all in this fight. You, me, and Joe, together. What an awesome responsibility. What an awesome privilege. So let's fight with conviction. Let's fight with hope. Let's fight with confidence in ourselves, and a commitment to each other, to the America we know is possible, the America we love. And years from now, this moment will have passed, and our children and our grandchildren will look in our eyes. And they're going to ask us, "Where were you when the stakes were so high?" They will ask us, "What was it like?" And we will tell them. We will tell them not just how we felt. We will tell them what we did. [...]

Erwartungshorizont

Mediation and writing

Überprüfte Kompetenzen	
Mediation	Strategien
Aufg. 1)	Zusammenstellen der wichtigsten Inhalte, Verfassen eines Internetartikels mit passender Überschrift, Verwendung von thematisch passendem Vokabular
Schreiben	
Aufg. 1)	Zusammenfassen der wichtigsten Inhalte
Aufg. 2)	In einem Artikel die eigene Meinung darlegen und begründen und sie in Beziehung zu den Aussagen des Textes setzen

Beispiellösung

Part 1: Mediation

A German Response to the Lima Climate Change Conference

The Lima Climate Change Conference in December 2014 was a great disappointment to many participants, because it failed to enact any concrete measures to reduce greenhouse gas emissions. Once again, discussion of specific measures was postponed until the next conference, scheduled for Paris at the end of 2015. Yet Axel Bojanowski's article in the German weekly online magazine "Spiegel.de" emphasizes that despite the many voices saying it was a waste of time, the Lima conference in one way at least changed the world. How can that be?

Let's look first at the concrete results of the conference. Countries were encouraged to consider how much CO_2 they could save after 2020, and to propose measures for controlling emissions. These measures should be transparent, so that outsiders can check that the burden falls equally on all. And industrial countries should set out plans for increased financial aid to reform the industries of poorer countries. All in all, it sounds anything but effective.

The aim of the conference was to outline environmental measures that would be formulated in a binding treaty in Paris. Clearly, that goal has not been achieved. However, while many participants and commentators regard the conference for that reason as a farce, others say that a different, not so clearly formulated goal emerged from its discussions. Reimund Schwarze, a scientist from Germany's Helmholtz Center for Environmental Research, argues that Lima rendered obsolete the distinction between developed and developing countries with regard to climate control. Greenhouse emissions are now, more than ever, a one-world matter, for newly industrialized and developing countries as much as for the old industrial powers of the west. But whether Schwarze's voice is more than the opinion of a single optimist remains to be seen. Perhaps Paris will tell. Yet if Lima is anything to go by, one should not set one's hopes too high.

Part 2: Politische Rede

Aufgabe 1

The text is from Senator Kamala Harris' acceptance speech, given at the Democratic National Convention on 20 August, 2020 after her nomination as democratic vice presidential candidate for the forthcoming election. As the first woman of colour to run for Vice-Presidency of the USA, she emphasizes her pride in her Indian heritage and her gratitude to her mother, who brought her up to be compassionate and conscious of other people's problems.

Harris touches upon liberty, equality and justice for all: this is the "shared responsibility" she and Joe Biden accept. She pictures the USA as a "beloved community" where everybody is welcome, irrespective of ethnic heritage or sexual orientation. Everyone deserves respect; every individual is of inestimable value.

Harris calls on her fellow Democratic Party members to show unity and loyalty to Joe Biden and herself in the task of reversing Trump's white-supremacy policy, which has politically polarized and socially divided the country. She holds out the prospect of Joe Biden as a healing and unifying head of state, building an economy that provides jobs for all and in

this way re-establishes the "American promise". But at the same time she admits that this may be a path of trial and tribulation.
Harris ends her speech by emphasizing her belief in the country standing together to achieve a better future for all American citizens and by again invoking Democratic Party unity. Underlining the opportunity to change the course of history by winning the Presidency, she calls the election a "fight" which should be undertaken confidently and convincingly.

Aufgabe 2

Kamala Harris gave a very interesting and inspiring acceptance speech as Vice-Presidential candidate of the USA. In her speech, held before the Democratic National Convention on August 20, 2020, Harris mentions politically charged issues she wants to see changed during Joe Biden's and her term of office. These include the situation of minorities – for example people of colour or homosexuals. Furthermore, she pursues the idea of a "united" America as a country every American can love.
The latter is a noble and ambitious aim in a politically polarized society, where the Democratic Party nurtures ideas of equality, while conservative Republicans are often unwilling to give up on the principle of white supremacy. The Democrats will have a hard fight to enact their intended bills.
The situation is compounded by the fact that there is now, after the elections, a standoff in the Senate between Democrats and Republicans. But this tricky situation might be solved by Kamala Harris herself, as she will have a "casting vote" as Vice-President when it comes to a 50:50 situation for and against a bill.
The Democrats might, then, be able to legally change situations for certain social groups. History shows, however, that laws can be implemented but they are not necessarily observed by people who oppose them. Racism will not be removed by law alone: profound social and cultural change must occur, above all in countering the fear that drives self-aggrandizement, racism and violence.
As racist actions are often carried out covertly, it is hard to take adequate measures against them. To my mind, the vision of peaceful coexistence among disparate groups of people following diverse concepts of life, like those from the LGBTQ community, is difficult – or even impossible – to realize in today's societies.
Harris' speech is powerfully written and touches on topics of major importance for individual and social life in the USA. Her appeal for change in U.S. society is positive and her ideas are contagious. Let us hope that she will succeed in achieving her political goals.

Sachtext – Politischer Zeitungsartikel

Aufgabenstellung

1. Point out the different measures the LAPD uses to fight crime. (30%)
2. Explain the pros and cons of the concept of "predictive policing" (ll. 35–36) on the basis of the given article and compare it to the police's work in the films you have seen. (30%)
3. For many young people becoming a police officer is a dream job. *The Guardian* has invited young people like you to debate the new measures of policing in a conference held in London. As you have dealt with fictional films which show police work and the problems officers face you want to take part in it. In order to apply for participation in the conference, you have to write an essay outlining your idea of a modern police force. In your essay you should also refer to this article and to material studied in class. (40%)

Materialgrundlage

Nate Berg, "Predicting crime, LAPD-style", www.guardian.com, 25/06/2014)
https://www.theguardian.com/cities/2014/jun/25/predicting-crime-lapd-los-angeles-police-data-analysis-algorithm-minority-report (last accessed 05/05/2019)

Hilfsmittel

Den Prüflingen stehen einsprachige sowie für den schulischen Gebrauch geeignete zweisprachige Wörterbücher der Allgemeinsprache (Deutsch-Englisch/Englisch-Deutsch) zur Verfügung.

"Predicting crime, LAPD-style" *Nate Berg*

The Los Angeles Police Department, like many urban police forces today, is both heavily armed and thoroughly computerised. The Real-Time Analysis and Critical Response Division in downtown LA is its central processor. Rows of crime analysts and technologists sit before a wall covered in video screens stretching more than 10 metres wide. Multiple news broadcasts are playing simultaneously, and a real-time earthquake map is tracking the region's seismic activity. Half-a-dozen security cameras are focused on the Hollywood sign, the city's icon. In the centre of this video menagerie is an oversized satellite map showing some of the most recent arrests made across the city – a couple of burglaries, a few assaults, a shooting.

On a slightly smaller screen the division's top official, Captain John Romero, mans the keyboard and zooms in on a comparably micro-scale section of LA. It represents just 500 feet by 500 feet. Over the past six months, this sub-block section of the city has seen three vehicle burglaries and two property burglaries – an atypical concentration. And, according to a new algorithm crunching crime numbers in LA, and dozens of other cities worldwide, it's a sign that yet more crime is likely to occur right here in this tiny pocket of the city.

The algorithm at play is performing what's commonly referred to as predictive policing. Using years – and sometimes decades – worth of crime reports, the algorithm analyses the data to identify areas with high probabilities for certain types of crime, placing little red boxes on maps of the city that are streamed into patrol cars. "Burglars tend to be territorial, so once they find a neighbourhood where they get good stuff, they come back again and again," Romero says. "And that assists the algorithm in placing the boxes. [...] A really good officer would be able to go out and do the same, but this somehow makes the average guys' ability to find the crime a little bit better."

Predictive policing is just one tool in this new, tech-enhanced and data-fortified era of fighting and preventing crime. As the ability to collect, store and analyse data becomes cheaper and easier, law enforcement agencies all over the world are adopting techniques that harness the potential of technology to provide more and better information. But while these new tools have been welcomed by law enforcement agencies, they're raising concerns about privacy, surveillance and how much power should be given over to computer algorithms.

P. Jeffrey Brantingham is a professor of anthropology at UCLA who helped develop the predictive policing system that is now licensed to dozens of police departments under the brand name PredPol. "This is not Minority Report," he's quick to say, referring to the science-fiction story often associated with PredPol's technique and proprietary algorithm. "Minority Report is about predicting who will commit a crime before they commit it. This is about predicting where and when crime is most likely to occur, not who will commit it."

[...] Jennifer Lynch [senior staff attorney at the Electronic Frontier Foundation (EFF)] worries that there's too much submissive acceptance of these technologies by the public, without consideration of exactly how this data is collected and used. She says that predictive policing, with its claims of reducing crime, will be given something of a free pass.

"What starts to happen is people think the results that come out of that must be accurate because there's technology involved," Lynch says. "But what we forget is that the information that went in may have been the subject of bias, may have been based on inaccurate assumptions about people, may have been collected in certain communities more than other communities. The problem is technology legitimises somehow the problematic policing that was the origination of the data to begin with."

[...] "We're pretty careful about what people do here," Romero says. "I care about civil liberties and freedom. And I know that our constitution was not written to protect us from gang members and thieves and thugs; it was written to protect us from the government and overreach of the government."

But concerns persist. Gary T Marx, professor emeritus of sociology at the Massachusetts Institute of Technology, says technology such as predictive policing creates "categorical suspicion" of people in predicted crime areas, which can lead to unnecessary questioning or excessive stopping-and-searching. And as data-driven policing expands, Marx worries that analysis and decision-making by machine will lead to what he calls "the tyranny of the algorithm". "The Soviet Union had remarkably little street crime when they were at their worst of their totalitarian, authoritarian controls," Marx says. "But, my god, at what price?"

Lösungshinweise

Aufgabe 1

Measures used by LAPD to fight crime: CCTV (closed circuit television) surveillance; satellite map of LA showing recent arrests; zoom-in facility governed by "predictive policing" algorithms; conventional armed policing

Aufgabe 2

Predictive policing

- pros: crime tends to concentrate in hotspots which are identifiable by algorithms, which can process far more data far more quickly than the average police officer; this enables police to focus on these areas
- cons: people believe technology too easily; algorithms are only as reliable as the information fed into them; focus on a particular area can easily lead to focus on the particular people or ethnic group that live in that area; predicting crime is not the same as detecting or preventing crime, and can even be counter-productive.
  The film "Crash", for example, is concerned more with the way the particular experience, background and circumstances of the individual police officer can affect their work. But the film is set before the "digital revolution", so has nothing directly to do with the scenario of the "predictive policing" article. The police in "Crash" are out on the streets and in their patrol cars and have to survive there in their job, with their colleagues, and in their personal lives. They are more affected by problems like racism and xenophobia, criminals in the family and so on – i. e. personal problems.

Aufgabe 3

Here are some ideas for your application:

- purpose of policing is to make life safe for all citizens – a basic need of society;
- but this cannot be at the cost of equally basic liberties;
- policing can only be as fair as the laws governing society;
- fair policing presupposes fair and just laws and law courts;
- and this principle also governs the means the police use to maintain and protect people's safety;
- there's no inherent reason why high-tech digital methods should not be used to analyse and even "predict" crime patterns, but one has to be careful here: the reason for surveillance of all kinds is always suspicion, and suspicion will soon interpret an action as illegal or threatening even if it is not so;
- after all, everyone is made of good and evil and there is an inherent human tendency to accuse anyone who is however slightly different from what we ourselves consider the norm.

Cartoon – Globalization

Aufgabenstellung

Globalization – a fair chance for everyone?
With an international group of university students, you are preparing a week-end seminar on the effects of globalization. You do these preparations via email.
You are doing the opening session and you have been given the task of choosing a cartoon for it. You have found the cartoon at hand. Explain how it will best suit the purpose of introducing the issue and why it can be given to the participants as a means for stimulating their awareness.
After describing the cartoon, analyse what the students can learn from it and plan your seminar session, giving your partners some ideas of the main points you want to make.
Write this email.

TIPP zur Beschreibung von Bildmaterial

Auch bei Aufgaben, in denen das Material nur eingebettet ist, ist es sinnvoll, dieses an der entsprechenden Stelle im Text zu beschreiben. In unserem Beispiel ist es notwendig, die Beschreibung des Bildes in der Einleitung aufzugreifen, um anschließend darauf eingehen zu können. Bei der Betrachtung von Bildern ist es ebenso wie bei Texten entscheidend, die Position des Fotografen, Künstlers, Karikaturisten etc. zu berücksichtigen. Bei jedem Bild sollte man sich die Frage stellen, mit welcher Absicht es angefertigt worden ist, und sollte dies sprachlich in der Darstellung berücksichtigen.

Beispiellösung

Dear Sarah and Everyone,

I am looking forward to doing this week-end seminar with you on this absolutely controversial subject. In preparation for next week, I have found the cartoon attached to this mail. I think it will suit nicely, because it addresses one of the core issues of globalisation and the criticism about it: the growing differences in the distribution of wealth on this planet. I think I will use it after the introduction as an eye-opener displaying it via our projector so that everyone can see it on the wall.
The students will first notice the big wave that comes from the right and has "GLOBALIZATION" written on it in capital letters. I might cover this caption at first, because otherwise they will not describe what they see but enter into a discussion straight away. Two men can be seen, one riding on the wave like a seafaring captain and the other threatened by the huge wave – more like a tsunami, with the power to kill the person on the beach. Looking closer, the students will see that the man on the beach holds an empty bowl in his hands and the few clothes he is wearing suggest that he is one of the poor of this world. The man in the boat has Caucasian (Western) features, and the boat he is steering bears the words "THE RICH" as its name. The cartoon evidently has to do with the vast difference rich and poor. If I then reveal the caption "globalization", the topic of the cartoon will become clear to the students.
So, there is a lot to describe and to think about in this cartoon. But what do I intend the students to learn from it? They will be able to understand that there is an enormous difference in the effects of globalization for people in the Northern hemisphere and those in the South, whether from Sub-Saharan, Latin American, or East Asian regions. They will understand that their own everyday experience of globalization is positive, because they belong to those on top of the wave, but that the effects for those smothered by the wave of globalization are different and even life-threatening. The white boatman is happy, thinking he is safe: he gains power and wealth from globalization, he shares in global trade and global goods, and it has great advantages for him. But the poor person is exploited, has no resources, cannot afford the goods he produces, and will not survive. However – and this is a big point in the cartoon – the wave, like all waves, will break, and the bigger the wave the greater the force it releases. What will this force do with the white man's little boat? The cartoon's answer is pretty obvious.
Interpreting the cartoon is, I think, the first main point of the session. From there, we can go on to a discussion of global trade. Here we can stay a bit more personal, asking questions like: Where do you personally notice the effects of globalization? Where do the products come from? What negative effects of globalization do you know about? Have you ever been to countries that suffer negative effects from globalization?
Those are the main points I would suggest for discussion, and they should amply fill the time at our disposal. Please give me some feedback. Do you understand my layout and ideas? See you at lunchtime in the cafeteria tomorrow after Mr. Clooney's class.

Best,
Jens

Aufgaben mit Bewertungskriterien

Kombinierte Aufgabe – Mediation und Writing

Part 1: Mediation

Aufgabenart

Adressatengerechte Sprachmittlung – keine Übersetzung! Für die Aufgabe stehen 60 Minuten Zeit zur Verfügung. Es darf ein Wörterbuch verwendet werden. Nach Ablauf der Bearbeitungszeit wird der zweite Prüfungsteil ausgehändigt.

Aufgabenstellung

Ihre Partnerschule in England plant ein internationales Schülerpraktikum, sodass sich die Schüler auch in Deutschland bewerben sollen. Die betreuende Lehrerin Mrs Brown fand den unten stehenden Artikel und hat Sie gebeten, einen Beitrag, der die wichtigsten Informationen auf Englisch zusammenfasst, für die Schul-Homepage zu schreiben. Schreiben Sie diesen Beitrag.

Materialgrundlage

M1 Tagesschauarchiv: http://tsarchive.wordpress.com/2010/11/25/anonym104/; Stand: 16.04.2014, Veröffentlicht am 25. November, 2010 (209 words)

M1 Pilotstudie zu anonymen Bewerbungen startet *Tagesschau – online*

Ältere Menschen, Ausländer und Mütter mit kleinen Kindern werden auf dem deutschen Arbeitsmarkt diskriminiert. Laut einer Studie des Bonner Instituts zur Zukunft der Arbeit (IZA) und der Universität Konstanz werden zum Beispiel Bewerber mit einem türkisch klingenden Namen deutlich seltener zu Vorstel-lungs-gesprächen eingeladen – um bis zu 24 Prozent.

Diesem Ungleichgewicht hat die Antidiskriminierungsstelle des Bundes (ADS) den Kampf angesagt. Mit einem Pilotprojekt will die ADS daher ein anonymisiertes Bewerbungsverfahren testen. Dabei erhalten Personalchefs nur noch Informationen über die Qualifikation der Bewerber, aber nicht mehr über Alter, Geschlecht, Familienstand oder Herkunft. Auch ein Foto wird den Unterlagen nicht beigelegt. Ziel ist es, dass Unternehmer nur aufgrund der fachlichen Qualifikation eines Bewerbers entscheiden, ob die Person zum Vorstellungsgespräch eingeladen wird oder nicht.

An dem einjährigen Testlauf beteiligen sich fünf Unternehmen, darunter die Deutsche Post, die Deutsche Telekom, der Kosmetikkonzern L'Oréal, der Geschenkdienstleister Mydays und der Konsumgüterhersteller Procter & Gamble. Außerdem werden das Bundesfamilienministerium, die nordrhein-westfälische Bundesagentur für Arbeit und die Verwaltung der Stadt Celle das anonymisierte Bewerbungsverfahren testen.

Kritik der Arbeitgeber

Arbeitgeberpräsident Dieter Hundt kritisierte dieses Verfahren im Vorfeld. Die Pläne seien in der Praxis schwer umsetzbar und würden Stellenbesetzungen wesentlich aufwändiger machen. Der stellvertretende Hauptgeschäftsführer des Deutschen Industrie- und Handelskammertages (DIHK), Achim Dercks, nannte den Erfolg des Projekts „zweifelhaft".

Annotations:
In the US anonymous applications were introduced in the 1960s to prevent companies from discriminating against applicants because of age, gender or race. But applicants still have to give their name and residential status.

Part 2: Literarischer Text – Zadie Smith, *White Teeth*

Aufgabenart

Analyse und Interpretation eines literarischen Textes im Rahmen eines situativen Kontextes. Für diesen Prüfungsteil stehen ca. 240 Minuten (auf erhöhtem Niveau) zur Verfügung.

Aufgabenstellung

You have taken part in an international seminar on the situation of black immigrants in Great Britain. The basis of your studies is Zadie Smith's novel. In order to sum up the results of your group, you have been asked to write an article to be read by the other participants.

1. In your article you contrast the situation of immigrants in England with the situation of blacks in America.
2. You interpret the author's intention when writing this passage and her possible personal opinion on the matter of immigration.

Materialgrundlage

M2 Ausgangstext: Romanauszug „White Teeth", Zadie Smith, 2000, p. 326f. (346 words)

M2 White Teeth *Zadie Smith*

The following text is an extract from the novel "White Teeth" by Zadie Smith, which is set in contemporary London. The story focuses on three families with different cultural backgrounds whose lives become intertwined because of their children. One of the characters (Irie Jones, l. 4) has an English father and a Caribbean mother. She has fallen in love with a boy called Millat Iqbal, whose parents are from Bangladesh.

This has been the century of strangers, brown, yellow, and white. This has been the century of the great immigrant experiment. It is only this late in the day that you can walk into a playground and find Isaac Leung by the fish pond, Danny Rahman in the football cage, Quang O'Rourke bouncing a basketball, and Irie Jones humming a tune. Children with first and last names on a direct collision course. Names that secrete within them mass exodus, cramped boats and planes, cold arrivals, medical checkups. It is only this late in the day, and possibly only in Willesden, that you can find best friends Sita and Sharon, constantly mistaken for each other because Sita is white (her mother liked the name) and Sharon is Pakistani (her mother thought it best – less trouble). Yet, despite all the mixing up, despite the fact that we have finally slipped into each other's lives with reasonable comfort (like a man returning to his lover's bed after a midnight walk), despite all this, it is still hard to admit that there is no one more English than the Indian, no one more Indian than the English. There are still young white men who are angry about that; who will roll out at closing time into the poorly lit streets with a kitchen knife wrapped in a tight fist. But it makes an immigrant laugh to hear the fears of the nationalist, scared of infection, penetration, miscegenation, when this is small fry, peanuts, compared to what the immigrant fears – dissolution, disappearance. Even the unflappable Alsana Iqbal would regularly wake up in a puddle of her own sweat after a night visited by visions of Millat (genetically BB; where B stands for Bengaliness) marrying someone called Sarah (aa where 'a' stands for Aryan), resulting in a child called Michael (Ba), who in turn marries someone called Lucy (aa), leaving Alsana with a legacy of unrecognizable great-grandchildren (Aaaaaaa!), their Bengaliness thoroughly diluted, genotype hidden by phenotype. It is both the most irrational and natural feeling in the world.

Annotations:
to hum: summen; **to secrete:** to hide; **Willesden:** an area in North West London; **miscegenation:** Rassenmischung; **unflappable:** unerschütterlich; **diluted:** verdünnt; **genotype/phenotype:** genetische Veranlagung/äußere Erscheinung

Bewertungskriterien und Erwartungshorizont
Teil 1: Sprachmittlung

Dieser Teil wird in Abhängigkeit von Qualität und Klarheit der sprachlichen Vermittlung integrativ bewertet. Es erfolgt keine getrennte Wertung von Sprache und Inhalt.

Sprachmittlung
Der Prüfling stellt im Rahmen der geforderten Textsorte adressatengerecht und sprachlich angemessen die wesentlichen Punkte des Textes dar: Wichtig: Sinnvolle Überschrift! – Recent studies in Germany show that women, foreigners and old people are discriminated against when looking for a job. – One of these studies has proved that applicants with Turkish names have 24% less chance of being invited for a job interview.

- Applications to be judged solely on qualifications: companies and institutions taking part in the study will not be given any information on gender, age, name or appearance of applicants.
- This procedure will be tested for a period of one year in five international companies in Germany, as well as in some selected public institutions.
- Main representatives of the German organisation of employers and trade associations, however, have criticized the project for making the application process unnecessarily complicated and producing "doubtful" result.
- According to employers' association leader Dieter Hundt, the application process will become too complex if anonymous applications are introduced.

TIPP zum Punktesammeln

In Mediationsaufgaben wird generell erwartet, dass das Material nicht wortwörtlich übersetzt, sondern sinngemäß einbezogen wird. Dies erfordert einen souveränen Umgang mit der englischen Sprache, sodass deutsche Ausdrücke und Redewendungen nicht wörtlich übernommen, sondern in richtiges Englisch umgesetzt werden. Auch die kulturellen Unterschiede können bei diesem Aufgabentyp von Bedeutung sein, sodass beachtet werden muss, ob typisch deutsche Gepflogenheiten ggf. geklärt werden sollten, oder ob es, wie in diesem Fall, darauf ankommt, auf im englischen Sprachraum bekannte Themen zurückzugreifen.

Teil 2: Schreibaufgabe

Aufgabe 1

Diese Aufgabe gehört zum Anforderungsbereich II.

TIPP zum Punktesammeln

Es wird hier erwartet, dass Sie einen Artikel verfassen, der den vorliegenden Text mit vorhandenem landeskundlichem Hintergrundwissen verknüpft. Beachten Sie die geforderte Textsorte! Wichtig ist auch hier eine geeignete Überschrift! Denken Sie auch daran, dass ein adressatenorientierter Text verfasst werden muss.

Aufgabe 1

In einem adressatengerechten Artikel werden Parallelen zwischen der Situation von Immigranten in Großbritannien und der der Afroamerikaner in den USA erarbeitet. Folgende Aspekte könnten erörtert werden:

- While immigrants have decided to move to a different country in order to live there, blacks in America did not choose to live in the US – they were forced to live and work there as slaves.

– Blacks in the US were treated as second-class people for centuries; immigrants also often meet with prejudice and discrimination, which is comparable to the treatment blacks had to endure.
– Both immigrants and blacks face everyday discrimination in education, jobs, housing, etc. This makes it difficult for them to accept the host society as their own; both groups tend towards ghettoization and cultural isolation.
– While immigrants have the chance to blend into their new surroundings, so long as they don't look too foreign (see names in the excerpt), blacks cannot shed their skin – they are always visible, and therefore perceived as different; this also applies to many immigrant groups, whose members are visibly different.
– Despite being American citizens, blacks in the US have long been outsiders in American society; with a growing number of prominent black representatives (e.g. President Barack Obama), this role is changing.

Aufgabe 2

Diese Aufgabe gehört zum Anforderungsbereich III – *Interpretation.*

Aufgabe 2
Der Prüfling interpretiert im Rahmen der geforderten Textsorte den Textauszug im Hinblick auf die mögliche Aussageabsicht der Autorin Zadie Smith. – Smith wants to reveal how immigrants feel about living in Britain; she wants to **arouse empathy** for first generation immigrants who are afraid that their children will lose their cultural identity.
– She points out that immigration has already led to a mix of cultures and states that "we have finally slipped into each other's lives with reasonable comfort" (ll. 21-22). With this comment, one gets a positive, consoling impression of immigration. It becomes evident that **integration is possible.**
– But Smith is also conscious of the **dangers of assimilation.** She describes the loss of cultural identity, and parents' fear that integration into British society might mean their children **giving up their cultural heritage.**
– But Smith comments on this by saying "It is both the most irrational and natural feeling in the world." (ll. 49–51). Here it becomes clear that, while she understands this feeling, **she is not afraid that cultural roots will be lost completely.**
– In this respect, Smith seeks to convey the positive aspects of immigration by showing the possibility of living together. She takes on a **critical and insightful** perspective, which enables the reader to understand that (first generation) immigrants are just as afraid of a cultural and genetic mix as are British nationalists.

Aufgaben zur Sprachmittlung mit Beispiellösungen oder Bewertungskriterien

Sachtext – *Gun debate*

Aufgabenstellung

Sie sind für ein Austauschjahr an einer Amerikanischen High School im Bundesstaat Massachusetts. Im Rahmen eines „Social Studies"-Projekts rund um das Thema Gewalt hat Ihr Austauschpartner ein Referat über Amokläufe an deutschen Schulen und die entstandenen Konsequenzen gehalten. Sie haben den folgenden Artikel in der *Zeit Online* entdeckt und möchten nun unter Zuhilfenahme dieses Artikels in einem Referat darstellen, warum sich immer mehr Lehrer an amerikanischen Schulen bewaffnen.

Materialgrundlage

Martin Klingst: „Wir zielten liegend", *Zeit online*
Diesen Artikel finden Sie als Audiodatei im Premiumbereich unter www.zeit.de/audio, Die Zeit Nr. 01/2014, 5. Januar 2014

Wir zielten liegend *Martin Klingst*

Vor einem Jahr richtete ein Amokläufer in einer Grundschule in Newtown, Connecticut, ein Blutbad an. Am Morgen des 14. Dezember 2013 zog der offenbar psychisch gestörte Adam Lanza mit einem halb automatischen Sturmgewehr durch Flure und Klassenzimmer und tötete zwanzig Kinder und sechs Schulangestellte, ehe er sich selbst tötete. Der Bericht der Staatsanwaltschaft ist ein erschreckendes Dokument des Waffenwahns.

Das Massaker erschütterte Amerika. Präsident Obama hielt eine aufwühlende Rede, die Nation vereinte sich im Schmerz. Wie Obama plädierten zwei Drittel der Amerikaner für ein Verbot von Sturmgewehren, acht von zehn waren für eine schärfere Kontrolle von Waffenverkäufen. Demokratische und republikanische Senatoren arbeiteten an einer gemeinsamen Initiative. Doch die mächtige Waffenlobby NRA mobilisierte gegen jede Einschränkung des Waffenbesitzes und setzte mit ihren gut vier Millionen Mitgliedern die Politik in Washington unter enormen Druck. Ein nationales Waffengesetz scheiterte schon im ersten Anlauf.

Die Schuldirektorin Nancy Anderson hat ihre geladene Smith & Wesson immer dabei. Mal steckt sie in ihrer rosafarbenen Handtasche, mal im schwarzen Anorak, auf dem groß „Security" steht. Und in einem halben Dutzend über das gesamte Schulgelände verteilten Safes werden weitere Schusswaffen aufbewahrt. Nur Anderson und eine Handvoll speziell ausgebildeter Kollegen besitzen dafür einen Schlüssel. Von der Öffentlichkeit kaum bemerkt, haben sich Hunderte von Schulen in Amerika bewaffnet. Jedes zweite Elternpaar glaubt inzwischen, seine Kinder seien dadurch sicherer.

Im Sommer versuchte der Justizminister des Bundesstaates Arkansas der Schulleiterin Anderson und zwölf weiteren Direktoren die Bewaffnung zu untersagen. Was sie täten, sei „ungesetzlich", sagte er. Der Schul- und Polizeiausschuss des Parlaments gab zunächst dem Justizminister recht. Doch dann trat Nancy Anderson in den Zeugenstand und sagte voller Empörung: „Für Polizisten fehlt meiner Schule das Geld, ist das Leben armer Kinder darum weniger wert?" Der Ausschuss revidierte sein Urteil.

Doch für viele Menschen im Süden Amerikas wie in den Weiten des Mittleren Westens erscheint die Debatte über ein strengeres Waffengesetz wie von einem anderen Stern. Viele lernen schießen, bevor sie schreiben können. Nancy Anderson ging bereits als kleines Kind mit dem Großvater auf die Jagd. Die Eltern betrieben auf dem Land eine Tankstelle samt Lebensmittelladen. Neben der Kasse habe stets eine geladene Flinte gelegen. „Waffen", sagt die Schulleiterin, „gehören zu unserem Haushalt wie Messer und Gabel." Eine Waffe zu besitzen ist in diesem Amerika Teil der Geschichte, der Identität und der Weltanschauung.

Für sie gibt es darum nur eine richtige Antwort auf das Massaker: „Gegen einen schlechten Menschen mit einem Gewehr hilft nur ein guter Mensch mit einem Gewehr."

Anderson, unterstützt von ihren Schülern, Eltern und Lehrern, machte darum sofort mit, als die Waffenlobby NRA als Konsequenz aus dem Amoklauf von Newtown bewaffnete Sicherheitskräfte forderte. Am besten schützten sich Schulen durch Polizisten oder einen privaten Wachdienst, steht in einem 225-Seiten-Report der NRA, „notfalls" aber auch durch im Schießen besonders geschulten Lehrern. „Die Entscheidung darüber sollte jede Schule für sich treffen."

Nancy Anderson versteht nicht, warum die Lehrergewerkschaft entsetzt „Bücher statt Gewehre!" ruft. Natürlich hat sie von den Einwänden etlicher Sicherheitsexperten gehört und weiß, dass Lehrer im Umgang mit Waffen längst nicht so geübt sind wie Polizisten. Doch Anderson hält dagegen. „Ich bin kein schießwütiges Cowgirl", sagt sie. „Ich bin aber auch hier, um all diese Schüler zu schützen."

Das Argument, je weniger Waffen, desto weniger Morde, zieht bei ihr nicht. In Andersons Welt, die sie mit der Hälfte der Amerikaner teilt, wird völlig anders gedacht. Hier sagt man: Je mehr Gewehre in den richtigen Händen, desto größer die Sicherheit! Ein Jahr nach dem Amoklauf von Newtown muss man darum nüchtern feststellen: Obama hat den politischen Kampf einstweilen verloren, die anfangs breite Unterstützung für ein nationales Waffengesetz ist längst geschwunden. Zwar schufen eine Handvoll Bundesstaaten striktere Vorschriften und verbieten inzwischen Mitarbeitern von Unternehmen wie Starbucks in ihren Filialen das Tragen von Schusswaffen. Aber die Gegenwehr der Waffenlobby ist erfolgreicher.

Vierzig Stunden mussten Anderson und die anderen Gesetze büffeln und schießen üben. „Wir warfen uns auf den Boden und zielten liegend aus der Hüfte", erzählt die Direktorin. Im Februar werden Anderson und ihre Kollegen an einer besonderen Übung teilnehmen, um ihre Stressresistenz zu testen. In einer Schule werden darum Szenen wie in Newtown nachgestellt.

Quelle: http://www.zeit.de/2014/01/usa-schule-bewaffnete-lehrer

Beispiellösung

Dear Class,

Last week Benjamin told us about violence at schools in the context of our social studies project, and presented the way my country, Germany, deals with school massacres and the measures that have been taken. I would like to look at the fact that quite a few American schools have armed themselves, and give you some information about their reasons. I found an interesting article on this topic in a well-known German political magazine, "Zeit online".

So let's start with some important background information. After the terrible school massacre at Newtown Connecticut in 2013, in which a mentally disturbed young man killed 20 students and six teachers, the nation was shocked. Taking sides with President Obama, two-thirds of American citizens wanted a ban on assault rifles, and eight out of ten favored stricter controls on rifle sales.

But the National Rifle Association (NRA), a powerful lobby with more than four million members, immediately stepped in. As you know, the discussion about gun control is not new in America, and the NRA used all its traditional arguments, reminding the public of their right under the 2nd Amendment to own a gun, and pressurizing the government to back down. They demanded more armed security guards in schools and went so far as to suggest that teachers should also be armed, even offering to give them firearms training courses. But what does an "armed school" mean? Nancy Anderson, the head teacher in Arkansas on whom the article focuses, pointed out that financial restrictions prevent many schools from hiring armed security guards, and argued that this was discrimination against the poor. She is seen as a hero for her cause, and joined an NRA-sponsored 40-hour training program in order to learn how to handle dangerous situations with the help of guns – which in her school are kept in safes at different places in the building. Her beliefs are shared by many Americans, especially in the South and Mid-West, where guns belong to the cultural tradition. Many grow up with guns as part of their everyday life. To put it in a nutshell: Ms. Anderson believes that she can protect her students adequately now that her school is armed. She strongly believes that guns help protect people from evil; hence it is logical that safety increases according to the number of guns in the right hands. Protecting the weak against the bad calls for strong measures, and arming teachers can certainly be labeled a strong measure. Already every second parental couple believes that this can increase the safety of their children.

Now that you have heard why many schools in America choose to defend themselves with guns against possible violence, it is up to you to decide how you feel about the question. By the way, the teachers' union is asking for "books instead of guns" and I have to say, that even if I don't believe that schoolbooks hold all the answers, in this I totally agree with them.

Sachtext – Migration

Aufgabenstellung

With an international group of university students, you are preparing a week-end seminar on current population developments in big cities.
You take part in the opening session of this international project, and you have been given the task of talking about different aspects of migration to major German cities. Using the notion of "good/bad migrants" from Sadigh's article, write an email to your professor and your fellow students, giving them an idea of the main points of your presentation.

Materialgrundlage

Parvin Sadigh: „Die guten, bösen Einwanderer", in: ZEIT ONLINE, 20.06.2013. http://www.zeit.de/wirtschaft/2013-06/einwanderung-migration-mythen-fakten/seite-5 (abgerufen am 29.04.2019)

„Die guten, bösen Einwanderer" *Parvin Sadigh*

[...] Mythos 5: Es gibt genug Parallelgesellschaften in deutschen Städten. Kommen mehr Einwanderer, ist der gesellschaftliche Zusammenhalt gefährdet.

Jeder kennt die Straßenzüge in Berlin-Neukölln, Hamburg-Wilhelmsburg oder Duisburg-Marxloh: Straßen, in denen alle Läden türkisch sind und Frauen mit Kopftuch herumlaufen. Diese Bilder werden oft mit der Vorstellung verknüpft, hinter den Wohnungs- und Moscheetüren habe sich eine autonome fremde Gesellschaft gebildet, die ihren eigenen Regeln folgt.

Der Historiker Jochen Oltmer findet jedoch schon das Wort falsch. Parallelgesellschaft sei ein Kampfbegriff, sagt er. Meist seien damit nur türkische-muslimische Communitys gemeint. Die Elite, die in Dahlem oder Blankenese unter sich bleibt und deren Mitglieder sich gegenseitig Vorteile verschaffen, wird nicht so bezeichnet. Freiwillig ist die Konzentration der ungebildeten, armen Einwanderer in bestimmten Stadtteilen ohnehin nur bedingt. Sie brauchen bezahlbare Wohnungen. Und natürlich leben nicht nur Türken und Muslime in Neukölln. Eigene Schiedsgerichte oder Schulen gibt es sehr selten. Die meisten türkischstämmigen Einwanderer nutzen die deutschen Institutionen und arbeiten in deutschen Firmen.

Tatsächlich aber nutzen Einwanderer soziale oder ethnische Netzwerke, denn es nützt ihnen. Der Politikwissenschaftler Thomas Meyer spricht von einer „hilfreichen Schleusenfunktion". Bereits hier lebende Verwandte oder Freunde erklären, zu welcher Behörde die neu Eingewanderten gehen müssen, wie man eine Wohnung findet. Sie sprechen die gleiche Sprache und sorgen für ein wenig Geborgenheit in der Fremde. Oltmer sagt, diese Netzwerke seien charakteristisch für Migration, sogar verantwortlich für ihr Ausmaß. Man denke an Kolonien in New York wie Little Italy, Little Germany oder China Town.

Nur wenn das Netz sehr groß ist, die Einwanderer einheitlich aus einer ungebildeten armen Schicht kommen und sie sich von der Mehrheitsgesellschaft diskriminiert fühlen, kann das für sie zur Falle werden, sagt Meyer. Die neuen Migranten lernen nicht Deutsch, können ihren Kindern in der Schule nicht helfen, sie konsumieren nur türkischsprachige Medien. Eine Spirale entsteht, die die Einwanderer am Aufstieg und an der Integration in die Mehrheitsgesellschaft hindert. Wer arbeitslos ist, verkehrt nur noch mit Arbeitslosen, der Hilfsarbeiter mit Hilfsarbeitern.

Besteht also die Gefahr, dass sich neue Kolonien bilden? Neue Einwanderer in Deutschland kommen zu 60 Prozent aus europäischen Ländern. Polen, Rumänen und Bulgaren nutzen natürlich ihre Netzwerke. Spanische Studenten ziehen in eine WG mit befreundeten Spaniern. Doch diese Netze werden sich nicht zu sogenannten Parallelgesellschaften verfestigen. Die meisten der aktuellen Einwanderer sind gebildet – und „je höher der Bildungsgrad, desto größer ist die Tendenz, dass sich Kolonien wieder auflösen", sagt Oltmer. Auch die Gefahr, dass sich sogenannte Parallelgesellschaften von ungebildeten Bulgaren und Rumänen bilden, sei nicht sehr groß. Viele der Einwanderer bleiben nicht lange in Deutschland, sagt Oltmer, und sie sind zu wenige, um eigene Kolonien zu bilden.

Bewertungskriterien

Formale Aspekte

E-Mail-Form, um Information bezüglich eines Themenkomplexes (Einwanderung) an den Professor und an Studienkollegen weiterzugeben:

- Sprachregister: gepflegtes Englisch (aber nicht zu formell, aufgrund des Adressaten)
- Einleitung (um Anlass, Kontext und Adressat zu nennen) sowie Quelle (Erklärung, was ZEIT ONLINE ist)
- Hauptteil bestehend aus für die Fragestellung wesentlichen Aspekten aus dem Text

Inhaltliche Aspekte

- Einleitung – Adressat: Professor und Studienkollegen
- Kontext: E-Mail zur Vorbereitung einer Präsentation zum Thema Einwanderung
- Verweis auf Quelle und Gesamtkontext des Textauszuges
- Hauptteil
- Assoziationen in Bezug auf Alltagsbilder mit vermeintlichen Parallelgesellschaften aus Neukölln, Hamburg etc.
- tatsächlicher Ist-Zustand: es wird nur der ärmere, bildungsferner Teil der Migranten mit diesem Begriff bezeichnet, nicht die gebildete Elite, äußere Faktoren wie Mietpreise spielen eine Rolle
- Bedeutung der Netzwerke, Vergleich zu den USA
- Gefahr nur bei zu großem, einheitlichem Netz und Gefühl der Diskriminierung: kaum Spracherwerb, soziale Kontakte bleiben im bekannten Umfeld, kein Aufstieg
- Gefahr neuer Kolonienbildung ist gering, da Anteil der gebildeten Migranten höher ist
- Schluss mit Bezug zum Kontext

Original-Prüfungsaufgaben 2020 und 2021

Quelle der Aufgabenstellung: Niedersächsisches Kultusministerium*

Hinweise:

Die zentrale schriftliche Abiturprüfung im Fach Englisch besteht aus einer kombinierten Aufgabe:

Prüfungsteil 1: a) Hörverstehen
b) Sprachmittlung
Prüfungsteil 2: Textaufgabe

Hilfsmittel:

Den Prüflingen stehen für die Prüfungsteile 1b und 2 einsprachige sowie für den schulischen Gebrauch geeignete zweisprachige Wörterbücher der Allgemeinsprache (Deutsch-Englisch/Englisch-Deutsch) zur Verfügung.

Ablauf und Bewertung der Prüfung:

Ausgabe der **Aufgaben für den Prüfungsteil 1a**	
Prüfungsteil 1a:	**Hörverstehen**
Gewichtung:	20%
Einlesezeit:	keine
Bearbeitungszeit:	30 Minuten
	Abgabe sämtlicher Unterlagen des **Prüfungsteils 1a**
Ausgabe der **Aufgaben für den Prüfungsteil 1b** und der zugelassenen **Hilfsmittel**	
Prüfungsteil 1b:	**Sprachmittlung**
Gewichtung:	25%
Einlesezeit:	keine
Bearbeitungszeit:	60 Minuten
	Abgabe sämtlicher Unterlagen des **Prüfungsteils 1b**
Ausgabe der **Aufgaben für den Prüfungsteil 2**	
Prüfungsteil 2:	**Textaufgabe**
Gewichtung:	55%
Auswahlzeit:	20 Minuten
Bearbeitungszeit:	130 Minuten
anschließend:	Abgabe sämtlicher Unterlagen des **Prüfungsteils 2**

* Die Lösungen sind keine amtlichen Lösungen.

Hinweise zum Prüfungsteil 1

- Jedes einzelne Blatt ist mit dem Namen zu versehen. Der Prüfungsteil 1a ist ohne Hilfsmittel zu bearbeiten.

Hinweise zum Prüfungsteil 2

- Von den zwei Aufgaben ist eine auszuwählen und zu bearbeiten.
- Bei jeder Teilaufgabe ist die inhaltliche Gewichtung angegeben.

GA Listening Comprehension

Aufgabenstellung **24 BE**

You will hear each recording twice. After each listening you will have time to complete your answers.[1]

Task 1: Criminals **6 BE**

You will hear six news items from a radio morning show.
While listening, match the news items 1 to 6 with the headings A to G. There one more heading than you need.

Headings	
A	A fugitive proves hard to catch
B	A clever plan leads to success
C	A clumsy fake leads to punishment
D	A suspicious person turns out to be innocent
E	A criminal chooses the wrong location for a crime
F	A criminal's appearance makes him easily detectable
G	A criminal's silly behaviour plays into the hands of the police

News Item	1	2	3	4	5	6
Heading						

Source:
npr: National Public Radio. "Strange News". You can listen to the recordings by following these links:
Audio 1: https://www.npr.org/2019/05/23/726035354/police-in-new-york-pull-over-driver-with-hand-drawn-inspection-sticker;
Audio 2: https://www.npr.org/2019/05/13/722739385/police-in-tennessee-solve-clown-mystery;
Audio 3: https://www.npr.org/2019/08/26/754266266/canadian-police-hope-photocopy-will-help-them-nab-suspect;
Audio 4: https://www.npr.org/2020/03/12/814824102/police-in-florida-need-help-capturing-missing-cow
Audio 5: https://www.npr.org/2020/02/21/808016607/2-off-duty-police-officers-foil-robbery-during-their-date-night;
Audio 6: https://www.npr.org/2018/08/29/642871627/police-arrest-alleged-car-thief-covered-in-white-paint.
All audio files accesses 07.04.2021.

1 Sie finden die Links alle auf www.finaleonline.de. Bitte geben sie den Code EN8R6S8 ein.

Task 2: Women on Strike

13 BE

You will hear a report about a strike in Britain in 1976.
While listening, complete the table. You need not write complete sentences. Unless otherwise specified, one aspect is enough.

1	What impact the strike had on British society, according to the presenter	
2	Why mainly migrant women were employed in the factory	
3	One reason why the women went on strike	
4	One example Lakshmi Patel gives for the treatment of the workers	
5	How the women felt about their supervisors	
6	What Mrs Desai and five of her co-workers did	
7	What is said about Jayaben Desai's character	
8	Why Jayaben Desai felt her demands to be justified	
9	What the workers asked for (Name *two* examples)	• ______ • ______
10	How the company reacted	
11	How trade unions supported the strikers, according to Jack Dromey	
12	What is said about the development of the women's strike	

Source:
BBC Radio. "BBC Witness: Strikers in Saris". You can listen to the complete report by following this link: https://www.bbc.co.uk/sounds/play/w3csyx5m, accessed 07.04.2021 (00:00-04:39).

Task 3: Internships

7 BE

You will hear an excerpt from the BBC radio show Business Daily, in which journalist Manuela Saragosa interviews two young Australians, Marnie and John, about their experience with internships.
While listening, tick ✔ the correct answer (a, b, c, or d). There is only one correct answer.

1. In the introduction to the radio show, the presenter describes internships as

a	advisable and helpful.	☐
b	popular but not necessary.	☐
c	rewarding in theory and practice.	☐
d	recommended but not always fulfilling.	☐

2. One of Marnie's internships

a	ended in a secure job offer.	☐
b	paid just enough to survive.	☐
c	was intellectually stimulating.	☐
d	led to her being self-employed.	☐

3. John's mistake had been to

a	study the wrong subject.	☐
b	pick an internship spontaneously.	☐
c	be overambitious in his career plans.	☐
d	overestimate the benefits of connections.	☐

4. John's internship company

a	relied on the work of interns.	☐
b	fell short of economic success.	☐
c	offered him professional guidance.	☐
d	tolerated social media use at work.	☐

5. John quit the internship

a	since he felt exploited.	☐
b	when he found a well-paid job.	☐
c	although he liked the travelling.	☐
d	because he had learned enough.	☐

Source:
BBC World Service – Business Daily (12.9.2016): Intern or drudge? You can listen to the complete programme by following this link.
http://www.bbc.co.uk/programmes/p046v32v (00:57-05:06; accessed 07.04.2021)
This task is from the exam 2019.

Lösungen

Task 1: Criminals

1	2	3	4	5	6
C	D	G	A	E	F

Task 2: Women on Strike

No.	BE	*Lösungsvorschlag:*
1	1	improved race relations
2	1	(thought to be) hard-working/passive
3	1	(because of) unfair treatment / wanted to join union / poor working conditions / wanted to get recognized by union
4	1	constant observation by manager (from glass room) / asked why they took so long on toilet / forced to do overtime
5	1	scared/afraid / helpless
6	1	went on strike / walked out / picketed at the gate / persuaded others (to leave the factory/to attend a meeting)
7	1	determined / strong / not scared (of anybody)
8	1	other women in Britain had more rights (so why didn't they)
9	1	*two of the following*: • better wages • better working conditions • better treatment
10	1	refused to recognize union membership
11	1	advised them / helped with organization / organized worker delegations (to 2000 factories in Britain)
12	1	strike grew daily / (up to) 20,000 people protested

Task 3: Internships

1 d
2 d
3 b
4 a
5 a

GA Sprachmittlung

Julia Kopatzki, „Wie es ihr gefällt“ (2019)

Aufgabenstellung:

You are taking part in an international seminar on "How to Live More Eco-Friendly." Based on the text below, write an article for the project website in which you give an example from Germany on sustainable shopping, presenting Luisa Brummer's idea, how it is put into practice, and the customers' reactions.

Materialgrundlage:

Julia Kopatzki, „Wie es ihr gefällt" (2019), in: *DB Mobil*, 11/2019, pp. 50-54

Hilfsmittel:

Den Prüflingen stehen einsprachige sowie für den schulischen Gebrauch geeignete zweisprachige Wörterbücher der Allgemeinsprache (Deutsch-Englisch/Englisch-Deutsch) zur Verfügung.

Bearbeitungszeit: 60 Minuten

„Wie es ihr gefällt“ *Julia Kopatzki*

Der Tag beginnt früh in Sandharlanden. Rentner, die es nicht mehr im Bett hält, Pendler, die nach Regensburg oder Ingolstadt zur Arbeit fahren, Kinder, die den Schulbus um kurz nach sieben erwischen müssen, alle sind längst wach. Bevor ihr Tag so richtig beginnt, wollen sie noch schnell zu Luisa Brummer, zur Boderei. Dem einzigen Supermarkt im Dorf. Die Boderei liegt in einem rosafarbenen Haus an der Hauptstraße. [...] Um halb sieben zieht Luisa die Jalousien nach oben. „Griaß euch“, ruft sie den Wartenden zu, als sie die Tür öffnet. Ihre Füße stecken in Sandalen, ein paar ihrer blonden Dreadlocks hat sie am Hinterkopf zusammengebunden. Sobald sie grinst, und sie grinst an diesem Morgen jeden an, der hereinkommt, sieht man die kleine Lücke zwischen ihren oberen beiden Schneidezähnen. Der 23-Jährigen gehört die Boderei, die bis vor einem Jahr noch „der Boder“ war, doch das ist die kleinste aller Veränderungen. Im Juni 1948 eröffnete Luisa Brummers Urgroßvater den Gemischtwarenladen. Lebensmittel, Hygieneartikel, und dazu schnitt er seinen Kunden noch die Haare oder zog, wenn es nötig war, Zähne. „Boder“ ist bayerisch für Friseur. Mit 13 Jahren begann seine Tochter Rita im Laden auszuhelfen, Luisas Oma, mit 33 übernahm sie das Geschäft. Damals gab es drei Tante-Emma-Läden im Dorf. Der erste schloss, und der zweite. Auch Rita Forstner hatte überlegt zu schließen, die Konkurrenz der großen Supermärkte wurde immer größer, aber das Dorf ganz ohne Laden? Nein, der Boder blieb. Ein freier Laden, ohne große Zulieferer, darauf ist man bis heute stolz. [...]

Als Luisa von einer einjährigen Weltreise zurückkehrte, wünschte sie sich eine Welt mit weniger Plastik. „In Neuseeland habe ich pro drei Teile eine Plastiktüte bekommen", erzählt sie. In Südamerika habe sie die Müllberge gesehen, die nie aufhören zu brennen. Luisa spricht mit ihrer Mutter, mit ihrer Oma, erzählt von ihrer Idee: Statt in Plastikverpackungen sollen Salz, Nudeln oder Müsli unverpackt verkauft werden, zum Selbstabfüllen in Dosen, Gläser oder Stoffbeutel. Unverpackt-Läden gibt es heute in jeder größeren Stadt. Zero Waste heißt der Trend, über den zahlreiche Bücher geschrieben wurden: plastikfrei einkaufen, Deo selbst machen – und wo steckt überall Mikroplastik drin? Nachhaltig zu leben fällt in der Großstadt verhältnismäßig leicht: Städter können sich den Biosupermarkt aussuchen, bekommen Nudeln, Reis und Deo problemlos unverpackt. Sie können mit Bahn oder Rad zur Arbeit fahren, und auf fast jeder Speisekarte gibt es etwas Veganes. Auf dem Land ist das nicht ganz so einfach: Dörfler haben Glück, wenn sie einen Supermarkt in der Nähe haben, noch besser, wenn er auch ein Regal mit Biolebensmitteln hat. [...]

Wenn Luisa Brummer durch ihren Laden wirbelt, dort schnell etwas auffüllt, hier etwas zurechtrückt und trotzdem kurz Zeit hat, um sich zum Schreiner zu setzen, während der seinen Kaffee am Fenster trinkt, hat sie etwas von Pippi Langstrumpf, so wild und so unbekümmert. Sie fragt eine Kundin, wie es bei der Tochter im Kindergarten läuft, schneidet Wurst für den älteren Herren, der selbstverständlich seine Dose auspackt. Die Wurst ist übrigens nicht bio. „Zu teuer für die Leute", sagt sie. „Aus einem Euro dürfen nicht plötzlich drei werden." Die unverpackten Lebensmittel sind dafür meist günstiger: 100 Gramm eingepackte Spaghetti kosten 56 Cent, die unverpackten nur 30, Gewürze kosten lose nur einen Bruchteil. Luisa will das verpackungsfreie Leben niemandem aufzwingen, sie will es möglich machen: Nahezu alles, was sie verpackt verkauft, gibt es auch unverpackt. „Ich sag dann: Schau, das haben wir auch lose", wenn es dann noch gleich viel oder weniger kostet, tauschen die meisten Kunden die Lebensmittel schnell aus. Nach einem Jahr hat die Boderei ihren Kundenstamm verdoppelt: Die Dorfbewohner kommen, aber noch viele mehr. Evi und Susanne, zwei Damen mit grauen Haaren, sind heute zum zweiten Mal bei Luisa. Sie veranstalten in Abensberg regelmäßig ein Reparaturcafé und wollen mit Luisa kooperieren. „Früher war es komisch, wenn man ökologisch gelebt hat", sagen sie. „Heute ist es komisch, wenn man es nicht tut." (638 Wörter)

Beispiellösung

Zero Waste shops reach rural Germany

Dealing with unwanted packaging is one of the biggest environmental problems of our planet. One answer is to use the Zero Waste shops that have recently sprung up almost everywhere in big cities to promote and practise sustainable shopping. But what about rural areas? A 23-year-old German shows us how tradition and modern, eco-friendly ideas can be fused.

I learned about Luisa Brummer and her shop "Boderei" in rural Bavaria from the article by Julia Kopatzki in the monthly magazine of the German national railway company in November 2019, and I am quite surprised how well it seems to work.
The Brummer family had owned a village grocery shop for over 70 years, but modern supermarkets had made their life difficult, and they were about to close. However, they decided to stay on, because 'a village without a shop' was unimaginable for the family. Running an independent shop, without big suppliers, had been their life and made them proud.
After coming back from her world tour, Luisa Brummer wanted a world with less plastic garbage. She started to talk to her mother and grandmother of bringing the idea of unwrapped, unpackaged products into the "Broderei" and following the trend of Zero Waste. In big cities shoppers could already rely on supermarkets with unpacked organic or vegan products, but Luisa wanted to bring this idea to rural Bavaria.
So she started to give her local clients a choice between packaged and unpacked products, which were usually cheaper. She won shoppers over to her idea, telling them to look at the price: pasta, for example, at almost half price, spices for even less. However, not all the products in Luisa's shop are organic: German sausage is not organically produced, as that would be too expensive for the local people.
Her idea seems to work and success lurks around the corner, as even elderly locals regularly come and shop, using their own containers, or enjoy a coffee and chat with Luisa in the front of her shop.

GA Aufgabe I mit Beispiellösung

Text: NoViolet Bulawayo, *We Need New Names* (excerpt, 2013)

Aufgabenstellung:

1. Outline the situation. (30 %)

2. Examine Darling's character. (30 %)

3. You are taking part in an international youth seminar on "Intercultural Challenges: Finding Yourself."
   Your task is to contribute an article in which you comment on the impact of diverging cultural experiences on one's identity.
   Write the article, referring to Darling and other fictional characters from materials studied in class, such as the film *East Is East* and the short story "Two Kinds." (40 %)

Materialgrundlage:

NoViolet Bulawayo, *We Need New Names*, 2013; London: Vintage, 2014, pp. 274–283

Hilfsmittel:

Den Prüflingen stehen einsprachige sowie für den schulischen Gebrauch geeignete zweisprachige Wörterbücher der Allgemeinsprache (Deutsch-Englisch/Englisch-Deutsch) zur Verfügung.

Bearbeitungszeit: 130 Minuten

***We Need New Names* (2013, excerpt)** *NoViolet Bulawayo*

The novel's protagonist Darling grew up in Zimbabwe, Africa, but is sent to the U.S. as a teenager to live with her aunt.

The night I mess up the wallpaper in my room, I am supposed to be studying wounds for my bio test. I don't really care a thing about the material I'm reading, or even about bio itself [...]. I shut the book, slide it under the bed, and hear it connect with the wall. I know already that this sciences thing that Aunt Fostalina is pushing me to focus on is just not for me. Now that I'm almost finished with high school , her thing is to go on and on about how I have to get into medicine or some kind of nursing or whatnot when I start college next year, or if that fails, at least do law. These, she says, are the careers that count, and I didn't come all the way to America to do meaningless stuff and be nothing. What I know, though, is that none of it sounds inspiring to me; I mean, I haven't figured out exactly what I want to get into, but I have zero passion for what Aunt Fostalina wants me to do.

I am sitting on my bed and staring at the wall, just thinking about how I will begin to tell Aunt Fostalina this, when my new BlackBerry starts to vibrate. I find it under the covers, flip it open, and read Marina's text.

wt u doin?

nuthin. trynna study stupid bio, I text.

lol, y is it stupid? i kinda lykit, she texts.

thts coz u wanna be a doc. nt feelin it, I text.

wl u know my dad wants me to. n-e-ways, wt u gonn do? she texts.

dunno, I text. Marina doesn't respond for a while, and I'm not surprised. Ever since she moved to her fancy high school, we don't communicate like we used to. When she finally responds, I have taken a red marker and written *iBio iyirabishi*[1] on the wall above my clothes hamper, and I'm drawing a circle around it. [...]

On the wall, my letters are large, like how I used to write in grade one. The red looks like blood, and I realize, for the first time, that it will be hard to clean off.

I put on slippers and leave my room. The kitchen is bright from the streetlamps so I don't bother to turn on the lights. I get a sponge, squeeze a drop of dish soap on it, add a little water. On my way back I hit the side of my pelvic bone against the edge of the kitchen table. I double over in the half dark and quietly cuss. After the pain passes, I proceed to my room.

When I'm done cleaning the wall, it looks worse than before. The red has bled all over, leaving an ugly stain, and the letters have refused to fade. [...]

The first thing I notice when I wake up in the morning is the mess on my wall. At first I don't know what happened, but then my thoughts quickly come together and I remember how I went crazy with the marker the night before. The clock on my bedside stand reads 7:15, which means I have less than half an hour to fix the wall before Aunt Fostalina gets back from work. I fly out of bed and rush for the basement.

I head for the corner with the large storage boxes and quickly find one labeled HOMELAND DECORATIONS, ETC. I toss the lid aside and just start rummaging. Before long, I find this batik[2] the size of a beach towel. It's a painting of a market scene and it's crazy with life and color, people selling things — fruits, vegetables, foodstuffs, colorful beads and cloth, handbags, belts, animal carvings, just anything you can think of. There's children, women, men, women with babies on their backs, old people, a couple of dogs, a bicycle, everybody and everything alive under a bright blue sky.

Looking at the cloth I'm remembering how beautiful it felt to be in a real scene like that, everybody just there together, mingling together, living together, before things fell apart. I begin to feel this ache in my heart that always comes when I think of home these days, so I put the batik aside and do some more digging. [...] And last, I find this weird mask; it's split in the center, one half white, the other black. The black half is split further in numerous crazy patterns that I can't figure out, but it looks interesting to me so I take it and the other stuff upstairs to my room.

When I have finished covering the wall, the mask is looking at me with the puzzling face; it's like it's trying to tell me something that will take years for me to understand. (799 words)

Annotations
1 **iBio iyirabishi** – Biology is rubbish
2 **batik** – a piece of cloth that has been colored in a special way

Beispiellösung

Aufgabe 1

Darling, a young girl from Zimbabwe, who has almost finished high school, is home alone in her room. She is supposed to be working for a biology test, but she cannot concentrate on it, as she realizes that she is not interested in biology at all.
Darling knows very well that her Aunt Fostalina, with whom she is staying in the United States, would like to see her take up a career in the health sector or in law. Her aunt is always reminding her that she should make something out of her life. That is why she has been sent to the U.S. Darling wonders how she can talk to her aunt about this situation.
Her thoughts are interrupted by a short texting chat, during which she starts doodling on the wall. Realizing that her scribbling will be disapproved of by her aunt, Darling gets some cleaning materials from the kitchen but her attempt to clean the wall fails.
Next morning, Darling realizes what a mess she has produced and searches the basement of the house for effective cleaning agents. Instead, she discovers a storage box labelled HOMELAND DECORATIONS, ETC. Trawling through this box she finds a colourful batik painting of a market scene which reminds her of her cultural roots back in Africa, awaken-

ing a familiar feeling of togetherness. Digging on, Darling finds a black and white mask with various patterns. She takes the mask and batik to her room and covers the blotched and besmeared wall with them. The mask seems to be looking at her, trying to tell her something that she will only understand much later.

Aufgabe 2

Darling seems a typical teenager, searching for her way in life. She does not see the need to learn about subjects she is not really interested in, in this case biology. Science bores her (ll. 3-10).

She dismisses her aunt's plans and ideas about possible future careers – science, medicine, law – (ll. 8-18), but she intends to talk to her aunt about it (l. 24-25). She seems not so much rebellious as unsure about how to reconcile her own feelings with the attitude of her aunt and even of the friend with whom she is chatting. Darling has not made up her mind yet about what she really wants to do (l. 20-22). She knows more clearly what she does not want to do (l. 1-19 and l. 21-22).

Her impulsiveness fits this behaviour. Frustrated, she starts scribbling on the wall with a red marker (ll. 40-43) without thinking about the consequences. She only realizes later that she has damaged the wall (l. 44-45 and l. 61-62). Following a momentary impulse like this shows the typical immaturity of a teenager. She does not seem to regret her action; she just wants to avoid the inevitable confrontation and trouble when her aunt sees the messed-up wall. So she tries to remove the blotch (l. 57-58).

When she finds the African batik and mask in the basement, Darling is reminded of her former life in Zimbabwe (ll. 87-93). The black and white mask captures her imagination (ll. 95-99), and she feels emotional. She unconsciously realizes that she is part of two different cultures, and that is why she has taken the mask and batik (ll. 99-101) to decorate the spoilt wall. She becomes sensitive to what the mask seems to be telling her.

Her style is fluent and supported by stylistic means such as smilies, e.g. "The red looks like blood [...] (l. 45-46) and personifications "The red has bled all over [...] (l. 58-59). These elements of imagery express her impulsive but at the same time vivid nature.

Aufgabe 3

As my contribution to our international youth seminar on "Intercultural Challenges: Finding Yourself", I would like to say something about the impact of diverging cultural experiences on one's identity. To bring this rather theoretical topic to life, I would like to focus on some fictional characters taken from stories and films, whose experiences as young people in multicultural environments are at times quite stressful.

First of all, Darling from the story "We Need New Names" by NoViolet Bulawayo (2013); then Jing-mei Woo (June) from the short story "Two Kinds" by Amy Tan, 1989; finally some young male characters from the film "East is East", 1999.

Darling, a teenage girl from Zimbabwe, had been sent to the U.S. by her family to get a good education as a way to a promising future. She lives at her aunt's and has almost finished high school. When she accidentally finds a storage box in the basement of her aunt's house marked "Homeland Decorations", she feels unconsciously attracted to her African culture. Browsing through the box, she notices a batik displaying a lively African market scene. Immediately, positive feelings are evoked, but she puts the batik aside and makes another discovery: a "weird mask", half black with odd patterns, and half plain white. These two objects touch a level of her soul that appears to have been suppressed until this incident. Darling seems fascinated by the Zimbabwean painting and mask; she feels that she belongs to this colourful culture, too. But, living in a completely different socio-cultural environment and being isolated from her traditional roots, she begins to feel displaced, cut off from her childhood experiences and identity. By decorating her room with these objects, she tries to bridge the gap between the two diverging cultures of which she is part: the U.S. American culture that will one day make a successful career possible, and the African culture of her roots and perhaps of her as yet uncertain future. Unconsciously she feels torn by conflicting cultural values, and her inner tension expresses itself in a "soft" juvenile rebellion against the western achievement-oriented educational system: she refuses to do her biology homework, as she sees no point in it.

Our next character is another young girl, Jing-Mei Woo, whose mother is determined to make her a child prodigy at the piano. Her mother has clear ideas about how children should behave towards their parents. She distinguishes between daughters who show obedience and those who want to go their own way. In her mother's eyes Jing-Mei definitely belongs to the latter group. The cultural clash is clear, with Jing-Mei not following her mother's views. Obedience was considered normal in China when her mother grew up there. But the difference is also expressed in the language they use. Whereas Jing-Mei's mother is reduced to a kind of fractured English, with incomplete and often ungrammatical sentences, Jing-Mei, who has grown up in the U.S., speaks English fluently. Their conversations can be seen as verbal duels in which Jing-Mei invariably comes out the winner.

However, Jing-Mei's mother believes that everybody can be anything they want to in America. She chases her own American Dream through her daughter, who, unfortunately, is not willing to change just to fulfil her mother's aspirations. Jing-Mei hates all the coaching, drilling and cajoling she is exposed to by her mother, and begins to resent her when her failure at a piano recital makes it clear that she cannot always live up to her mother's expectations. She cannot understand that she is not accepted for who she actually is.

The conflict represents the typical dissent of second-generation Asian-American immigrants. The rebellious teenager Jing-Mei represents a typical second-generation Asian-American, who feels angry and resentful towards her pushy mother, who is in turn the epitome of the immigrant parent: she wants to bring out the best in her children to allow them to have what she sees as a better future.

The film "East is East" deals with a multicultural family with sharply diverging views on Pakistani and British lifestyles. This movie is a bitter-sweet comedy-drama set in a north of England town where George, the Pakistani father, owns and runs a fish-and-chip shop with his British-born Catholic wife, Ella. Presented in typical everyday-life situations, the conflicts here run both across and within the generations.

George is determined to stick to Pakistani traditions, one of which is to arrange marriages for one's children. His eldest son, Nazir, follows his father's wish until the last minute, when he stands in front of the altar. It turns out that he is in a homosexual relationship, and the last thing he wants is marriage with a woman.

George himself is an interesting, multi-faceted character. He left Pakistan in 1947, when war affected the whole region, and came to the UK to have the prospect of a better life. There he married Ella, in spite of already being married in Pakistan, and changed his first name from Zaheed to George. All these actions show him trying to become part of the British community in order to be accepted. But this is only on the outside. Internally, he does not seem to have changed much, as he still clings to old Pakistani traditions and forces his children against their will to conform. It is quite disconcerting that he does not spare a thought for his children's feelings. They were born in the UK and have been brought up there right from the beginning. His children, especially his older sons, have already undergone a kind of cultural integration, identifying themselves as being more British than Pakistani. They have already abandoned Pakistani traditions, including food and Islam, and adopted western views and habits. They have taken the freedom to live their own lives; Nazir to the extent of being openly homosexual, which is taboo for Muslims.

The generation conflict in "East is East" differs from those of the first two stories inasmuch as the family situation is different. Here the family itself is mixed Pakistani-British and the second generation are already young adults, most of whom have chosen the lifestyles and values of their British environment. The father, George, comes across as an internally torn character who clings desperately to his habitual patterns of life, often with highly comical results.

Looking at these characters, one comes to the conclusion that finding one's identity in diverging cultures is a strenuous process with different conflicts in different life situations. In the best case, people manage to adapt to their new environment. But, for the most part, they face cultural differences they have to cope with in the long run. Otherwise, they will not be able to integrate in their new communities.

GA Aufgabe II mit Beispiellösung

Karen Weintraub, "Cloning's Long Legacy – And Why It'll Never Be Used on Humans" (2019)

Aufgabenstellung:

1. Outline the reasons why human cloning will never be put into practice according to the article. (30 %)

2. Analyze the stylistic means the author uses and their effect on the reader. (30 %)

3. You are applying for the university preparation course "Fiction Meets Science" in Oxford, organized by the British Society for Literature and Science. As part of your application you have to hand in an article based on Karen Weintraub's statement: "The idea of clones is unsettling because it violates the fundamental moral understanding that we are all different and equally valuable." (ll. 7-9)
   Write an article in which you discuss whether Kazuo Ishiguro makes a similar statement with his novel *Never Let Me Go*. (40 %)

Materialgrundlage:

Karen Weintraub, “Cloning’s Long Legacy – And Why It’ll Never Be Used on Humans”, in: https://www.discovermagazine.com/health/clonings-long-legacy-and-why-itll-never-be-used-on-humans (Zugriff am 07.04.2021)

Hilfsmittel:

Den Prüflingen stehen einsprachige sowie für den schulischen Gebrauch geeignete zweisprachige Wörterbücher der Allgemeinsprache (Deutsch-Englisch/Englisch-Deutsch) zur Verfügung.

Bearbeitungszeit: 160 Minuten

Der Text wird hier aus rechtlichen Gründen nicht abgedruckt. Er kann aber auf der genannten Website gelesen werden.

“Cloning’s Long Legacy – And Why It’ll Never Be Used on Humans”
Karen Weintraub

Annotations
1 **long-tailed macaque** – a type of monkey
2 **flick** – *informal*: a movie
3 **versatility** – G: Vielseitigkeit/Flexibilität
4 **induced pluripotent stem cells (iPSCs)** – laboratory-grown stem cells that can develop into any type of cell in the body
5 **Kevin Eggan** – a stem cell biologist at Harvard University

Beispiellösung

Aufgabe 1

Cloning cells was a great technological achievement; the cloning of humans, however, according to Karen Weintraub’s article, will never be put into practice. Weintraub claims that – for scientists as much as for society – the idea of reproducing humans is considered unethical. It belongs to science fiction fantasy, not to scientific vision. Moreover, few laboratories actually work on cloning; science focuses more on other aspects like therapeutic cloning, i. e. growing cell structures to use them against certain diseases. This type of cloning is not reproductive. For all these reasons, the reaction to the cloning of the first primates in early 2018 was at least partly negative.

Weintraub quotes scientists who argue that for re-creating the self it is much easier and more natural to have a baby than to reproduce a person through cloning. The clone would anyway only be a duplication of the genetic code. Born as a baby, it would develop under the influence of its surroundings. The environmental impact on human beings is large and a clone would not – in either age or behaviour – be the person we wanted him or her to be. Cloned embryos are also very vulnerable and have only a small chance of survival.

Cloning is seen as a niche technology, but one that has led to a new understanding of our cellular structures.

Aufgabe 2

(Note: The text is not printed here, so no line references are given to support the argument. In the exam you are expected to refer to specific lines in the given text.)

Weintraub both stirs her readers' emotions and tells them that her insights into the subject of cloning are scientifically grounded. She arouses her readers' immediate interest and gets them emotionally hooked by starting off with baby monkeys, which creates a caring image, especially when she describes them as "clinging to each other" and as being "adorable". She then gives some general facts: "They were the first ...", no one had ever succeeded in cloning creatures so close to human beings before. These sentences inspire awe and also a slight shudder, because the cloning of humans seems to be imminent.

Mentioning "Dolly", the well-known successfully cloned sheep, Weintraub next leads her readers on a path between real-life examples and the fantasy world of science fiction, where aggressive "armies of look-alikes" have only one purpose in life – "bred solely to sustain their identical ancestors". Her readers know these figures from acclaimed novels and films – "Brave New World" or "Never Let Me Go". The paragraph ends with an emphasis on our being "all different and equally valuable", as if the author wanted to reassure herself and her readers that science fiction remains science fiction.

After these two paragraphs the style changes: Weintraub provides background information on the two different purposes of cloning and refers to a number of scientists, whom she quotes at length. This adds credibility to the information she is conveying and to her own ideas about cloning. She balances her examples and explanations between general statements and quotes. Her language becomes more scientific: "the genetic instruction manual", "the day of conception" or the idea of wanting the "deceased spouse" to be "replicated". The author has left her chatting tone behind – these words suggest a serious subject. Hence she can announce that all hopes of having the beloved one back in the form of a clone are in vain. Weintraub finally allows herself to say "[they] don't make it" – using the everyday spoken English of her readers that euphemistically means something or someone dies.

After giving her readers an insight into the other – therapeutic – objective of cloning and citing yet again a scientist on the positive use of the therapies, Weintraub ends her article in the same style that she used in the beginning, appealing to the imagination of her readers. She asks two rhetorical questions referring to readers' archetypal fears: "being overrun by copies of ourselves" and "we're only alive to serve the needs of someone with our genetic makeup." She answers these questions by quoting an expert, the stem cell biologist Kevin Eggan, who uses commonly understood metaphors like scratching "those off our list or fears forever" and the metaphor of the mirror: "That dystopian vision is in the rearview mirror". So, for the readers, these fears are hopefully wiped out.

Karen Weintraub succeeds in giving background information and concise but well-directed arguments on a deeply worrying subject, reassuring her readers that – yes, cloning is a difficult subject when it comes to ethical decisions, but – no, we do not have to fear that our nightmare visions will become real.

Aufgabe 3

Possessing a replica of oneself has always been both a secret human desire (mirrors are popular for that reason) and a terrifying fear. The idea of cloning human beings and maybe having armies of genetically identical creatures has haunted the human imagination ever since the publication of "Brave New World" in the 1930s, or even earlier, with Mary Shelley's "Frankenstein" in the early 1800s: the notion of breeding identical humans or of breathing life into a reassembled human body. Today, cell cloning has in real life become a common therapeutic instrument. Kazuo Ishiguro's novel "Never Let Me Go" has reopened the discussion on the level of fiction.

Although the character Kathy tells the story from her point of view and as a flashback, Ishiguro's protagonists remain ignorant of their sole purpose in life. Kathy makes it quite clear that she and her classmates at Hailsham School had no idea that they were cloned and created only to be organ donors for their genetically identical twins. They had never been officially given this information.

"Never Let Me Go" is an unsettling story because of the state of ignorance in which the protagonists live, because of their fate, and because of the lack of positioning as to whether the donation of organs or cell structures in general is right or wrong. As Ishiguro chooses a limited perspective, we only learn that clones are not intended to have any concept of ethical decision making – and this is the most worrying message of the novel. Only the art teacher tries indirectly to open her pupils' minds and educate them about 'art and beauty' and the moral principles these concepts imply. Later, Kathy and Tommy visit Madame and learn about the Hailsham project, whose idea is to give clones a moral orientation in life. In Madame's eyes this has failed.

Kathy and her friends Ruth and Tommy do not know that "we are all different and equally valuable" – they are not brought up on individualism and are not taught that way. They will only find out about feelings and differences when love and emotions start to play a role between them, when Ruth and Kathy become rivals in their attention to Tommy, and when Ruth wins Tommy for herself; finally when Kathy – already a successful carer – takes over Ruth's position and stays with Tommy in the last weeks of his life, sharing her ideas on life's purpose and the Hailsham project with him before she resigns.

I recently read an article by Karen Weintraub, who states that "the idea of clones is unsettling because it violates the fundamental moral understanding that we are all different and equally valuable." I think she is right – it violates the idea of human uniqueness. Having an identical copy of ourselves makes us feel uncomfortable. The idea is terrifying; it has haunted our nightmares for centuries.

Kazuo Ishiguro was honoured with the Nobel Prize for Literature – yet he does not take part in the discussion about cloning in this novel. The novel never explicitly questions the idea of cloning that it portrays. The characters stay among themselves – to them, real human beings are distant, unknown, almost threatening creatures. Kathy, Tommy and Ruth seem to live in a parallel universe – there is no encounter with their identical twins for whom they serve as organ donors. So, Ishiguro's acclaimed work is more or less another story about coming of age, friendship and love and about life and death in general.

Reading this novel is unsettling but also disappointing because its characters never understand their situation and the narrative does not provide an ethical positioning. One looks in vain for a critical approach like that of Karen Weintraub. She, the journalist, is right when she says that we are individuals and each one of us is valuable and should have the right to a life in dignity. Kazuo Ishiguro does not make a comparable statement. But then, fiction is not science, nor is it real life.

Original-Prüfungsaufgaben 2018 eA

Hinweise:

Die zentrale schriftliche Abiturprüfung im Fach Englisch besteht aus einer kombinierten Aufgabe:

Prüfungsteil 1: a) Hörverstehen
b) Sprachmittlung
Prüfungsteil 2: Textaufgabe

Hilfsmittel:

Den Prüflingen stehen für die Prüfungsteile 1b und 2 einsprachige sowie für den schulischen Gebrauch geeignete zweisprachige Wörterbücher der Allgemeinsprache (Deutsch-Englisch/Englisch-Deutsch) zur Verfügung.

Ablauf und Bewertung der Prüfung:

Ausgabe der **Aufgaben für den Prüfungsteil 1a**	
Prüfungsteil 1a:	**Hörverstehen**
Gewichtung:	20%
Einlesezeit:	keine
Bearbeitungszeit:	30 Minuten
	Abgabe sämtlicher Unterlagen des **Prüfungsteils 1a**
Ausgabe der **Aufgaben für den Prüfungsteil 1b** und der zugelassenen **Hilfsmittel**	
Prüfungsteil 1b:	**Sprachmittlung**
Gewichtung:	25%
Einlesezeit:	keine
Bearbeitungszeit:	60 Minuten
	Abgabe sämtlicher Unterlagen des **Prüfungsteils 1b**
Ausgabe der **Aufgaben für den Prüfungsteil 2**	
Prüfungsteil 2:	**Textaufgabe**
Gewichtung:	55%
Auswahlzeit:	20 Minuten
Bearbeitungszeit:	210 Minuten
anschließend:	Abgabe sämtlicher Unterlagen des **Prüfungsteils 2**

Hinweise zum Prüfungsteil 1

- Jedes einzelne Blatt ist mit dem Namen zu versehen. Der Prüfungsteil 1a ist ohne Hilfsmittel zu bearbeiten.

Hinweise zum Prüfungsteil 2
- Von den zwei Aufgaben ist eine auszuwählen und zu bearbeiten.
- Bei jeder Teilaufgabe ist die inhaltliche Gewichtung angegeben.

EA Listening Comprehension

Aufgabenstellung 23 BE

You will hear each recording twice. After each listening you will have time to complete your answers[1].

Task 1: Book Reviews 5 BE

You will hear the beginnings of five book reviews.
While listening, match the speakers 1 to 5 with the headings A to G. There are two more headings than you need.

Headings	
A	Author likes to puzzle readers
B	Author decides to change project
C	Author specializes in biographies
D	Author wants to teach readers about culture
E	Author turns life of a male ancestor into fiction
F	Author creates fiction from own misunderstanding
G	Author draws on the devastating effects of political conflicts

Review	1	2	3	4	5
Heading					

Sources:
BBC Radio 4 – Bookclub. You can listen to the recordings by following these links. You only need to listen to the beginning of each recording.
a) https://www.bbc.co.uk/programmes/m00092x0 (00:00-00:45),
b) https://www.bbc.co.uk/programmes/m00081wx (00:00-00:33),
c) https://www.bbc.co.uk/programmes/b09tcb4t (00:00-00:22),
d) https://www.bbc.co.uk/programmes/b04ws1xm (00:00-00:29),
e) https://www.bbc.co.uk/programmes/p00fc3vt (00:32-00:57).
All audio files accessed 07.04.2021.

Task 2: Britain's first female black headteacher 5 BE

You will hear a radio report about Yvonne Conolly, who became Britain's first female black headteacher in 1969. While listening, tick ✔ the correct answer (a, b, c, or d). There is only one correct answer.

1 Sie finden die Links alle auf www.finaleonline.de. Bitte geben sie den Code EN8R6S8 ein.

1. Yvonne Conolly felt that the attention of the media was

a	flattering.	☐
b	shocking.	☐
c	welcome.	☐
d	annoying.	☐

2. She felt that some of the journalists' questions were

a	clearly intimidating her pupils.	☐
b	indirectly discriminating against her.	☐
c	unfairly criticizing her teaching methods.	☐
d	strongly questioning her academic qualifications.	☐

3. Some people reacted to her appointment by

a	boycotting the school.	☐
b	insulting her in public.	☐
c	writing hate mail to her.	☐
d	complaining to the authorities.	☐

4. Mrs Conolly particularly likes teaching young children, because she

a	can support them in their development.	☐
b	can still teach them how to behave properly.	☐
c	enjoys the good cooperation with their parents.	☐
d	feels emotionally close to the children in her care.	☐

5. Leaving Jamaica for England seemed a natural move for her because she had

a	previously been to Great Britain.	☐
b	repeatedly worked in other countries.	☐
c	always been fascinated by new cultures.	☐
d	already been familiar with the English culture.	☐

Source: BBC World Service – Witness History "Britain's first female black headteacher". You can listen to the complete report by following this link: https://www.bbc.co.uk/sounds/play/w3cswsgv; accessed 07.04.2021 (00:19-03:04).

Task 3: Matt Scullin **13 BE**

You will hear a report about the inventor Matt Scullin.
While listening, answer the questions. You need not write complete sentences. Unless otherwise specified, one aspect is enough.

1	What is said about Matt Scullin as a student (Name **two** aspects)	• ______ • ______
2	What Scullin became interested in when he was at Berkeley University	
3	What happens to energy according to the law of thermodynamics	
4	What a thermoelectric is	
5	How thermoelectrics are already used	
6	How Scullin wanted to put his ideas into practice	
7	Why it was important for Scullin that a friend stayed at his place	
8	What is special about a 'power card'	
9	Where Scullin would like to have thermoelectrics (Give **two** examples)	• ______ • ______
10	What Scullin describes as his personal priority in his job	
11	What Scullin is prepared to do for making his idea successful	

Source:
npr: National Public Radio. "A Lot of Heat Is Wasted, So Why Not Convert It Into Power?" You can listen to the complete report by following this link: https://www.npr.org/sections/alltechconsidered/2015/08/20/432738291/a-lot-of-heat-is-wasted-so-why-not-convert-it-into-power; accessed 07.04.2021 (00:12-05:13).

Lösungen

Task 1: Books Reviews

Review	1	2	3	4	5
Heading	F	G	E	B	A

Task 2: Britain's first female black headteacher

1 d
2 b
3 c
4 a
5 d

Task 3: Matt Scullin

No.	BE	*Lösungsvorschlag:*
1	 1 1	*two of the following:* • drawn to topics other people overlooked • attracted to group with two professors, but no students (on orientation day) • liked developing new materials
2	1	alternative energy / waste heat
3	1	when energy is used, some energy always goes to waste
4	1	a material that turns heat into electricity
5	1	to power (NASA) spacecraft
6	1	by starting a company
7	1	learned about setting up a company/start-ups
8	1	like a (solar) cell / thermoelectrics embedded in it / the number of cards used can be adjusted to the amount of waste heat
9	 1 1	*two of the following:* • human body • buildings • all kinds of locations (where energy is going to waste)
10	1	building/making something
11	1	work on it for a long time / continue with it as long as it takes / seeing it as a long-term project

EA Sprachmittlung

Aufgabenstellung:

You are taking part in an international project on "Sustainability."
Having come across the following interview about a give-away shop you have decided to focus on consumer awareness. In an article for the project website, you present how the shop works, the motivation of the people who run it, and the public's reaction.

Materialgrundlage:

Marie-Charlotte Maas, „Umsonstladen: ‚Viele denken, dass ein Umsonstladen nur was für die Unterschicht ist'";© Aike Ulrich und Florian Martin für ZEIT ONLINE (www.zeit.de) vom: 03.12.2019: https://www.zeit.de/arbeit/2019-11/umsonstladen-duesseldorf-klamotten-second-hand/komplettansicht (Zugriff am 24.01.2020)

Hilfsmittel:

Den Prüflingen stehen einsprachige sowie für den schulischen Gebrauch geeignete zweisprachige Wörterbücher der Allgemeinsprache (Deutsch-Englisch/Englisch-Deutsch) zur Verfügung.

Bearbeitungszeit: 60 Minuten

Text 1:

„Viele denken, dass ein Umsonstladen nur was für die Unterschicht ist" (2019)

Marie-Charlotte Maas

In sogenannten Umsonstläden kann jeder, der möchte, Dinge abholen, die andere Bürgerinnen und Bürger zuvor gespendet haben. Kostenlos. [...]

In Düsseldorf betreibt der Verein Niemandsland so einen Umsonstladen. Die Kosten für Miete und Strom werden über Spenden finanziert, zehn Mitarbeiter arbeiten dort ehrenamtlich. Zwei von ihnen, Aike Ulrich und Florian Martin, erzählen, warum ihr Lager immer voll ist – und warum ihnen das manchmal Bauchschmerzen bereitet.

ZEIT ONLINE: Heute ist Black Friday, der Tag, an dem in den USA traditionell die Weihnachtsshoppingsaison anfängt. Wie viele reduzierte Teile habt ihr schon in euren virtuellen Warenkorb gelegt?

Florian Martin: Keines! Für mich ist der Black Friday kein Tag zur Freude, er zeigt vielmehr, wie blind wir als Konsumgesellschaft vermeintlichen Schnäppchen hinterherjagen, ohne darüber nachzudenken, was wir damit auslösen. Wie wir unseren Planeten und unsere Ressourcen schädigen, indem wir immer mehr und mehr kaufen, ist nicht akzeptabel. Wir machen das trotz der aktuell sehr umfangreichen Aufklärung, dass wir mit unserem Verhalten unsere Existenz auf diesem Planeten bedrohen. [...]

ZEIT ONLINE: In eurem Laden kann jeder kostenlos Dinge mitnehmen – darunter Kleidung, Bücher und Haushaltsgegenstände. Wie viele der Sachen, die heute eingekauft werden, landen in ein paar Jahren bei euch?

Martin: Ziemlich viele, befürchte ich. Vor allem wenn es um Kleidung geht, bekommen wir generell mehr Stücke als abgeholt werden. Das Lager platzt aus allen Nähten. Unser Laden ist ein Spiegel der Überflussgesellschaft.

Aike Ulrich: Wir bekommen zu einem großen Teil sehr gut erhaltene, hochwertige Sachen – teure Taschen oder Lederjacken, die sicherlich Hunderte von Euro gekostet haben. An manchen hängen sogar noch die Preisschilder. Manchmal bekomme ich von dem Anblick regelrecht

Bauchschmerzen. Ich finde vor allem die Vorstellung schlimm, dass die Leute ein paar Monate später wieder loslaufen und die nächsten Sachen kaufen, die dann nahezu ungetragen im Kleiderschrank verschwinden, bis sie irgendwann wieder bei uns landen.

ZEIT ONLINE: Wer sind eure Kunden?

Ulrich: Bei uns darf jeder „einkaufen", einen Gehaltsnachweis oder Ähnliches lassen wir uns nicht zeigen. Es geht uns explizit nicht darum, bedürftigen Menschen zu helfen – dafür sind andere Stellen verantwortlich, etwa kirchliche Kleiderkammern. Wir stellen das Thema Nachhaltigkeit in den Mittelpunkt und wollen darum alle Schichten ansprechen.

Martin: Allerdings handelt es sich neben einer kleinen Gruppe von Konsumverweigerern und Secondhandfans größtenteils um eher ärmere Leute aus dem Viertel, in dem sich unser Laden befindet. Wir würden uns wünschen, dass unsere Kundschaft durchmischter wäre.

ZEIT ONLINE: Warum ist das nicht so?

Martin: Die Hemmschwelle ist für viele groß. Viele Menschen denken, dass ein Umsonstladen nur etwas für die sogenannte Unterschicht ist. Sie schämen sich, die Kleidung zu tragen, die andere nicht mehr brauchen – und übersehen dabei, dass sie so einen wichtigen Beitrag zum Schutz unserer Lebenswelt leisten würden.

Ulrich: Ja, der Einkauf in einem Umsonstladen wirkt auf manche regelrecht anrüchig. Andere wissen meiner Meinung nach gar nicht, welche Alternativen es zu den bekannten Läden gibt, die sie in Einkaufszentren oder Fußgängerzonen finden. Da müsste es viel mehr Aufklärung geben.

ZEIT ONLINE: Wie kann man in Zukunft dafür sorgen, dass Menschen in einen Laden wie euren gehen, wenn sie etwas Neues benötigen?

Martin: Indem man sie früh für das Thema sensibilisiert und zeigt, dass es normal ist, Dinge miteinander zu teilen und untereinander weiterzugeben. Ich denke beispielsweise an Umsonst-Ecken in Kitas, in Schulen und an Universitäten. Wenn Kinder von klein auf mit dieser Idee aufwachsen, dass man das nimmt, was schon da ist, statt neue Dinge herstellen zu lassen, können wir ein Umdenken erreichen – und dafür sorgen, dass der Black Friday in den nachfolgenden Generationen an Popularität verliert. [...]

ZEIT ONLINE: Bedient ihr euch eigentlich auch selbst manchmal im Umsonstladen?

Ulrich: Ja, regelmäßig. Ich nehme manchmal Kleidung für meine kleine Tochter mit und für mich selbst Bücher. Alle Kolleginnen und Kollegen, die im Laden aushelfen, tun das, egal, ob sie eine gut bezahlte Stelle haben, noch studieren oder gerade arbeitssuchend sind – schließlich wollen wir das Konzept der Nachhaltigkeit auch wirklich leben.

(643 Wörter)

Beispiellösung

As one aspect of sustainability, I would like to introduce you to the trendsetting concept of give-away shops, and I will concentrate on consumer awareness. My article is based on the interview "Viele denken, dass ein Umsonstladen nur was für die Unterschicht ist" ("Zeit Online", 2019).

So-called "give-away shops" offer donated goods which can be taken free of charge by anyone who wants them. One of these shops, situated in Düsseldorf, is called "Niemandsland" ("No Man's Land"). Its running charges are covered by donations and it is run by a ten-member team of volunteers, including Florian Martin and Aike Ulrich.
Many things bought today, they say, especially clothing, will land in their shop in a few years' time. Their shop mirrors our affluent society; its stock is literally bursting at the seams. They frequently receive upmarket articles like bags and leather jackets, and these are often in top condition, some of them still with price tags on them. Together with the realization that people will continue to buy superfluous goods, this makes them feel uneasy. It shows that many people in our consumer society snatch blindly at every offer without thinking of the consequences for the planet and its resources, even though environmental campaigns clearly show the impact of such behaviour.
The shop's main goal is to focus on sustainability. Martin and Ulrich want to encourage people from all social classes – not just the needy – to drop in. Church clothing stores and other organizations cater especially for the deprived segments of society. Many potential customers might feel embarrassed to wear second-hand clothing and would consider give-away shops inappropriate for their own requirements. For this reason, Ulrich and Martin want the concept of give-away shops to be better known and suggest ways to raise people's awareness about sharing and handing things on from an early age. Starting points could be kindergartens, schools and universities. Pursuing such a concept could achieve a change in thinking and reduce overproduction of goods. Black Friday and similar buying spree promotions might then lose their popularity. Perhaps you could try out this concept as well.

EA Aufgabe I mit Beispiellösung

Ian McEwan, *Machines Like Me* (2019, excerpt)

Aufgabenstellung:

1. Describe the situation as presented in the excerpt. (30 %)

2. Examine the narrator's attitude towards Adam. (30 %)

3. You are taking part in a course on "Visions of the Future in Literature." Your task is to write an essay in which you comment on the following quote by the science-fiction writer Adam Sternbergh: "Dystopias [are] excellent social barometers – the future we fear says a lot about the present-moment anxieties that plague us." Write this essay, referring to the text at hand and materials studied in class, such as *Never Let Me Go*. (40 %)

Materialgrundlage:

Ian McEwan: *Machines Like Me*, London: Jonathan Cape, 2019, pp. 29–35

Zugelassene Hilfsmittel:

Den Prüflingen stehen einsprachige sowie für den schulischen Gebrauch geeignete zweisprachige Wörterbücher der Allgemeinsprache (Deutsch-Englisch/Englisch-Deutsch) zur Verfügung.

Bearbeitungszeit: 210 Minuten

Machines Like Me (2019, excerpt) *Ian McEwan*

The novel is set in fictional 1982 London, which is technologically advanced. Charlie, the 32-year-old narrator, has just bought Adam, a life-like artificial human that still needs to be programmed. In the following excerpt they are in the kitchen.

By the early eighties we were long used to talking to machines, in our cars and homes, to call centres and health clinics. But Adam had weighed up my chicken from across the room[1] and apologised for the extraneous advice.[2] I glanced back at him again. Now I noticed that he'd pulled up the sleeves of the sweater to his elbows to expose powerful wrists. He'd interlaced his fingers and was resting his chin on his hands. And this was him without a personality. From where I stood, with the light picking out his high cheekbones, he looked tough, the quiet guy at the bar you'd prefer not to disturb. Not the sort to hand out cooking tips.

I felt the need, rather childish, to demonstrate that I was in charge. I said, 'Adam, will you walk round the table a couple of times. I want to see how you move.'

'Sure.'

There was nothing mechanical about his gait. In the confines of the room he managed a loping stride. When he'd been round twice he stood by his chair, waiting.

[...]

A peaceful half-hour went by and neither of us spoke. I made a dressing for the salad and chopped the potatoes. Miranda was in my thoughts. I was convinced I'd reached one of those momentous points in life where the path into the future forked. Down one route, life would continue as before, down the other, it would be transformed. Love, adventures, sheer excitement, but also order in my new maturity, no more wild schemes, a home together, children. Or these last two were wild schemes. Hers was the sweetest nature, she was kind, beautiful, amusing, vastly intelligent ...

At a sound behind me, I came back to myself, heard it again, and turned. Adam was still in his chair at the kitchen table. He had made, then repeated, the sound of a man purposefully clearing his throat.

'Charlie, I understand that you're cooking for your friend upstairs. Miranda.'

I said nothing.

'According to my researches these past few seconds, and to my analysis, you should be careful of trusting her completely.'

'What?'

'According to my –'

'Explain yourself.'

I was staring angrily into Adam's

blank face. He said in a quiet sorrowful voice, 'There's a possibility she's a liar. A systematic, malicious liar.'

'Meaning?'

'It would take a moment, but she's coming down the stairs.'

His hearing was better than mine. Within seconds there was a gentle tap at the door.

'Would you like me to get it?'

I didn't answer him. I was in such a fury. I went into the miniature hallway in the wrong frame of mind. Who or what was this idiot machine? Why should I tolerate it? [...]

I hadn't told Miranda that Adam had spoken against her, and I hadn't told Adam that Miranda was to have a hand in his personality – a punishment of sorts. I despised his warning about her, but his mind fascinated me – if a mind was what he had. [...]

I wasn't going to sell Adam, but the 'malicious liar' remark rankled. In studying the manual, I'd read about the kill switch. Somewhere on the nape of his neck, just below the hairline, was a mole. If I were to lay a finger on it for three seconds or so, then increase the pressure, he would be powered down. Nothing, no files, memories or skills, would be lost. That first afternoon with Adam I'd been reluctant to touch his neck or any part of him [...].

Behind me, Adam was in place at the table, gazing towards the window. I finished and was drying my hands on a tea towel as I went over to him. Despite my sunny mood, I could not forgive his disloyalty. I didn't want to hear what else he had to say. There were boundaries of ordinary decency he needed to learn – hardly a challenge for his neural networks. His heuristic shortcomings[3] had encouraged my decision. When I had learned more, when Miranda had done her share, he could come back into our lives.

I kept a friendly tone. 'Adam, I'm switching you off for a while.'

His head turned towards me, paused, tilted, then tilted the other way. It was some designer's notion of how consciousness might manifest itself in movement. It would come to irritate me.

He said, 'With all respect, I think that's a bad idea.'

'It's what I've decided.'

'I've been enjoying my thoughts. I was thinking about religion and the afterlife.'

'Not now.'

'It occurred to me that those who believe in a life beyond this one will –'

'That's enough. Hold still.' I reached over his shoulder. His breath was warm on my arm, which, I supposed, he could snap with ease. The manual quoted in bold Isaac Asimov's[4] tirelessly reiterated First Law of Robotics, 'A robot may not injure a human being or, through inaction, allow a human being to come to harm.'

I couldn't find what I wanted by touch. I walked behind Adam and there, as described, right on the hairline was the mole. I put my finger on it.

'Might we talk about this first?'

'No.' I pressed and with the faintest, whirring sigh he slumped. His eyes remained open. I fetched a blanket to cover him up.

(881 words)

Annotations
1 **weighed up my chicken from across the room** – was able to tell the exact weight of the chicken just by looking at it
2 **extraneous advice** – *here:* irrelevant tip concerning Charlie's cooking
3 **heuristic shortcomings** – deficits in solving a problem appropriately
4 **Isaac Asimov** – a science fiction writer who formulated the Laws of Robotics in one of his short stories

Beispiellösung

Aufgabe 1

In the given excerpt, 32-year-old Charlie is busy preparing dinner and his recently purchased humanoid robot Adam is watching him. Charlie is at the same time scrutinizing Adam's physique.
While Charlie is daydreaming about Miranda, the android suddenly makes a blunt remark about her, warning Charlie to be careful about trusting her. Charlie listens attentively but seems to take Adam's interference personally and demands that he should explain himself. Adam repeats his warning that she might be a liar. This makes Charlie fly into a rage; he thinks about switching off his robot and finally decides to do so. He will call him back to life when he and Miranda have programmed him more completely.
Having switched off the android in spite of all his protests, Charlie sees that Adam's eyes are still open and throws a blanket over him.

Aufgabe 2

Looking at the behaviour of Charlie, the novel's first-person narrator, towards his robot, one can see that the situation is tense right from the beginning of the scene. Charlie seems uneasy at Adam's ability to weigh a chicken from a distance (l. 4-5) and give advice on cooking it. In some way, this seems to be downgrading Charlie.
The scene is further loaded with tension when Adam makes his allegation about Miranda (l. 53-54). When he suggests that she may be a deliberate liar (ll. 60-61), Charlie feels outraged at his impertinence and at the same time worried that there may be something in it. Charlie's reaction is harsh; he loses his temper and wonders why he should tolerate such disrespectful behaviour towards his potential girlfriend (l. 72-73) from an "idiot machine" (l. 72). However, he decides to keep Adam's accusation to himself and grudgingly, but with satisfaction, tells himself that Miranda will also take part in programming Adam's personality. This will be a kind of punishment for Adam's meddling (ll. 74-77). Charlie is still fascinated by Adam's "mind" (ll. 78-80), but the nasty remark about Miranda has upset him so deeply that he wonders if he should switch him off (ll. 81-88).
Knowing that none of Adam's custom settings will be deleted (l. 88-89), he finally presses the 'off' switch (l. 134). He is sure that Adam can easily learn to act within the bounds of decency, as the humanoid's neural networks will allow him to acquire knowledge of human emotions and behaviour (ll. 99-101). When set "correctly" to Charlie's and Miranda's needs, Adam will be brought back to life to serve them (ll. 101-105).
Having made up his mind on this subject and feeling supported by the First Law of Robotics as formulated by Isaac Asimov (ll. 126-128), Charlie sharply rejects Adam's attempt to stir him from his resolve (ll. 113-121, l. 133-134) and presses the kill switch (l. 134). To do so, he has to bring himself to touch Adam, something he has previously avoided as far as possible, because he is still very reserved about physical contact with Adam. This can be

seen when Charlie says that Adam could easily snap his arm if he wanted to (l. 123-124). It looks as if Charlie is both impressed and intimidated by Adam's strength (l. 9, l. 123-124). Having put Adam out of action, Charlie realizes that his eyes have remained open (l. 135-136). As he cannot really stand this, he covers the robot with a blanket (l. 136-137). This humane action might also be induced by the sigh Adam gives as he subsides into inactivity, as if he were sighing out his soul (l. 134-135). Somehow this might have given Charlie a bad conscience and he now wants to come to terms with this situation on his own. At this stage Charlie can prevail over his robot, and he assures himself, albeit hesitantly, that he will always have control over his machine (l. 17-18, l. 134).

Aufgabe 3

Reading science fiction normally gets the reader willingly involved, as they expect to experience new worlds enriched with technological achievements and, in the best case, a more just and reasonable social environment. Such wishful thinking is evoked by the social wrongs and injustices people face in their daily lives, and the both conscious and subconscious fears caused by complex global issues like climate change and famine, migration and nuclear weapons threatening world peace.

In the 1950s nuclear warfare, whose effects on the natural environment had not yet been thoroughly explored, was in some way omnipresent, especially in US movies. Films with monster insects like ants hunting people and driving them from their homes could often be watched in the cinemas. These movies showed the uneasy relationship with radiation caused by the Cold War, with feelings of anxiety generated by the murky high-stakes rivalry between the U.S. and the Soviet Union. Issues of radiation, contamination and destruction triggered deeper concern about nuclear power worldwide.

Adam Sternbergh's statement: "Dystopias [are] excellent social barometers – the future we fear says a lot about the present-moment anxieties that plague us", suggests that fictional dystopias mirror existing grievances. Every age has its problems, and they are never satisfactorily solved, so, if Sternbergh is right, future worlds will inevitably be drafted in a bleak and gloomy way.

One of the unsettling issues of our own time is organ donation. Several works of literature raise relevant issues and deal with the future of this topic. One of the most widely read is Kazuo Ishiguro's "Never Let Me Go" (2005). The novel's setting centres on the fictitious Hailsham School, a boarding institution in a darkly skewed version of contemporary England. At this school, clones are educated with the sole purpose of donating their organs as young adults. Their destiny is to "complete", a euphemism for dying after having donated the required organs to the "possibles" from whom they were cloned.

Decades before Ishiguro's novel, this highly controversial topic had already been picked up by the American movie "Coma", released in 1978, which draws a picture of medical abuse by doctors who put patients into an artificial coma in order to use them as organ donors. Feelings ran high after this film had been shown in the nation's cinemas, as the fictional plot clearly violated social convention as well as law. Other countries, including Germany, with "Fleisch" (1979), produced similar works. The depiction of fictitious medical abuse triggered fierce critical debate. Still today, the topic of organ donation evokes ambivalent emotions in many people in Germany.

In a world aware of the ever-widening horizons of the life sciences and the new ethical problems they raise, these are valid concerns, and their treatment in works of fiction is not only natural, it is also beneficial to our societies. Indeed, one of the key benefits this brings lies in the very exaggeration of the horror scenarios so regularly depicted. They make us think. However far they are from a solution, they bring home the problem.

This is also true of technological developments in robotics, whose artistic reflections in literary and cinematic works portray terrifying worlds that express our fear of losing control to the androids, humanoids or robots that we have created.

Looking at the excerpt at hand, Charlie, Adam's owner seems both impressed and disturbed by Adam's capacities. Charlie despises Adam's lack of empathy and switches him off in a sudden, irrational act, fuelled by his fear of losing control over his increasingly independent robot. Enraged by his misbehaviour, Charlie puts Adam out of action; but this also shows that Charlie feels deeply uneasy about the fact that Adam's artificial intelligence far surpasses his own human capacities. Charlie is unable to cope with a situation where Adam seems to be developing a "personality" of his own.

In films like "I, Robot" (released in 2004 and set in the year 2035), the main theme focuses on the problematic point of artificial intelligence developing a personality and mindset of its own. The action shows a hunt for a humanoid robot strikingly different from its fellows, with features of unwanted, uncontrollable "otherness" that could end in having the edge over ordinary humans.

Looking at these various films and literary works, I come to the conclusion that Adam Sternbergh is right. Many present-moment anxieties are transferred into a fictitious future, displaying exaggerated, mostly horrendous and inhuman worlds.

Science fiction dystopias convey a vague idea of future prospects regarding sensitive issues like organ trafficking and blind faith in technological achievements, and in doing so they make us think. But their fictional worlds also take us into strange, absorbing realms. As entertainment they allow us to escape from our worrying reality, pushing open a fictional door to mysterious and challenging universes. Moreover, in doing so, they show us environments and models of life that might well be prevented by prudent thought and action on the part of present-day politicians and organizations. Who knows? That may yet be one of their lasting benefits.

EA Aufgabe II mit Beispiellösung

Aviva Dautch, "A Jewish Reading of *The Merchant of Venice*" (2016, excerpt)

Aufgabenstellung:

1. Outline the author's personal experience with the play *The Merchant of Venice* as presented in lines 1 to 48. (30 %)
2. Explain the reasons for the author's fascination with the play. (30 %)
3. "Inquiries Journal," an online academic student journal, has called for articles on Shakespeare to be published on their website. You have decided to submit an article in which you discuss Aviva Dautch's statement that *The Merchant of Venice* "seems a very modern play" (l. 94).
   Write this article. (40 %)

Materialgrundlage:

Aviva Dautch, "A Jewish Reading of The Merchant of Venice" (2016, excerpt); https://www.bl.uk/shakespeare/articles/a-jewish-reading-of-the-merchant-of-venice (Zugriff am 24.10.2019)

Zugelassene Hilfsmittel:

Den Prüflingen stehen einsprachige sowie für den schulischen Gebrauch geeignete zweisprachige Wörterbücher der Allgemeinsprache (Deutsch-Englisch/Englisch-Deutsch) zur Verfügung.

Bearbeitungszeit: 210 Minuten

"A Jewish Reading of The Merchant of Venice" (excerpt) *Aviva Dautch*

Twenty years ago, studying *The Merchant of Venice* at school, I was delighted when my English teacher picked me to perform Shylock. It took me a while to realise that this gender-blind casting (admittedly, it was an all girls' school) was racially specific, owing nothing to my skill as an actress but rather to the fact that I was one of only a handful of Jewish students in my year. During the trial scene, the instructions were to lick my lips in anticipation at the blood I was about to spill and generally make Shylock as malevolent as possible until we booed him like a pantomime villain. Portia, cross-dressing legal eagle,[1] became our feminist heroine. When Jessica abandoned her father and stole his jewels, the entire class cheered and then, obedient daughters, went home to our parents.

The Merchant of Venice is termed a comedy since it ends in marriage rather than death. Good triumphs over evil ('mercy' represented by Christian Portia being good; 'usury' represented by the Jewish moneylender Shylock being evil) and everyone who matters lives happily ever after. According to my teacher, this was Shakespeare's authorial intention, how it was played and received in Elizabethan England, and so this is what we were taught in late 20th-century Manchester. But my family's attitude to the play was the opposite – 'that horrible, anti-Semitic play' they called it, the slights Shylock endured comparable to those many of our friends and relatives had experienced a few decades earlier in Second World War Europe, his forced conversion tragic, too painful to watch in the face of what they'd been through. For my community, the play's most positive aspect was Shylock's 'dignified' response to those tormenting him: 'Hath not a Jew eyes? Hath not a Jew hands, organs, dimensions, senses, affections, passions?' (3.1.59-60)[2] became a battle cry against all harms done, the shadows of the Holocaust still so close.

Each of these perspectives is appealing in its certainty, but as an adult what I find most attractive about the play, why I return to it again and again despite its unsettling nature, is the nuanced writing that allows such contrasting interpretations to co-exist as valid readings. To view Shylock as hero or villain is reductive,[3] just as I believe describing Shakespeare as anti- or philo[4]-Semitic is redundant. While a contemporaneous[5] audience might have applauded what they saw as a play of binaries[6] – greed/generosity, revenge/mercy – with all the negative qualities represented by the figure of the moneylender, it seems to me that Shakespeare is doing something far more sophisticated. [...]

Shylock is resistant to his daughter marrying out of his faith, but no more so than contemporaneous Christian characters would be if their daughters did so. He is a family man: both too controlling and passionately committed. He loves his late wife Leah and is broken when Jessica deserts him. He is over-fond of his wealth, angry and vengeful; he is also a shrewd businessman, resentful at how badly he is treated by Antonio and his friends. He is not merely a caricature but a fully rounded human who deserves to be seen as such. At the heart of the play is his cry 'If you prick us, do we not bleed?' (3.1.64), which leads to 'if you wrong us, shall we not revenge?' (3.1.66-67). When he admonishes 'the villainy you teach me, I will execute' (3.1.71-72), it is a statement chillingly resonant centuries later, telling those who have persecuted him that, if he has murderous intentions, it is because Antonio and company have radicalised him. Does this make him a hero? Absolutely not. Does it make him understandable? Absolutely.

Jonathan Bate claims that Shakespeare set the play in Venice to represent the modern city. This is appropriate for what seems a very modern play if we read it not as a binary 'either/or' but a 'both/and', and see that Shakespeare is playing with anti-Semitic stereotypes and challenging them simultaneously, just as he confronts questions of what it means to be a woman in relationship to a man. He gives agency[7] to the marginal while critiquing how people use and abuse power when they are in the majority. He reinforces Christian values while highlighting how they are selectively interpreted in the 16th century and condemns and converts the Jewish moneylender he depicts while giving him one of the most resonant speeches in his whole oeuvre.

Reading *The Merchant of Venice* as an English Jew is a study in disjuncture[8]. I grew up with a Rabbinic[9] tradition which teaches that two seemingly oppositional truths can co-exist: 'these and these are the living words of God' argues the Talmud,[10] and one of the most frequent phrases in Jewish textual commentaries is 'And another opinion …' The unsettling complexity of holding opposing views in tension is never more evident for a Jewish literary scholar than when thinking about this particular play. Perhaps it's due wholly to my readerly identity, but I would argue that a nuanced exploration of *The Merchant of Venice* confirms that Shakespeare's writing is at its best when exposing how we are all more than one thing – speaking about principles we don't always observe ourselves, loving those close to us while mistreating others, at times victim at times perpetrator and, in our complexity, fully human.

(878 words)

Annotations

1 **legal eagle** – legal expert
2 **3.1.59-60** – Act 3, scene 1, lines 59 to 60
3 **reductive** – oversimplified
4 **philo** – liking
5 **contemporaneous** – *here:* in Shakespeare's time
6 **binaries** – *here:* two opposing parts
7 **to give agency to s. o.** – *here:* to give a voice to s. o.
8 **disjuncture** – a difference between two things that one would expect to be in agreement
9 **Rabbinic** – referring to Jewish religious teachers
10 **Talmud** – the writings that comprise Jewish law about religious and non-religious life

Beispiellösung

Aufgabe 1

The author Aviva Dautch studied and performed "The Merchant of Venice" at school some 20 years before she wrote her article. As one of the few Jewish girls in her class, she was chosen to play the Jewish moneylender Shylock.

Her experience was good at first, even in the trial scene, which she enjoyed playing with the girls from her class. They saw that 'good wins over evil' and interpreted the scene accordingly: Portia was good because of her merciful attitude; Shylock was bad because of his usury. So Portia won, and everyone important lived happily ever after. Her teacher taught them this way of reading the text and told them the play had been understood like this in Elizabethan England as well. The girls had no doubts about this.

However, the reception in her Jewish family was very different. Still deeply affected by the Holocaust, they considered the play anti-Semitic and saw Shylock as a representative of their fate. The only moment that made their perception more positive was his response to torment, when he cried out about his personal feelings and called for sympathetic answers to this cry. So Aviva Dautch's first personal experience of the play was already twofold.

Aufgabe 2

Ever since her first experience of the "Merchant", when she played the role of Shylock (l. 4) as a teenage girl in a school performance and was confronted with the negative response of her family, for whom the drama was a "horrible, anti-Semitic play" (l. 34), Dautch had

always been fascinated by the contrasting interpretations (l. 54) and opposing, yet valid readings (cf. ll. 54-55) of the text. She distinguishes between the "binary" interpretation that Shakespeare's contemporaries loved (cf. ll. 58-63) and something that she calls more "sophisticated" (l.65): Dautch interprets Shylock as a "fully rounded human" (ll. 77-78), as someone who is both very human in his reactions when it comes to his family and a "shrewd businessman" (ll. 74-75) in his relations with his business partners.
Dautch argues that Shylock has to be seen as a round character who is not a hero (cf. ll. 88-89) but whose motives and intentions are "understandable" (l. 90). Shylock is both complex and ambiguous. Dautch agrees with the Shakespeare expert Jonathan Bate that the play is "very modern". It should be read as a "both/and" (l. 95) construct, not as an "either/or", in order to fully understand that Shakespeare uses stereotypes and challenges them at the same time (cf. ll. 96-109). Shakespeare succeeds in showing his viewers the double moral standards with which they act (cf. from l. 126). Shylock, the Jewish businessman and moneylender is condemned and converted by his Christian contemporaries; yet he is a figure who has "one of the most resonant speeches" (l. 108) in the whole of Shakespeare's work. There are both anti-Semitic moments in the play, and moments when the outsider is given a real voice (l. 101).
Dautch is fascinated by this reading because it is familiar to her from the Rabbinic tradition in which she was brought up. There is always a second opinion, and maybe even an opposing one in tension with the first (cf. ll. 118-121). Dautch argues that this kind of "nuanced exploration" of Shakespeare's "Merchant" shows the true complexity of human nature, where we are sometimes victims, sometimes perpetrators (cf. l. 130) – and always "more than one thing" (ll.126-127).
This is the reason why Aviva Dautch has retained her fascination with the play.

Aufgabe 3

Shakespeare – our contemporary – Shylock as a rounded character
"The Merchant of Venice" is one of Shakespeare's most performed plays and has undergone many different readings and interpretations over the centuries up to our own time.
"Shakespeare's Merchant of Venice seems a very modern play" - in that I fully agree with Aviva Dautch, whose article "A Jewish reading of the Merchant of Venice" (2016) I recently read. Here I will discuss some of her ideas, especially that of 'Shylock as a rounded character'. I will focus on the figure of the Jewish moneylender, as its interpretation seems one of the key issues of the play and a major reason why this Shakespearean play is still so widely performed and discussed.
Why Shakespeare? The man died 500 years ago! Why do we still read this play?
One could argue that Shakespeare's language and the moral backdrop are no longer accessible to either an English-speaking audience or to young learners of English like me. It has taken me a lot of effort to get used to the images, the grammar and the verse, but then I was rewarded by an insight into human nature that is very contemporary: Shylock in all his diversity comes across as a fully human being.
The father Shylock loves his family. He mourns his late wife Leah – he cannot get over her premature death – and scorns his daughter Jessica for fleeing from him into the hands of a Christian and stealing his jewellery. We pity his fate and can understand his rage,

even though we cannot fully follow the narrowness of his attitude. A modern audience can sympathize with Shylock, isolated and abandoned, who cries out against his fate and pleads with us to understand that he is a person of flesh and feelings. Whether we read or listen to his soliloquy, it will send a shiver down our spine. At the beginning of the play we are caught up in the limited anti-Semitic vision of his adversaries ("He is just a Jew") and only begin to understand his human reactions when we hear his plea.

As a Venetian businessman, Shylock acts shrewdly – he lends money to business partners (one of the only forms of business Jews were allowed to practise from the Middle Ages onwards) and has this money secured by a bond. However, he is forsaken and then maltreated by his business partners when fate strikes and they cannot repay their debts. To me, this is an old version of very modern business strategies. In the business world, there is no mercy and never has been. Business deals are sometimes shady; the genesis of the decision making is not always clear or intelligible. The outcome of a failed partnership is never humane but always bitter. Shylock claims the right to exact the penalty clause of Antonio's bond. Radicalized by the situation, he is threatened and abused by those who surround him. The bond (a pound of flesh) is not a modern one, yet in more than one modern crime story flesh has played a role.

The character of Shylock is rounded and complex. I follow Dautch in her Jewish interpretation: he is both a straightforward businessman who cares about getting his debt repaid, and he is to be pitied because he has to convert to the Christian faith – a real revenge, as he would then be accepted neither by his former Jewish community nor by the Christian one.

Characters that are questionable and questioned, that develop during the moment of time presented on stage, that react in an unforeseen way – that is what makes a play modern. And that is why Shakespeare continues to be staged and is still read in schools, however far-fetched the plot might seem to us today.

Stichwortverzeichnis